A NEW INTRODUCTION TO
MORAL THEOLOGY

A NEW INTRODUCTION TO MORAL THEOLOGY

*

HERBERT WADDAMS

THE SEABURY PRESS · NEW YORK

First Seabury Paperback *edition published 1965*

© 1964 BY SCM PRESS, LTD.
LIBRARY OF CONGRESS CATALOG CARD NUMBER: 65-22258
509-665-C-5
PRINTED IN THE UNITED STATES OF AMERICA

To the Staff and Students,
Past and Present, of the
Montreal Diocesan Theological College

CONTENTS

PREFACE

THIS book was first conceived when I was working as a parish priest in the diocese of Ottawa, Canada. The problems of everyday Christian living raise a great many moral questions, and it is important that intelligent Christian people should be able to think about them coherently and constructively. Some treatment of the subject matter of moral theology could serve to help them in this task. I was also asked to deliver a course of lectures on moral theology by Dr E. G. Jay, then Principal of the Montreal Diocesan Theological College, for his students. This and subsequent invitations to lecture encouraged me to gather material which might be published and which would, I hoped, be found useful for clergy and theological students as well as for the laity.

As will be seen from the contents, the book covers the main ground of moral theology. It is an attempt to use the insights of past studies and to apply them to the moral situation of the present day. Modern society has become complex, and moral problems reflect this complexity. It is more than ever necessary that Christians should be able to think clearly about the issues which face them in the moral field. A book of this character cannot deal in detail with more than a very few actual examples, but it can provide the framework and principles which should support and govern right thinking, and it can show how they may be applied to actual conditions.

Moral theology does not lack detractors, especially in the Protestant traditions. The opening chapter has therefore been devoted to examining some of the objections brought against moral theology as a legitimate part of Christian study. Exponents of moral theology, however, cannot merely sit back and behave as though the traditional way of dealing with it has been unaffected by recent thought. Like all true Christian thinking, it must take new insights into consideration and be ready to grapple as effectively with new conditions as it has dealt with those of the past.

I should like to express my sincere thanks for the assistance and encouragement of the Rev. David L. Edwards of the SCM Press, in preparing the typescript for publication, and also for the help of Bishop Kenneth Warner.

12 *The Precincts,*   HERBERT WADDAMS
Canterbury

  March 1964

I

IS MORAL THEOLOGY UNCHRISTIAN?

IT IS OBVIOUS that in a book on moral theology the answer to
the above question will be that moral theology is not unchristian.
It might therefore seem that the question was unnecessary in the
first place. But it is being asked and answered in the affirmative by
a number of writers. From several different sources we hear that
there are no such things as moral laws, that it is impossible to say
that any action is right or wrong in itself, and that the whole idea
of casuistry is based on assumptions which have no place in the
religion of Christ. It is desirable, before going further, to consider
some of these objections.

Lutheran Objections

Lutheran teaching has almost always been opposed to Roman
Catholic moral theology on the grounds that it does not adequately
deal with the sinfulness of man in the face of God. Lutheranism
has always stressed the truth that man can only be justified in the
sight of God by God's own act, which receives him, sinner though
he is, and breaks down the wall of partition between man and God.
In a recent work on *Theological Ethics*[1] Dr Helmut Thielicke,
Rector of Hamburg University, has expounded the Lutheran
approach with force and lucidity. It would be impossible, and also
insulting, to try to sum up his argument in a few pages, but we
may perhaps be allowed to take up one or two of his points. After
doing so, we shall look at two other publications, which may be
taken as typical of one recent trend in criticizing moral theology
and its methods.

There is no difficulty in accepting the main contentions of
Professor Thielicke. He has emphasized that 'Evangelical Ethics'
move only within the framework of personal relations, primarily

[1] *Theologische Ethik*, Turbingen 1955 (English translation in preparation).

the relations between man and God and secondarily those between men in the light of God's action. He does not admit the possibility of considering any action in the abstract, for that withdraws it from the personal relationship in which it alone has meaning. No consideration of Christian behaviour can take place outside the actual situation in which the choice of action has to be made. In his view a method of thought or analysis which suggests that action can be isolated from the personal elements of the living choice is bound to lead to confusion. His objection is based on a theological principle that it is impossible to give to man any status which belongs to him as man, and thus suggest that he has certain qualities which do not depend on the relationship which has been established with God by his act in his saving work. If, Thielicke holds, a study of morals begins from the assumption that man retains certain inherent characteristics, this is tantamount to admitting that God's saving work was not really essential.

The problem of Christian growth or sanctification, Thielicke writes, can only be seen in the context of justification, that is, of what God has done. We cannot even think of showing the fruits of a Christian life without seeing that this depends entirely on the state of being a forgiven sinner, which God's love has accorded to us. When this truth of forgiveness or justification takes its grip on us, then the fruits will follow automatically, even though there continues to be sin. Yet this sin does not alter our status as forgiven sinners: we are, as Luther said, *simul justus et peccator* (at one and the same time justified and a sinner).

Dr Thielicke also maintains that it is a serious mistake to make love appear as *the* essence of God. Within God himself there is a tension between his holiness and his love which should not be minimized. It is from this fact that the quality of miracle belonging to God's action in saving the world comes. 'The point at issue is to safeguard the miracle of the Gospel by which God overcomes himself, by which his love saves us from the threat of his holiness.' Connected with this tension between love and holiness in God is the irreconcilable opposition between Law and Gospel on earth. If this opposition is done away the whole meaning of the Gospel is lost in Thielicke's opinion. The Gospel overcomes and does away with the Law, and, if any kind of law is allowed to come back into the Christian religion, it is a guarantee that the true understanding of the Gospel has been lost.

With care and thoroughness Professor Thielicke goes on to argue
that the concept of natural law, as presented in Roman Catholic
theology, cannot be fitted in to a proper Christian understanding
of the Faith. For, he holds, it gives to unredeemed mankind a
status independent of God's action by recognizing the general
quality in man of a sense of moral values. This in his view undermines the greatness of the Gospel and the saving work of Jesus
Christ. His point is that we cannot establish any goodness in man
because to do so makes man independent of God in a certain sense.
When this occurs the Gospel instead of being a radical change of
relationships with and by God is replaced by a system of building
on the natural moral qualities which man already possesses.

The criticisms which Thielicke makes of Roman Catholic moral
theology can be justified when the moral theology is of the kind
which he dislikes. But moral theology is not necessarily bound up
with the legalistic system which he criticizes. It is perfectly possible
to use the insights of traditional moral theology without in the least
including the features which are objectionable to a proper Christian
understanding of the work of salvation. And even the scholastic
theologians, most objectionable to Thielicke, grasped certain truths
which we ought to be able to use.

It is possible to hold that man retains a moral sense without at
the same time making it a diminishment of the work of God. For
this sense is a gift of God given to man in creation and still remain-
ing in him because God has not ceased to love him. This applies
as much to the heathen and rebel as to the converted Christian:
it is the actual fact that God loves every man and that Jesus Christ
died to save him that endows him with those qualities which are
part of God's gift and God's love. The retention of those qualities
in man by God's grace is indeed part of the redeeming love of God
as well as of his love in creation, if it is possible to make such a
distinction between the two kinds of love, for they both come
direct from the nature of our loving God. To ascribe to man the
power of alienating himself altogether from God is tantamount to
saying that God himself is not the God of heaven and earth 'in
whom all things consist.'

But one must completely agree with Thielicke in seeing that the
natural law does not and cannot provide a whole system of
casuistry, which gives answers to all questions and makes a man
guiltless if he follows the rules. That would indeed be a betrayal

of the Gospel, for it would assume that man can work out his own
salvation without anything more than a handbook of morals,
together with some assistance from God. As Thielicke clearly sees,
such an approach is a denial of the basic message of the Gospel
which concerns only relationship with God. The sense of right and
wrong, which reflects the reality of the natural law, is a means of
guiding and helping those who are in moral perplexity, and who
may suffer from a wrong sense of guilt. It is like Thielicke's view
of the Law as a sheepdog, which has the duty of keeping the sheep
from straying from the right path and falling over precipices or
into the jaws of wild beasts.

This sense of right and wrong is what is called 'conscience' by
Thielicke, though it is not the only meaning which 'conscience'
can bear. He examines the various conditions of conscience and
how it functions, though he does not attempt to define it. 'The
opposite of an unsettled conscience is not a good conscience; it is
a conscience reconciled to God.' This is profoundly true, but
nevertheless when it comes to practical guidance for the ordinary
Christian it is not enough merely to give him theological truths.
He needs help in practical ways, as he tries to pick his path between
alternative courses of action. This can only be done by considering
the actual circumstances which confront him, and the study of
general moral principles is undertaken so as to provide some
pointers to help him, when he is not sure in which direction he
should go. These pointers should never be mistaken for unvarying
rules, for every problem has its own circumstances peculiar to
itself and must be solved in the light of them.

The study of moral theology is therefore aimed, not at providing
moral certainty that any choice is right, but at helping Christians
to relate their own circumstances to what is known of the will of
God in the Scriptures and in the history of the Christian Church.
The danger of Thielicke's approach, and the Protestant approach
generally, is that it leaves all moral problems merely to the subjective emotions of the person involved, and these are very often
the worst possible guide. One of the things which psychological
study has clearly revealed is that the heart of man is even fuller of
deceit than we thought, and that therefore he is often inclined to
do things without even knowing what are the motivating forces
within him. Moreover, as educated Christians acquire a smattering
of psychological knowledge, they find themselves in even more

confusion than before, for they begin to distrust all their motives. There is nothing that can more certainly inhibit the Christian Gospel than a refusal to trust one's own motives, for a man can then find himself in a psychological state in which the act of faith is virtually impossible.

When Thielicke comes to discuss actual situations, as he does in the second of his volumes, we find that his analysis and examination are exactly of the same kind as would be undertaken by any moral theologian. He has waged a fierce war on casuistry (which is, after all, merely the consideration of specific cases), but he does himself examine a number of cases. His analysis of them is lucid and profound, for example, in the matter of telling the truth about a dying patient, or on the subject of resistance to an evil government. They would be an asset in any book of moral theology. But as a result of his presuppositions he does not give any guidance except by implication. He explains how it is that the requirements of a 'just war' in traditional moral theology are so difficult and complicated that it is in fact impossible for anyone to be certain that a war is just. But what the Christian wants to know are the principles on which he should begin to think about the matter. It is guidance that he needs rather than certainty. And it has always been a prime principle of moral theology that a man has to make up his own mind in the end and to follow his conscience.

Some of the things which Thielicke brings out in his analyses do by implication refer to principles similar to those which moral theology tries to make explicit. It is not at all necessary to abandon the whole operation merely because one particular way of conducting it has been shown to have serious shortcomings. In every moral situation one consideration has to be weighed against another in the light of our reconciliation with God and in the light of the personal factors involved, but within this framework there is room for a proper discussion of principles and their application. For, as Thielicke himself shows, there are definite prohibitions in the New Testament and the Old which deal with behaviour which is inconsistent with a right relationship with God. This is surely another way of saying that there are some things which are wrong, and, even if Thielicke will not go so far as to say that this means that there are some things which are right, it does mark out a sphere where the consideration of alternative actions which are not forbidden would seem to be perfectly natural and legitimate.

'Koinonia' Ethics

The second recent work on which some comment should be made is *Ethics in a Christian Context* by Professor Paul L. Lehmann of Union Theological Seminary, New York.[1] The burden of this book is that the only kind of Christian ethics which ought to be accepted is what is called *koinonia* ethics. *Koinonia* is the Greek word meaning 'fellowship' which is used of the new community created by the Gospel into which Christians come at their baptism. 'The ethical question—in the *koinonia*—is not "What *ought* I to do?" but "What *am* I to do?" because in the *koinonia* one is always fundamentally in an *indicative* rather than in an *imperative* situation.' This statement and many others like it make a distinction which is valid and important, but it is taken here to extreme lengths. It is desirable that Christians should start from what has been done for them by God and proceed from this present fact, rather than starting from some theoretical moral obligation. But this does not abolish the moral claim upon us, nor do away with the sense of moral obligation which has everywhere been accepted as having a valid content for man. It would be impossible to try to evacuate the New Testament of this claim, for it is an ever-present assumption of everything which Jesus and the Apostles do. The appeals which Jesus makes to his hearers are not relevant, if the moral sense is thought to be absent or to be something which ought to be ignored.

The emphasis which Lehmann puts on ethics is very much the same as that of Thielicke, and we do not need to repeat what has already been said. But Lehmann takes his ideas as justifying an abandonment of the use of moral principles in any recognizable form. He criticizes tabu law, fear and conformity as reasons for moral behaviour—quite rightly—but he then goes on to conclude that moral laws have no use at all, a conclusion which does not follow. One of the reasons why he wishes to abandon traditional Christian teaching about sexuality (though it is not clear exactly what part of it he does wish to abandon) is that it 'is also steadily losing effectiveness' (p. 136). His idea of the Christian ethical tradition seems to be overmuch affected by its aberrations and failures rather than its positive aspects. But this is not the place to discuss detailed aspects of morals. It is necessary to point out that

[1] SCM Press, London, and Harper and Row, New York, 1963.

a proper freedom of choice in no way affects the aim which should govern all sexual teaching, namely that its fulfilment can only be found in conforming to the will of God, and that this will has been plainly stated by Jesus himself in the New Testament as being permanent lifelong marriage with one partner. There *is* guidance in the shape of a moral principle, and it is plainly incorrect to suggest that there is not.

Professor Lehmann thinks that 'it is much easier, ethically speaking, to be a Roman Catholic or a Christian Scientist than it is to be an evangelical Christian' (p. 142). He bases this statement, at least as far as Roman Catholics are concerned, on a caricature of their moral theology. In his own discussion of just and unjust wars he engages in the same type of discussion as a moral theologian would conduct, but with less pertinence, as he has refused to use what guidance is available. It is only too easy to misrepresent one's opponent in order to appear to destroy his case, and Lehmann is not free from this kind of action.

A section of the book is devoted to a criticism of moral theology, but in this criticism the writer assumes that the aim of moral theology 'is to free the believer from the ethical predicament by conducting him out of the ethical situation to which the problem of the right or good action is intrinsic. Such an attempt is an ethical *tour de force* because it assumes *de facto* that the moral counsellor is in a *different* situation from that of the man under instruction and guidance.' This may be true of some kinds of moral theology, but it is certainly not true of moral theology properly understood. Its aim is not to free anyone from the ethical predicament, it is to help the man in the ethical predicament to think rightly about the situation in which he finds himself. It is difficult to see how the author can object to this when he himself has written a whole book with precisely this aim, but in doing so he has misrepresented the function of moral theology. Nor does it assume that the person giving advice is in a different situation in a basic sense, even though obviously he will often be in a different situation so far as the ethical problem itself is concerned.

The examples which Professor Lehmann provides of advice from moral theology are a deplorable exercise in putting up his own targets in the shape of Aunt Sallys and knocking them down. He merely identifies the imaginary moral theologian with the man who does the wrong thing, and thinks that this condemns moral theology. He later opines: 'The ethical predicament has been overcome—not piecemeal but by a total renewal of our humanity. Moral theology obscures this act of God' (p. 321). This is tantamount to saying that moral theology takes a view which cannot be fitted in with a true understanding of the action of God in the life of man, a statement which only has to be made to be seen to be absurd.

In short Lehmann has maintained that a *koinonia* ethic, which according to his view is the only fully Christian ethic, is concerned with relations and functions, not with principles and precepts (p. 124). But there is no necessary enmity between these two groups. So long as principles and precepts (in a general sense) are subordinate to personal relationships with God on the one hand, and with other persons on the other, they can be of the greatest service and help to people in making the choices which inevitably face them in everyday life. At the risk of being considered over simple we may take the example, which everyone knows, of the human family. The important and overriding aim of the family must be to promote the best possible personal relations between all its members, and everything must be seen within that overall framework and objective. Nevertheless there are rules within the family which provide guidance for the children as well as for the adults. There are principles in the family which are to be applied in relationships outside the family also. These can be, and usually are, laid down in some way by the parents, who may discuss with the children how they apply to their relations with others. The purpose of this is to help them in the practical choices which they have to make. In doing this parents and children are engaged in the work of moral theology, which is a form of teaching and learning derived from Christian experience and thought in the past.

Lehmann is correct in stressing the fact that each moral situation has to be dealt with as it arises and that each is unique, but he ought also to recognize that, although each moral situation differs from every other, there is much in common between one and another. No one who has been engaged in trying to help people in their personal problems can fail to see that both sides are true. Moral questions have to be decided in the context of the Church, as Lehmann states, but this means not only the local congregation, which he mentions, but also the Church at large and throughout history. History can never be ignored in Christian life, for the historic events of the Gospel stand at its centre.

Professor C. F. D. Moule of Cambridge University in an article in the *Expository Times* (September 1963) unhappily gives currency to the same misconceptions as those which we have already considered. He again repeats the accusation that moral theology claims to answer the question 'What precisely are we to do in the more problematic cases?', and one wonders what moral theology he has read which has given him this false impression. To give guidance and to provide detailed answers in advance are two vastly different things. He seems to think that virtues are quite outmoded and even writes: 'Faith, hope and charity are not virtues at all; still less are they the *cardo* or hinge on which conduct turns.' He appears to have confused the cardinal virtues (prudence, justice, fortitude, temperance) with the theological virtues (faith, hope and love). Whether they are virtues or not depends on what meaning one gives to the word 'virtue'. It does not contribute towards clear thinking to indulge in such sweeping statements without careful definition. If virtues are to be described as 'qualities concerned with relationship-conditions', then faith, hope and love would be virtues according to his own definition.

The positive statements which Moule makes about the New Testament will be generally agreed by all, but the negative conclusions which he draws from them are far from obvious. It is difficult to see, for example, why, if the New Testament is concerned with a relationship, there should be no moral laws or principles. It depends how they are regarded, whether they fit in with such a relationship or not. Everyone knows, of course, that the Holy Spirit is the source of the true answers to the problems of life, but is the Holy Spirit confined to the single person in a situation of temptation? And is it contended that moral theology rules out the activity of the Holy Spirit? We all live in the Church, which is above all the place where the Holy Spirit is active and where God reveals himself.

Moule sums up his presentation by saying that 'Christian moral guidance is the *Christian worshipping congregation listening critically*' and underlines the fact that each of the last five words of the phrase is vital to the definition. Moral theology is an intensely practical study and will at once ask how this truth works out for the individual person when he is faced with temptation. Is he to resort to the local congregation for advice and help? If so, what will he get? And to whom is the Christian worshipping congregation listening?

It is presumably listening to God as he speaks to their own consciences. But he speaks in other ways too—to other congregations,
to the Church as a whole, to the Church in history, through the
New Testament in the Church. Moral theology takes the wisdom
derived from these various sources and puts it into a context where
it can be useful as a guide to those who are face to face with moral
problems. It is in this sense and this sense only that there are
principles and rules and standards, which have to be brought into
relation to the particular problem at stake. As a practical method
of action Moule's guidance can in fact only be secured in the form
of general principles, since obviously the whole congregation
cannot consider every one of the individual moral problems with
which each of its members is faced day by day. It is exactly this
function which moral theology is designed to discharge.

It is rash to cross swords with an expert on the New Testament,
but, nevertheless, one cannot help thinking that the exegesis and
interpretation which Moule gives of I Corinthians 7 hardly gives
the impression of meeting the requirements which he has laid
down. There is not much evidence of the congregation having
decided anything; on the contrary, St Paul uses the first person
singular very freely in the instructions which he is giving.

Professor Moule is quite right in desiring to avoid 'the constant
danger of confusing law and gospel or trying to legalize the gospel',
but he has, in giving his warnings, provided a caricature of what
the moral law is and what it claims to do. One cannot evade the
conclusion that he has not given a balanced picture of what the
New Testament itself writes. The passages which tell against him
are omitted, and he is too apt to take the scholar's view of the New
Testament, which includes the tacit assumption that nobody has
ever given serious attention to the problem before present-day
writers. Early in his article Moule expresses the fear that it may
be taken as an attack upon the foundations of morality. It need not
be so regarded, but these points should be made clear: the approach
which he favours leads to a sort of moral antinomianism at a time
when the world in general is inclined to make morals relative in
every way; it thus weakens those who most wish for guidance and
help; and, in doing so, it clearly abandons an attitude which runs
all through the New Testament. Within its limits moral theology
has an important and practical part to play in the ordinary life of
Christian people.

2

THE SETTING OF MORAL THEOLOGY

Did Jesus Lay Down Laws?

IN 1904 BISHOP Charles Gore wrote: 'No one, with his eye
on the New Testament and the earliest records of the Church, can
deny that the Church was, and was by Christ intended to be, a
society with a common moral law, which was to be constantly and
authoritatively reapplied by way of legislation in general principle,
and applied by way of discipline to individuals, in admitting them
or refusing to admit them into the Christian Society, retaining or
refusing to retain them in membership.[1]

The actual behaviour of the Church, Bishop Gore continued,
had often obscured this function, both Roman Catholics and
Anglicans having been remiss in different ways. He went on to
refer to the teaching of Jesus, and to point out that he emphasizes
character before conduct, as in the Sermon on the Mount, but
that he 'lays down laws for a kingdom, a society' and applies them
to a number of particular cases, some imaginary (if any man would
take thy coat, let him have thy cloke also), and some of them actual
(go sell what thou hast and give to the poor). The power of binding
and loosing, given by Jesus to the Church, is the power to apply
these moral laws to the members of the Church.

Some modern scholars would reject *in toto* Gore's interpretation
and maintain that Jesus had no idea or intention of laying down
laws. Are we to believe these scholars? If so, which scholar do we
accept and which do we reject? This question brings us into the
field of higher criticism of the New Testament text. There are
very few conclusions on which all scholars are agreed in deciding
which text should be taken and which left. Every scholar decides
according to his own presuppositions. If he assumes that Jesus did

---

[1] *The Social Doctrine of the Sermon on the Mount,* published by the Christian
Social Union, Oxford 1904.

not lay down laws, he explains them away. If he takes the opposite view, he finds good reason for regarding them as authentic. And all that leaves the ordinary Christian just where he was.

What then should be done? One solution, to which many Christians feel themselves driven, is to take refuge in a biblical literalism, commonly called fundamentalism. This approach is a 'take it or leave it' mentality. Either everything is strictly and literally true *au pied de la lettre*, or the whole thing is worthless. It is almost certainly the critics who have produced the great revival of fundamentalism in the twentieth century, by appearing to force this dilemma upon simple Christians.

But there is another point of view which is not only reasonable but which has behind it the authority of Christian tradition. We may listen to the critics who divide up the New Testament text and dispose of large pieces of it, saying that they do not represent what Jesus actually said. And when they have finished, we can say: 'That is all very fine. You may be right or wrong: I do not have the equipment to cross swords with you. But whatever may be the textual facts on these points, there can be no doubt that the New Testament represents what the Early Church thought that Jesus had said and taught. The omission of certain texts does not prove the Early Church wrong.' At first sight this may seem a somewhat negative attitude. But in fact it is similar to the attitude of the Christians in early times who had no New Testament. They were taught, and learned, and lived the Christian Faith in and through the fellowship of the Church. Perhaps God is teaching us through the critics that we ought never to have exalted the text alone of the New Testament to the pedestal on which we have put it, as something which gives us easy answers, but that we must see it only in conjunction with the living person of Christ at work in the Church.

In other words there is no need to throw out the passages which critics say have been inserted into the text later. If we are told that Jesus did not forbid remarriage after divorce, we must ask ourselves how it was that the Christians soon after his time were convinced that he did. For there can be no doubt that the New Testament text as we have it does include those elements of moral law and of its application, of which Bishop Gore wrote. We are in no position to set up our standards as to what Jesus ought to have taught and to make them a test of his teaching. This is to turn things upside down with a vengeance. Nor is it necessary to hold that the early Christians never made mistakes. We do not set them up as right in everything they thought. For example, they were clearly wrong in expecting the end of the world in their own lifetime. But it is necessary, if we are to have any coherent or reasonable outlook at all, to hold that, without utterly convincing reasons to the contrary, we must take the content of the New Testament to be what Jesus substantially taught.

At this point we ought to add that the work of the higher critics is and has been of very great value in establishing the possible dates and processes by which the documents are to be judged— as documents. But the individual theories of New Testament professors about what Jesus taught and about the meaning of his Person must be judged by the same standards as those of anyone else, for it is only within the life of the Church that they can be properly evaluated, that is, the Christian life of the centuries from the first up to and including the twentieth, and this life is not primarily intellectual but spiritual and moral.

In this study, therefore, we shall assume that the New Testament documents can be taken as representing the teaching of Jesus. No attempts will be made to impose a theory on the New Testament which would result in removing anything of substance from the text. This attitude rests on the grounds that the belief of the Early Church that Jesus said something or taught in such a manner is better evidence for it than the theories of modern scholars. Even if some texts were shown not to be the *ipsissima verba* of Jesus, the removal of words from the text by scholars is not evidence that Jesus did not say something very similar or even the very words themselves, unless they can be shown to be contradictory to and incompatible with other authentic words of his. But this cannot be done in any important matter.

This means that Gore's statement, quoted at the start of this section, is substantially true. We shall take the New Testament as it is, rather than as it might have been or as we would like it to be. In doing so we assume that Jesus and the Apostles not only taught what was good for the Church, but that, in doing so, enunciated the truths about God and man in which alone all men can find true fulfilment and happiness.

'Christian Ethics' and 'Moral Theology'

Before going further a preliminary question arises as to whether there is any difference between moral theology and what is usually called 'Christian Ethics'. Protestant theologians more commonly use the term 'Christian Ethics', and those of the Catholic tradition 'moral theology', and there is no doubt that the treatment of the two subjects has usually varied. It is fair to say that Christian ethics has for the most part concerned itself with general principles, and moral theology with their application to specific cases. But both studies deal with behaviour, that is, the way in which Christians should act in a naughty world. In some cases 'Christian Ethics' has been used merely to cover the most general principles, and on the other hand 'moral theology' has often become bogged down in deplorable petty legalisms. But the two belong together and should be two parts of one study dealing with Christian principles of behaviour and their application—there is no basic opposition between them. Moral theology takes the principles and tries to relate them to concrete situations.

Moral theology is a distinct subject of its own and it must be clearly delineated in its aim. But at the same time it must not be separated completely from other aspects of truth with which it is bound up. Moral theology suffers from two dangers to which it has often fallen victim. The first is a separation from other parts of the Christian life, so that the study of moral theology has often become a highly technical discussion of the application of moral principles to particular cases, without reference to the other aspects of the Christian life. When such separation occurs it always means that moral theology becomes legalistic, and that it puts too much emphasis on finding out what are the minimum requirements of the Christian moral law, and how much can be evaded. Thus the general impression is given that moral theology is concerned with teaching people what they can 'get away with', rather than with inculcating the true spirit of Christian living.

The late Dr Kirk in an essay on moral theology in the composite volume called *The Study of Theology*[1] defended the thesis that it was right for moral theology to be concerned with minima. He recognized that to many people such an idea is repellent, but he went on to point out that in practice it is essential to have minimum

---

[1] Hodder and Stoughton, 1939.

standards. Even those who most dislike the idea do in fact have to decide what are the minimum requirements which are needed for Baptism. Such minimum standards are an inescapable part of having a visible society called the Church and of belonging to it. Dr Kirk went on to say that for this reason moral theology is mixed up with Canon law, though it is wider than Canon law in some respects.

There is, however, some doubt whether the minimal approach, if we may call it such, is either necessary or desirable. There are occasions when laws have to be made about such things as church discipline, and when they are being considered, moral theology is the study which should make the largest contribution to their framing. For it is the business of moral theology to translate Christian beliefs into the common coin of everyday behaviour. In disciplinary matters, therefore, moral theology will have much to say as to the standards which the Church ought to uphold, and on the basis of its considerations those who frame the laws of the Church will come to their conclusions.

But, apart from the framing of Canon law and other regulations, there are many occasions when the parish priest has to make a decision as to moral standards. He may have to answer the question as to whether he should present a person to the Bishop for Confirmation, when the candidate is in fact engaged in activities which are generally thought to be dishonest. The activities in question may be perfectly 'respectable' from the point of view of the world, but at the same time repugnant to the Christian spirit. Moral theology has as its duty the guidance of priests and others who are faced with this kind of problem. But it is doubtful whether it is a good thing to proceed on the basis of laying down minimum moral conditions.

If we take the problem of a man engaged, let us say, in using methods of high-pressure salesmanship to persuade people to commit themselves to paying more than they can afford for goods which they have on hire-purchase, the problem before us is not easy. One way of dealing with it, and this is the traditional method of moral theology, is to settle certain external standards which the man in question must not transgress, and to say that, so long as he does not do so, there is no fault for which he can be blamed. Such standards in the case we are considering might be that he must not use improper pressure: improper pressure could be

defined as threats or lies. So long then as he were careful not to
do this, he would be 'in the clear'. But there are a great many
other things which would not fall within such a definition as we
have just used, but would certainly be out of keeping with a fully
Christian attitude. For example, it would not be a Christian thing
for him to encourage envy or covetousness, or to use means which
implied that his goods were necessary for unworthy reasons of
social status.

All these fuller considerations should be taken into consideration
when the priest is deciding if he should present a man for Confirmation or not. No doubt one of the facts which will weigh in his
mind is that a man who approaches Confirmation without earnestly
desiring to devote his whole life to God's will is hardly in a fit
state to be presented. Perhaps he might think that in the absence
of strong evidence to the contrary he ought to give the man the
benefit of the doubt and assume that his motives are worthy
enough. But the introduction of the word 'enough' at once throws
us back on to the idea of the acceptable minimum.

It is such problems as the one we have just sketched which
are the proper subjects of moral theology. We see from this that
moral theology cannot avoid some treatment of minimum standards
in the Christian life, but that this should be seen as a sort of incidental matter in a much broader field, namely the general problem
of Christian behaviour in an imperfect world. The case just discussed has not been exhaustively examined, and important moral
problems have been omitted. In any full consideration of such a
case it would be necessary to bring into the balance the effect of
the economic methods of the society in which the man is living,
his need to support himself and his wife and family, his chance
of finding any other job, the accepted moral framework within
which he is acting in selling goods, and similar matters. The
question is by no means simple if it is to be thoroughly examined,
and it may be added that this sort of problem is typical of the
problems which face Christians every day of their lives in the
present age.

Therefore, although the minimum standard must play some part
in moral theology, it must be set in the whole perspective of
Christian life and vocation. When moral problems are seen in
proportion, we also immediately realize why moral theology cannot
be separated from other Christian disciplines and subjects of study.

For one's moral attitudes and decisions depend on what one believes, or to put it shortly in theological terms—morals depend on dogma. If a man believes that God forbids the deliberate taking of human life in any circumstances, his moral attitudes will reflect this belief. Obviously he would be against capital punishment, he would be a pacifist, he would oppose the killing of thalidomide babies or old people suffering from incurable diseases, he would not kill a madman who was threatening to murder innocent women and children. These are simple examples. But if he believes that killing is permissible in certain circumstances, he will want to know the principles on which such an opinion is to be based. It works both ways. Our moral attitudes reflect our beliefs, and it is therefore important that our beliefs should be true. On the other hand many people adopt moral stances without having any clear beliefs at all, but their moral attitudes do in fact imply beliefs, so that, even if they have not thought them out, the beliefs could be said to be operative in the deepest sense. It is important, therefore, that moral behaviour should be related to underlying beliefs so as to expose them clearly if they are not already known. If this is done, moral behaviour can be helped to rest on truth rather than on sentiment, a highly desirable arrangement, for sentiment is the most uncertain of all human motives for action.

Moral theology must also be linked to sacramental and pastoral theology, for it is they which deal with the basic question of how a Christian finds the means to live a Christian life, and how God assists him in doing his will. That is no doubt the reason why many Roman Catholic books on moral theology include a section on Sacramental Theology. It is plainly useless to study what Christian behaviour ought to be, without relating it to the only means by which a Christian can find the inspiration and the power to put it into practice.

For a similar reason moral theology is not detached from ascetical theology, which is the study of spiritual growth in prayer. The development of the prayer life is most intimately bound up with the whole gamut of Christian behaviour. Man is a unity of body, mind and spirit, and the study of any one aspect of his life must never be undertaken in such a way as to suggest that this unity does not exist. Moreover moral theology, in wrestling with actual problems, must avoid the impression that it is setting standards which are in any way different from those set by Jesus himself, who told his followers to be perfect as his Father in heaven is perfect.

The practical result of such thoughts as those we have just set out is that in studying moral theology we must take these other studies for granted. All the dogmatic background is assumed to be accepted before moral theology begins its work. There are from time to time difficult moral disputes where it is necessary to go back and to reconsider first principles, but for the most part it is not practicable nor necessary to deal with them, for they form the subject of systematic theology, and must be established there. But even that assumption is not enough and can easily depersonalize moral theology. It can hardly be stated too strongly that moral theology is basically dealing with our life as it is lived in union with Christ. As a recent work has put it:

> The principle, the norm, the centre, and the goal of Christian Moral Theology is Christ. The law of the Christian is Christ Himself in Person. He alone is our Lord, our Saviour. In Him we have life and therefore also the law of our life.[1]

When therefore we come to study Christian behaviour, there are several different elements involved. Unhappily it is always necessary in such a theoretical study to examine the conditions without considering the person, who provides the most important and indispensable element. It is conceivable, and indeed it happens not infrequently, that an act which is quite all right for one person is all wrong for another, just because the persons concerned are in a different state of the Christian life, a different stage of spiritual development or have different responsibilities. This might lead the cynic to conclude that moral theology is a waste of time and merely an excuse for theologians to occupy their energies. But he would be wrong, because moral theology provides guidance for the thinking of those who want to take their Christian living seriously.

Perhaps in a perfect world there would be not enough for moral theology to do because the conditions would make it easy for a sincere Christian to find where his path lay. But in a world as evil as ours there are innumerable occasions when there is sincere puzzlement, and at the same time anxiety to avoid doing wrong or spreading harm. But 'only if it is imbued with religion, centered

[1] B. Häring, *The Law of Christ, I,* Newman Press, Maryland, 1961 p. vii.

in the religious, can morality be rightly judged. The more fully it conforms to the basic laws of the religious, the more it is animated by the essential spirit of the religious, the more sound and wholesome will it be.'[1] We are left with a sort of tension between our moral calculations and our religious calling which we must never try to abolish, because in it is the guarantee of our right balance and our constant sense of the presence and calling of God to us in everyday life.

The second danger which moral theology faces is that of being so closely related to the rest of the Christian life that it loses its separate usefulness and becomes mixed up with ethical and philosophical questions. As we have seen, it is closely connected with other disciplines, but at the same time it must be studied in distinction from them, if it is to be of maximum usefulness. Quite often the subject entitled 'Christian Ethics' is moral theology which has lost its incisiveness. Moral philosophy is a separate subject from moral theology, and it deals with questions of language and basic concepts: often it starts from a point at which there are supposed to be no presuppositions (though the absence of suppositions is itself an important presupposition). Christian Ethics not infrequently becomes a Christianized moral philosophy, and is more concerned with general concepts than with particular cases.

'Christian Ethics' usually describes an approach to the subject of Christian behaviour much more general than that of moral theology, for moral theology, while certainly dealing with principles, is also much concerned with the study of the application of those principles to cases. This study of cases is technically known as casuistry, a word which has been given a bad name, but which nevertheless is an inescapable occupation for anyone who wishes to do right and avoid wrong. Casuistry merely means the study of particular cases, an activity in which every person engages when he asks himself whether he ought to spend his money on something he wants to do or buy. The book *Christian Ethics* (edited by Waldo Beach and Richard Niebuhr, Ronald Press, New York 1955) contains a large number of valuable extracts from writers throughout Christian history, which deal with the general approach to life in the world. It does not contain a single extract dealing with specific moral problems, nor does it include an extract from

[1] Häring, *op. cit.*, I, p. 38.

any Anglican or Roman Catholic writer who could be called a moral theologian in the accurate sense of the word. It is in no spirit of criticism that these observations are made, but with the sole object of making it clear that there is a difference between moral theology and what is usually called Christian Ethics.

Dr Kirk was probably right when he held that the danger of modern religion was not over-analysis, but vagueness, at any rate in England. Failure to define is as bad as over-definition and is inclined to lead to a lack of clear principles, which in turn inevitably leads to the attitude that it does not matter what anyone believes or does as long as he is sincere. That point of view may be all right when it does not lead to personal inconvenience, but it is difficult to maintain it *ex animo* when one is at the receiving end of a Hitler's tortures or boiling in the pot of a cannibal king. Kirk maintained that this kind of woolliness could only be overcome by a new investigation into 'the principles of human action, the nature of conscience, the character of divine law, the distinction between virtue and sin; and a reassertion of whatever certainties can be discovered as to the nature and rules of Christian life'.[1] This quotation brings out well the central purpose of moral theology.

The Development of Moral Theology

Moral theology falls into two distinct parts. The first is the discussion of the principles which affect human behaviour, themselves derived from the revelation of Jesus Christ in his lifetime and their subsequent development in his Church. Moral principles include the great dogmatic affirmations of the Christian Faith and their implications for the nature of man and his relation to God, on which are based in turn the study of cases of conscience, of problems of right and wrong and of similar questions in the moral field. It is the study of the application of these principles to cases which makes up the second main division of moral theology, properly called casuistry.

In the New Testament itself there are indications both of the exposition of principle (Rom. 2.14, 15) and of the application of Christian principles to cases of difficulty which arose, for example, in the case of remarriage of widows (I Cor. 7.8) and when the question arose about whether or not to eat meat sacrificed to idols (I Cor. 8.10). It is precisely the kind of problem arising from such

[1] *Some Principles of Moral Theology*, Longmans 1957, p. 6.

questions that makes the study of moral theology not only desirable, but necessary. Although the New Testament does not provide any systematic treatise of moral theology, any more than it provides such a treatise on doctrine or any other subject, yet moral theology, no less than other branches of theology, can rightly claim that it rests its own study on elements which are clearly found there.

The *Encyclopaedia of Religion and Ethics* deals with moral theology entirely under the heading 'casuistry'. As we have seen, this is somewhat misleading, but there can be no dispute that it is with the development of casuistry that moral theology has historically been mainly concerned, and in which it has got itself a bad name. In the development of moral theology in the Roman Catholic Church, in which casuistry has been studied in great detail, there have been two main landmarks which have promoted its study. The first was the Lateran Council of 1215 which made auricular confession compulsory at least once a year; the second was the Council of Trent (1545-63) which was dealing with the vigorous Protestant movements and which attempted to deal with the many problems engendered by them. Questions of discipline bulked large during the whole of the Counter-Reformation period, and these came within the province of moral theology.

Two names stand out above the rest in their influence in the study of these problems within the Roman Catholic Church. The first is that of St Thomas Aquinas, who provided in his *Summa Theologica* a remarkable analysis of the basic doctrine and principles on which a detailed casuistry could be founded. He lived (1225-74) just at the time that the increased importance of Penance made demands on those hearing confessions, which could be satisfied by such a work as his. The second name is that of St Alphonsus Liguori (1696-1787), who became the greatest authority for Roman casuistry and the model for subsequent writers. His influence can be gauged by the fact that he is one of the few to have been given the rank of Doctor of the Church, and that this honour was bestowed on him by Pius IX as late as 1871.

The Counter-Reformation was marked in the Roman Church by the rise of the Jesuits, who were formed for the main purpose of defeating Protestantism and of regaining lost ground by any methods which promised success. The Jesuits were also prominent in developing the new moral theology, especially in Spain, and its

shape was much affected by the desire to reconcile penitents to
the Church as speedily and effectively as possible. In pursuing
their ends the Jesuits replaced the internal moral considerations
by external rules and subtleties, which sometimes had the effect
of reversing true Christian values altogether.

Blaise Pascal in his *Provincial Letters* exposed the absurd lengths
to which this kind of moral theology had gone, and his *Provincial
Letters* brought criticism both within and without the Church to
a head. A typical example of Pascal's style may be quoted from
Letter XII addressed 'To the Reverend Fathers the Jesuits', dated
9th September, 1656, on the subject of simony, murder and other
matters.

> Seriously, fathers, it would be extremely easy to hold you up to
> ridicule in this matter, and I am at a loss to know why you expose
> yourself to such treatment. To produce this effect, I have nothing
> more to do than simply to quote Escobar,[1] in his *Practice of Simony
> according to the Society of Jesus*. 'Is it simony when two Churchmen
> become mutually pledged thus: Give me your vote for my election as
> Provincial, and I shall give you mine for your election as prior? By
> no means.' Or take another: 'It is not simony to get possession of a
> benefice by promising a sum of money, when one has no intention of
> actually paying the money; for this is merely making a show of
> simony, and is as far from being real simony as counterfeit gold is
> from the genuine.' By this quirk of conscience, he has contrived
> means, in the way of adding swindling to simony, for obtaining
> benefices without simony and without money.[2]

The slashing attacks of Pascal have lived in men's memories and
go far to explain the condemnation of all casuistry, which is often
made without any reasoned justification. Nor can there be any
doubt that the attacks were soundly based. But Pascal's attacks
did not succeed in changing the course of Roman moral theology,
although they helped to prune it of its worst excrescences. He
could not do away with the legalistic and external aspect of Roman
treatment. Not only was moral theology closely connected with the
confessional, envisaged as a judgment-seat in a juridical sense, but
it was also inevitably linked with the whole subject of Canon law
and the various and numerous regulations contained in it. Indeed
it might be said that Roman theology sees moral theology and
Canon law as two aspects of the same thing, Canon law being

[1] Escobar y Mendoza (1589-1669) was one of the most prominent and
influential of the Jesuit writers.
[2] Modern Library, New York, 1941, p. 495.

externally identical with moral law. The difference would be that moral theology deals with the subjective aspect of moral behaviour, and Canon law with the objective. This seems to be borne out by H. Davis, S.J.[1]

> Canon Law is the body of church law which regulates man's conduct as a member of the visible society of the Church, that is, it imposes a certain discipline on man in his external relations within that society. Human acts must conform to the laws of the Church, since it is, for man, a divinely appointed teacher and ruler. But it is only in this external relationship, in the *forum externum*, as it is termed, that Canon law imposes specific lines of conduct, whereas Moral Theology considers the obligation in conscience, termed the *forum internum*, that arises whensoever the Church, through its canons, imposes such definite rules of conduct.

No one would claim, of course, that Canon law covers all moral duties, but merely that where it deals with a matter of human behaviour that becomes a moral law *in foro externo*.

The result of identifying Canon law with moral obligation is twofold. It has the effect of introducing an additional legalistic element into moral calculation, since the Canon law has to be interpreted in any point of vagueness before it can be discovered what the obligation is. This may and does give rise to quibbles which distract from the purely moral consideration of the problem. And in the second place the exaltation of the Canon law to a moral obligation has the effect of adding significantly to the moral demands which are made on the individual Christian, for every regulation in Canon law makes another obligation for him. Presumably in theory every layman should be conversant with the Canon law, so far as it concerns him, for otherwise he might well be guilty of transgressing it without knowing it.

The complications of a judicial attitude in the confessional and a legalistic attitude in Canon law have made moral theology in the Roman Church a legalistic exercise, and have removed it far from the other related subjects of ascetic, sacramental and pastoral theology. Recently, however, there have been significant signs among Roman Catholics of an attempt to return to a wholeness of approach in moral theology which would escape these dangers. Two works may be mentioned as indicating this new trend: B. Häring's *Das Gesetz Christi* [*The Law of Christ*] and G. Gilleman's

---

[1] *Moral and Pastoral Theology*, I, Sheed and Ward 1935, p. 2.

The Primacy of Charity in Moral Theology.[1] The former is a Redemptorist and the latter a Jesuit.

It is important that we should be aware of the general background of moral theology in the Roman Church. Roman theologians have studied the subject far more thoroughly than any other Christians during the last three centuries: we can therefore learn much from them of ways of treating the subject, and can derive from them much guidance as to significant ways of approaching moral distinctions. On the other hand we can also learn from their mistakes, so as not to become sunk in the quicksands of legalism, and not to try to go too much into detail when analysing what are imaginary cases, invented for the purpose of illustration. Ecumenical experiences in all fields ought surely to lead us to read much more of one another's writings, and should encourage students of one church tradition to find the underlying strength and truth of those of others.

Moral theology in the Anglican churches had a period of serious writing during the seventeenth century, when Joseph Hall, Jeremy Taylor and Robert Sanderson were the outstanding writers. In their approach to cases of conscience they adopted the general framework of the Schoolmen and were much indebted to St Thomas Aquinas. But they developed their own conclusions, working freely on the basis of the general principles they had adopted. Hooker earlier had also dealt with aspects of moral theology and had firmly refused to separate it from what we now call pastoral and ascetical theology, that is, those parts of theology which are concerned with man's relation to God.[2]

Side by side with the divines who may properly be called Anglican the study of moral theology was also undertaken by Puritans such as Richard Baxter, whose best-known work was *The Christian Directory*. Although there were differences in view about ecclesiastical polity, there was a general agreement upon the demands of the moral life, and the resemblances between Baxter and Taylor, for example, are more striking than their differences. But after this period of flowering the subject ceased to produce books. The main reason for its cessation was almost certainly the change in the general religious atmosphere. The seventeenth

[1] In French, 1947. Eng. tr., Burns and Oates 1960.
[2] H. R. McAdoo, *The Structure of Caroline Moral Theology*, Longmans Green 1949, p. 26.

century, like its predecessor, was a time of religious ferment, when men fought and died for their religious convictions. In England the struggle between Crown and Commonwealth, which erupted into civil war and eventually ended in the restoration of the monarchy, had rent the people in two: the struggle was semi-religious in character, involving deep emotional and psychic forces. When its end came with the restoration of Charles II in 1660—or perhaps its true end should be identified with the abdication of James II in 1688—men were mortally tired of internal strife, both political and religious. Religion ceased to be the subject of public debate and discussion in the same way, and moral theology gave way in religious interest to other subjects, some of them more fundamental. There continued to be a deep piety among Christians, but their attention in public debate moved to discussion of the nature of God in the light of Deist theories. Moral theology in a time when books were expensive and hard to publish could only flourish when public interest was concerned with Christian behaviour within a generally accepted framework of Christian belief. The concentration of debate upon defence of the Christian idea of God did not leave room for work on moral theology, and this would seem the natural explanation of its temporary disappearance.

It was not until the nineteenth century that the Oxford Movement and its successors revived interest in the subject. The new interest was certainly connected with the revival of the use of sacramental confession and the need to provide guidance to priests who were called upon to hear confessions. Priests needed to have some principles by which they could discern and also explain degrees of culpability, and thus give sound advice to those who had come to them. There was a natural tendency to turn to Continental moralists in this situation and to adapt them for Anglican purposes. Pusey himself rewrote Gaume's *Manuel des Confesseurs* in the form of *Advice for those who exercise the ministry of reconciliation through Confession and Absolution*, published in 1878.

A revival of the comprehensive study of moral theology in the Church of England did not come until after the First World War when Dr Kenneth Kirk, afterwards Bishop of Oxford, undertook it. His best-known work is his Bampton Lectures of 1928 published under the title of *The Vision of God*, in which he maintains the earlier tradition of bringing together moral theology, strictly so called, with the whole Christian life and its progress in the ways of God. In other books and frequent lectures he did much to spread interest in the subject, and it is to be regretted that there have been few successors of his calibre, though there have been various minor studies of problems of human conduct.

In Protestant circles where the study of moral theology in the sense we have been considering has not been undertaken at all for a long time, there are signs that it is provoking more interest, though the subject is approached mainly from the social angle. Moral theology in the traditional sense has started from the examination of the principles, theological and otherwise, which should guide human conduct, and has proceeded from them to study individual cases. Protestant theology in the twentieth century has tried to find Christian principles to help solve human problems, and international affairs have provoked special interest. It is significant that the Commission of the Churches on International Affairs has existed as a semi-independent body from the time of the formation of the World Council of Churches in 1948. The Protestant approach to moral problems is not unconnected with the Social Gospel which was characteristic of much Liberal Protestantism, and aroused interest in the possibility of improving social conditions on Christian moral principles. If such interests are pursued to their logical conclusions they are bound to coincide over large areas with the casuistry of moral theology proper.

There is therefore some hope, not unfounded, that studies by Roman Catholics and Protestants, and also by Anglicans who here take an independent position which coincides with neither, may bring those undertaking them to find common ground, and that this may be one more field where ecumenical co-operation and understanding will strengthen the contribution which Christianity has to make towards the guidance of mankind.

Moral Theology Today

The general position of moral theology in relation to the movements of opinion of the time has been set out in an excellent essay by G. F. Woods, entitled 'The Grounds of Christian Moral Judgments', considering the situation in relation to non-Christian approaches to moral questions.[1] He points out that the old method of using New Testament texts to support detailed moral behaviour has become more and more difficult to use, with the historical examination of the make-up of the New Testament itself. While the authority of the New Testament has in some respects been strengthened rather than weakened, and while the person of Jesus Christ is no less decisive for moral and spiritual standards, it has become impossible to isolate small portions of the New Testament writings to prove some moral point.

The new attitude to biblical texts is an important change in the attitude of many Christians, though there are still very many who have not adapted themselves to the latest state of knowledge and understanding. It affects Protestant approaches to Christian ethics, but it must also have its effect on Roman Catholic treatment, which has been marked by a conservatism in its attitude to the text of the New Testament similar to that of the Protestant fundamentalists. The question at issue is not one of making moral standards acceptable to the non-Christian, but primarily of being faithful to the best understanding of the New Testament which modern critical research has made possible. For although many ill-informed spectators regard biblical criticism as mainly destructive, the opposite is the truth. A much deeper understanding of the New Testament has come from modern study, and this will continue to be true of all the best research of the future.

G. F. Woods noted the modern tendency in certain circles to put all the emphasis upon sincerity and integrity and to ignore the possibility of objective moral standards. This is a mark of existentialism, though it betrays a lack of clear thought, for it is impossible even to define sincerity and integrity without some outside measuring rod, even if it is no more than the absolutizing of human nature. Mr Woods rightly wrote:

> A sheer emphasis upon sincerity and integrity, while supremely relevant in assessing praiseworthiness and blameworthiness, does not provide any clear ground for distinguishing between acts which are good and those which are bad.[2]

There is no doubt that one of the changes in mental climate which has most affected attitudes towards moral standards has been the diminishing appeal of the idea of the natural law, held

---

[1] In *Soundings* ed. A. R. Vidler, Cambridge 1962.   [2] *Op. cit.*, p. 207.

to be knowable by the unaided reason of man. Dr R. C. Mortimer
has written:

> The natural law, then, is the pattern of conduct laid down for men
> by the Creator, which they must follow if they would attain to their
> true end. It is perceptible by reason.[1]

This is a time-honoured method of dealing with the basic ideas
of moral theology, but it has been much weakened by the evident
fact in the modern world that this law is actually not perceived by
the reason of men who would normally be considered intelligent
and reasonable by any standards, apart from their failure to hold
the Christian faith.

In an age like Hooker's or that of St Thomas Aquinas there was
universal acceptance of the basic Christian teaching that the world
was created by God, and the general attitudes of men to natural
law derived from that atmosphere of thought and belief. In the
twentieth century the movement of opinion has been away from
such assumptions, or at least it has refused to accept such assumptions as axioms of thought. Large numbers of reasonable men in
this century do not find it easy to establish or accept a framework
of moral principles merely by the exercise of their natural reason,
unless they have already adopted a belief about the origin of the
world which makes such a framework a corollary to that belief.
As G. F. Woods writes in the essay already mentioned, 'The view
taken of the facts of any moral case is bound to differ when the
observers take different views of the world' (p. 213). Such differences run right through men's moral attitudes.

But if it is difficult, and perhaps impossible, to say that there
are any moral laws which all men of reason, whatever their beliefs,
will accept as binding, it is possible still to maintain that every
man has some sense of right and wrong which he cannot altogether
escape. This is perhaps the most important basic truth of human
morals. It is interesting to see how those who have completely
deserted Christian morals still appeal to the sense of right and
wrong to maintain their own societies and to justify their actions.
The most conspicuous example is the Communist world, where a
whole new set of moral standards, radically different from those
of the Christian world, has been adopted. The Communists, however, do not urge action because it is convenient, but because it is
right. In some ways this appeal to their own moral standards is

[1] *The Elements of Moral Theology*, A. and C. Black 1953, p. 9.

more evident among them than elsewhere. By this attitude Communists bear unintending witness to the moral sense which has been implanted in them by the Creator of all men.

It is not infrequent to find that people are misled about the general acceptance of moral laws by statements which are meaningless when analysed. A simple but common example is found when it is said 'But everyone agrees that murder is always wrong'. The fallacy is obvious. 'Murder' is a word which implies and includes the meaning of wrongness when it is done. Murder in short is to kill a person wrongly. To say therefore that murder is always wrong is merely to say that killing people wrongly is wrong. The deep differences of opinion on the subject of taking human life were vividly brought out in 1962 by a trial in Liège, Belgium, of a mother who had killed her baby, born without arms and legs as a consequence of drugs taken by the mother during pregnancy. This case will be discussed more fully at a later stage.

We find, therefore, that it is almost impossible to answer the question, 'What are the natural moral laws which every reasonable man agrees upon?' Hooker's suggestions, 'God to be worshipped; parents to be honoured; others to be used by us as we ourselves would be by them' do not sound very convincing as a basis on which all men are likely to agree, whether they be Christians or not. But we can still claim that the sense of right and wrong remains, in spite of a good many attempts to rationalize it away.

Modern life has introduced other complications into moral issues. It is a commonplace remark, and it seems to be true, that modern life is immensely more complex than that of previous centuries. This is certainly the case for the ordinary man. In former times most men were spared the need to know about the infinitely detailed and puzzling facts of national and international life. Until quite recently large numbers of men could not read, or, if they could read, they did not have access to sources which provided the facts. Now not only can they read, but into almost every home the news about national and international affairs is introduced through sight and sound broadcasting. It is difficult for ordinary people, who have little experience beyond their own social circles, to make value-judgements of any reliability about the thousands of facts, personalities and events which crowd upon them.

For those who try to take an intelligent interest in events moral judgements are made far more difficult by the complication of the issues. Such difficulty springs from the introduction of an immense number of uncertainties in each situation. In the past there were presumably just as many uncertainties facing, for example, those in charge of foreign policy. But now the ordinary man is asked, implicitly and often explicitly, to make up his mind on such far-reaching issues as whether the Anglo-French invasion of Suez was right or not in 1956 or whether the U.S.A. was right to create a naval blockade of Cuba in 1962.

The increase of complications in such moral decisions as these arises largely from the fact that a 'right' course of foreign policy must depend on whether it is likely to achieve its object or not (assuming that the object is in itself morally acceptable). In other words it must rest on calculation, the calculation of probable reactions from other people and other countries to the course of action which is proposed. Of course it is possible to rule out some courses of action as morally impermissible in any circumstances, but these are not the issues which are now being considered. The detailed study of moral standards and problems in international affairs must be left until later. Here it is important only to note that in general the element of calculation has come to play a much greater part in such decisions than has usually been recognized in the past. Because of this moral judgements have become much less certain that hitherto.

An important result of the situation is that the help of experts is often needed to a much greater degree than is commonly recognized. Christians especially who find themselves in a moral dilemma about such things as a crisis in international affairs are often tempted to try to establish some so-called moral principle as a short cut through the difficult thinking and wrestling which has to be undertaken. This is a form of moral irresponsibility. 'Frequently the expert advice will be taken from experts who make no profession of the Christian faith,'[1] a necessity which some Christians find unpalatable, though they only do so because they have an inadequate understanding of the ways of God.

It cannot be too strongly stated that Christianity and moral theology do not claim to be able to provide easy or straightforward answers to moral problems of great complexity. Moral theology has the much more limited task of trying to teach Christians to think

[1] Woods, *op. cit.*, p. 213.

clearly and correctly about moral problems, and thus to enable them to approach the actual decisions which have to be made with a better hope of being able to find their own right decision and to help other people along the same path. Great harm has been done, and continues to be done, by the idea that Christianity can put the world to rights by giving clear and simple answers to complex problems.

It is, of course, true that Christian moral theology deals with the end of man, that is, the purpose for which he is made and his own proper fulfilment, known respectively to moral theology as the objective and subjective ends of man. Moral theology claims to be searching into the ways of God and learning to do his will. This carries the inevitable implication that there is a will for man outside himself, which is in the mind and intention of God. There is also the very deep truth, not always sufficiently stressed, that the fulfilment of man depends on his seeking to find God's will and to obey it. The matter can be approached from either end, and each approach meets at the centre, the will of God. But this fulfilment and how it is to be sought, brings us back again to the point, earlier mentioned, of the full Christian life and associated pastoral, sacramental and ascetical studies.

Another important development which has affected moral theology is the modern study of psychology. There are a number of different schools which explain their findings in different ways, but among them there are some well-established facts, which have a direct bearing on the considerations of moral theology. The most important of these is perhaps the diminution of moral responsibility caused by emotional and psychological forces which are found in the personality, but which are not the direct responsibility of the person concerned. The traumatic effects of shocks experienced in early childhood which come out in almost irresistible impulses in later life are examples of this kind.

There is a school of psychology which takes a deterministic view of the psyche in an extreme form, suggesting that all our actions are caused by uncontrollable elements within us. It is difficult on this theory to see how such theorists can possibly recommend their own conclusions to others or put any value upon them themselves. For even the most rigid theorist of this kind does in fact order his life on opposite principles: he behaves as though he were a free man, able to make decisions for himself. The deterministic school cannot, of course, be accepted by a Christian, and it seems as though its influence is beginning to wane even in the U.S.A. where it had a number of strongholds.

Psychological knowledge has not affected the most important principles of moral theology, but it has made it necessary to change certain distinctions, such as that between mortal and venial sin. This will be more fully discussed later on: all that needs saying here is that, although it may still be possible to maintain a theoretical distinction between mortal and venial sin, in practice it has become quite impossible to apply it. It ought therefore to to be completely abolished. Even before psychological knowledge made it senseless, there were many objections to it. The distinction has mainly been used in Roman Catholic moral theology, though some Anglicans have also used it. It is hoped that it will now fall into well-deserved desuetude.

3

THE NATURAL LAW

'Natural Law' and the Christian

THE EXPRESSION 'NATURAL law' has a number of different meanings. It may mean the laws of nature as they are actually observed to occur in the world, especially in the physical world. On an assumption of unalterable natural law the development of modern science has largely been founded. This approach to the natural law postulates an unbreakable chain of cause and effect which can therefore be investigated by scientific methods. Such a concept has been applied to psychological phenomena and has encouraged deterministic theories in that field.

The natural law has historically played an important part in moral theology, and it still does so, especially within the Roman Catholic Church. It needs, however, to be carefully examined before it can be used, for in many of its manifestations it has done more harm than good. It is commonly supposed to be the foundation of scholastic moral theology, and St Thomas Aquinas to have been the most influential thinker in introducing it into Christian theology. Thus Professor Boorman writes:[1] 'The Thomistic system is rooted not in the Gospel but in natural or moral law, that is, in the affirmation of "common and indemonstrable principles" which are apprehended by man's natural reason'. He quotes with approval Paul Ramsey's question,[2]

> By what is Christian ethics to be distinguished from generally valid natural morality, if some theory of natural law becomes an authentic part and to any degree the *primary* foundation of Christian morality?

There have been many Protestant theologians who refuse to have anything to do with the concept of natural law in Christian morals, but there is a growing tendency among present-day

[1] *Canadian Journal of Theology*, vol. VI, no. 3.
[2] *Basic Christian Ethics*, New York and London 1950, p. 86.

Protestants to accept some limited place for the idea of natural law within the context of the Christian revelation and Gospel. As we have observed, there can be no satisfactory foundation for Christian conduct which is based on less than the message of Christ and his personal saving work. Otherwise Christ becomes for men an optional extra, with disastrous results, for it is only in and through Christ that the possibilities of human nature can be fully realized, since the gap between man and God is closed by God's own action through Christ.

In the above paragraphs the term 'natural law' has been used in two distinct senses. It has meant (*a*) the order of nature as created by God and observed by man, and (*b*) the sense of right and wrong supposed to exist on a certain number of moral propositions which can be understood by man's reason alone. It is important for our clarity of thought that when the phrase is used we should be clear which use of it we are taking.

Let us consider each in turn and take the second of the two first. We have earlier pointed out that the general acceptance of Christian attitudes which was common in earlier centuries does not now exist. In former times nobody thought of questioning the divine origin of the world or the general basic Christian teaching about it, and theologians were thus encouraged to base upon this supposed moral agreement more than it will in fact bear. It has become clear in recent years that there are very few, if any, principles of natural moral law on which everyone is agreed. It is still possible to claim that the universal and inherent sense of right and wrong indicates that there are moral distinctions which men are meant to observe. But this sense cannot be made the foundation of any moral superstructure of natural moral law. Moreover the growth in the twentieth century of political systems and beliefs which have altogether abandoned Christian principles has made it clear that men's moral outlooks depend much more than was formerly supposed on their underlying beliefs as to what is true in the religious field.

But even were it possible to establish a substantial natural moral law, it would not be satisfactory from a Christian point of view, for the Christian teaching of the love of God has radically changed the value of such general moral principles. When moral values are transferred from outside Christianity to within it, they become completely different in their meaning and content. There may, it is true, be a certain external resemblance, but it is the inner content which alone finally matters. The external in Christianity is always secondary, the inner man is always primary. The teaching of Jesus Christ gives plain witness to this again and again, the best examples being in the Sermon on the Mount in St Matthew's Gospel, chapters 5 to 7.

The general acceptance of a natural moral theology led theologians into the mistake of giving far too much attention to it in their schemes of treatment. This tendency was increased by the fact that it became the custom, following St Thomas, to base a discussion of the virtues on the Stoic quartet of the 'cardinal' virtues (from *cardo* = hinge)—prudence, temperance, justice and fortitude. In some Christian writers it is suggested that these virtues may be distinguished from the theological virtues (faith, hope and love) on account of the fact that they are able to be achieved by the natural man, they are natural virtues, while the three theological virtues are supernatural virtues, only to be achieved through the grace of God. A similar division has also sometimes been made in ascetical theology between the acquired and infused parts of prayer. In both cases the divisions are abhorrent to the true nature of Christianity, for if God does not inform every part of the Christian life and transform it, then the message of Christ is radically altered.

But, it may be said, there are many people who are not Christians who do in fact exhibit the cardinal virtues, often more perfectly than Christians. Are we to conclude that such persons are not virtuous after all? It is not necessary to answer this question in the negative. Heroic virtue is found among those who are not Christian, but it is not the same in its inner nature as the virtue practised by a Christian. The difference can be seen most clearly in the attitude of a man before and after conversion to Christ. There are many men who lived a virtuous life before being brought to put their faith in Christ. After their conversion they continue to live a virtuous life, which so far as those particular virtues are concerned, does not appear to differ much, if at all, from their life before conversion. But its inner nature has been changed by submission to Christ, and their outlook upon everything they do has been changed too. Behaving well to his neighbour no longer expresses merely a moral standard of desirable behaviour for idealistic or for other reasons, it becomes now a form of the expression of the love of God shown in Christ and spread abroad in his heart. The outside observer may say that this cannot be proved, and he is right. He must rely on the unanimous testimony of all those Christians who have in fact gone through this experience, that this is what occurs. The inner man is changed, enlightened by love and empowered by unity in Christ.

What then is the status of the virtuous non-Christian? He has some light from his human nature, for that also is the creation of a loving God. From this light, if he tries to live according to it, he finds a real though limited satisfaction, for he is trying to live in the way and for the ends for which he has been made. But he can never know the fulness of life which comes only through Christ. In countries where Christianity has long influenced the ideals and standards of society a man also shares in a sort of reflected Christian light, and to that degree his attitude is informed by Christian experience in the society and family life in which he partakes.

A Christian will thank God for the good which is in the world in spite of the power of evil, but he must never so speak or act as to make people so satisfied with such an interim condition that they cease to suppose that the full acceptance of Christianity is important. For as Jesus himself says, 'I am the way, the truth and the life', and, as that is true, there can be no complete fulfilment except in him. 'No man cometh to the Father but by me.'

It is impossible to come to any useful final conclusions by the *external* comparison of one life with another. Christians as well as others are constantly committing this mistake. Each man differs from his fellow in numerous ways. Each begins with his own natural endowments, which may be rich or poor; he is affected deeply by his relationship with his parents and other members of his family, as well as by other aspects of his environment; he may be strong or weak in health; he may be exposed to severe trials or to few. All such differences make it impossible for one person to judge another in the sense of reaching any final conclusion about his innermost character. This surely is what Jesus meant when he said, 'Judge not and ye shall not be judged.'

Yet the external measurement is not without value, since the ideals of the Christian life, and even of the moral non-Christian world, provide a stimulus to men to try to attain them, and they do in fact represent what is the only ideal in which fulfilment for mankind can be found. Even though the cardinal virtues without Christianity cannot give fulness of life, yet they can help men to approximate to what God wants them to be. Like the Old Testament they can be schoolmasters to bring us to Christ (Gal. 3.24).

It is important here to understand that Christians do not look down on those who have not found the key to fulfilment in Christ. They may in one sense look up to those who have made heroic efforts to obey a high moral code, far more heroic perhaps than most Christians could achieve. A Christian attitude is one of love, which wishes to share with them the secret of life which alone can meet all those hidden and known desires which God has planted in them, for the Christian knows the truth of the famous words of St Augustine in the first chapter of his *Confessions*: 'Thou madest us for Thyself, and our heart is restless, until it repose in Thee.'

But the cardinal virtues are not in themselves the first stage of the Christian life, though in cases of virtuous non-Christians, who are afterwards converted to the Christian faith, they may in fact play a preliminary part, as we have already suggested. It is important that Christians should not view them as the first stages of *Christian* activity in Christians. When a man is trying to live in Christ, the cardinal virtues, like every other part of his behaviour, are transformed by that life. They do not come *before* the theological virtues; they are, so to speak, aspects of the life of faith, hope and love as seen in relation to particular problems and people. Thus justice is not something which to a Christian is an independent virtue on its own: it is the expression of the love of Christ as it is seen in personal relations between one man and another in society. Prudence is not some kind of wisdom detached from any other consideration: it is the judgement of man enlightened by the mind of Christ. Temperance similarly is the attitude to the use of things which is informed by the teaching of Christ and illuminated by his life, while fortitude is that readiness to sacrifice oneself in the cause of Christ, which springs from sharing with him the life of sacrifice, passion and crucifixion.

The natural law, therefore, does not exist as a separate entity for a man who is a Christian, for everything is transfigured by Christ. Nevertheless he is ready to meet other people where they are, and to do whatever is possible with non-Christians to order human affairs as nearly as is possible to what he understands to be the will of God. For that too is an expression of Christian love. A Christian loves his neighbour, he appreciates all the good in him, thanking God for all of it, and he is ready to work with him for the good of mankind. We cannot base Christian morals on a concept of the natural law, but we can see how the idea of the natural law influences the lives of our non-Christian fellow men; and, because of it, we see in their strivings towards a better world the reflection of the love of God who made them and put into their hearts such hopes for higher things.

The acceptance of a natural moral theology has usually been associated with Roman Catholic moralists, and Protestant theologians have often made this a cause of serious complaint. They have seen it as one more piece of evidence that the Roman Catholics want to exalt works and to avoid the true doctrine that we are saved by faith and God's grace alone. Yet curiously enough there is also a strong stream of natural moralism in the Protestant churches, and, as it is often not balanced by an adequate sacramental doctrine and practice, it is apt to be even more 'natural' than that of the Roman Catholics. It is evident in the outlook of the English-speaking peoples, which is often more moralistic than religious. Religion itself is often seen and interpreted in exclusively moralistic terms.

But the most striking example of natural morality in modern times is the movement called Moral Re-Armament (M.R.A.), originally the Oxford Group Movement, led by Dr Frank Buchman until his death in 1962. The movement began by being avowedly Christian, but now welcomes adherents of any religion or none. It bases its appeal largely on a claim to be a successful ideology against Communism, and it takes considerable credit for successes in the secular field, the evidence for which is not always convincing to the outsider. The central affirmation of M.R.A. is the acceptance in the lives of its members of what are known as the four 'absolutes' of honesty, purity, unselfishness and love.

M.R.A. is a typical product of the Protestant American world, its founder having originally been a Baptist minister in the U.S.A. In pursuing the four absolutes it does not disdain religion, and the movement's concept of guidance is an integral part of its activities, though theologically questionable in practice. Among M.R.A. members are many keen Christians, and it may be readily admitted that the movement has been the means of rejuvenating and reinspiring the Christian lives of many who, before contact with M.R.A., were merely nominal Christians. But this Christian element is incidental to its general programme and it must be judged on what is common to all its members rather than on what is peculiar to one section of them. And when it is examined from this point of view, it is found to have an exclusively moralistic programme.

It is not our purpose here to examine or pass judgement on the movement of M.R.A. as a whole, but we merely take notice of it as an interesting phenomenon based on a natural morality, in which the person of Christ and Christian teaching are optional extras for its members.

What is Natural

We come then to the second sense in which 'natural law' is used. Hitherto we have been discussing the theory that man can within certain limits know what is right and what is wrong by the unaided use of his reason and an ingrained moral sense. We have seen that this sense is so limited as to be of little practical use when it comes to deciding moral issues, though we have recognized that the sense of right and wrong itself is so universally known as to give some reason for thinking that it is an integral part of human nature as such.

Connected with this moral sense, but different from it, is the attempt to establish moral norms by reference to what is also termed the 'natural law' in the sense that the natural law can be discovered by observation and deduction from nature itself. In other words the will of God can be found by observing the way in which the world and human nature works. This approach plays a part of importance in Roman Catholic morality, and it must be carefully examined to see whether it is soundly based. The establishment of moral law by a process of reasoning only makes sense if the previously discussed use of the term 'natural law' is accepted, namely that it is possible to reach a definite conclusion by reason alone.

No theologian will deny that man's reason is given him by God. Any such denial would put the theologian out of business. And, although in the past the doctrine of total depravity has sometimes been maintained, it is rare to hear it upheld nowadays, perhaps for the same cause that theologians do not deny the use of reason. If man's reason is totally depraved it is not of much use to try to exercise it, nor is it worth the trouble to examine what comes out as a result of such exercise. The reasoning faculty is, when rightly exercised, a reflection of God's own nature to the small degree that men and women can share in it. But it cannot be detached from God's revelation without being twisted and made unreliable. Man is not altogether without the light, but he suffers from his own lack of wholeness and from that of the world in which he lives. It is therefore dangerous to maintain that the natural exercise of reason can be decisive in the moral field, not because it undermines the Christian faith (though it does so), but because, if the Christian faith is true, it is more likely than not to lead to fatally wrong conclusions.

If we believe that the world is created by God, we must also believe that within it he established an order which was intended to bring everything within it to fulfilment. This order has been twisted and disordered by sin. While therefore it is possible to make some deductions from the natural order, they can only rightly be made within the context of what Christ has taught us through his own life and death. A higher law than that of nature has been revealed to us through Christ, and this means that the true meaning of nature can only be properly seen in the light of this higher law. We have therefore to be very careful not to allow our reasoning process to exclude Christ until the end of the process, when it is too late for him to affect its main content.

To see the limitations of human reasoning is not to lower the standards which the will of God requires. It guarantees and reinforces those standards as part of his revelation to mankind by using reason in the right perspective. Let us then examine one field in which the appeal of reason to the natural law plays an important part in Roman Catholic moral theology, that of sexual relations. Many of the laws which have been adopted by the Roman Church in sexual matters are based on the claim that they give expression to the natural law. For example, the use of contraceptives in married sexual intercourse is forbidden by that Church on the grounds that such use is against the natural law. The general point of view has been expressed, in connection with a similar matter, by Fr H. Davis, S.J., as follows:[1]

> Man and woman, being subject to the Natural law in respect of procreation, may not positively thwart the primary intentions of nature, that is of God, whilst using the powers which nature has given them for a definite purpose and for that purpose alone.

[1] *Moral and Pastoral Theology*, I, p. 131.

The Roman view of contraception within marriage is that it does in fact thwart the primary intentions of nature and therefore must always be forbidden, since it cannot be essential to have sexual intercourse. This makes two important assumptions. It assumes that we can in fact discover the primary intentions of nature, and it assumes that these intentions are the same as those of God. Neither of these assumptions is self-evident.

The phrase 'primary intentions of nature' is somewhat ambiguous. 'Primary' may mean first in time, or first in importance, with others which follow in time or importance almost on the same level; or it may be used in the sense of the only intentions which matter, or to which attention should be paid. It seems that its use here, and very frequently in Roman Catholic treatment, is a mixture of the two. Fr Davis begins by using 'primary' in the sense of being rather more important than others, and, having had its use accepted in this sense, goes on to use it in the more restrictive sense of the only thing which ought to be allowed.

If we consider the physical aspect of life alone, it will be generally agreed that the main purpose of sexual intercourse between human beings is the procreation of children. This is certainly true of animals, in which it serves the propagation of the species. In men and women, when their animal qualities are abstracted from the rest of their lives, the same thing can be said. But when we have accepted this fact, it does not get us any nearer to moral judgements than we were before we began, for the whole point about human beings is that they are moral beings and animals are not: this is another way of saying that they are not exclusively physical, and physical considerations alone cannot possibly be taken as establishing a norm for moral behaviour.

But there is another confusion besides the use of the word 'primary'. It is this: the phrase 'natural law' is used in two different senses. It is first used to describe the physical conditions which we have just mentioned, and in the physical sphere it could reasonably be said that the procreation of children is the natural result of sexual intercourse, or, that it is the result according to the 'natural law' (in this sense). The phrase 'the natural law', which has been used in an exclusively physical sense, is then given a moral connotation and used in a moral sense. So the argument goes as follows: physically, sexual intercourse is connected with the procreation of children according to the natural law; but we are

morally bound to obey the natural law; therefore sexual intercourse
which is disassociated from the procreation of children is a moral
offence. The fault in this argument is that we are only bound to
obey the natural law when it is the natural *moral* law, established
unalterably by moral principles. We are not bound to obey the
natural physical law as such.

It is hardly necessary to buttress this statement with further
examples, but the whole way we deal with medicine and surgery is
an example of thwarting the natural results of physical events, and
thus changing the physical natural law. Of course all such acts are
serving a higher purpose of life and health, and that is their moral
justification. The point is that the natural law in the physical
sphere has no moral claim on man *of itself*: it is morally neutral
until it is related to other aspects of man's moral, intellectual and
spiritual life.

It is, as we have said, his moral sense which makes man different
from animals. It would therefore be the height of absurdity to
argue that he is bound to act as though he had no moral sense, or
as though his moral sense had no relevance or importance in regard
to his actions. But that is just what the argument from physical
natural law implies. For if man is bound morally without further
consideration by what takes place physically, or seems to be in
accord with physical arrangements, it makes nonsense of his
reason and of his spiritual status.

We are therefore driven to the conclusion that what we discover
about the physical laws of man's nature has to be used and directed
by moral principles. This is in any case the way in which we normally act over a large range of human life. The moral call to man
to relieve suffering, to assist health, to educate children and to prolong life all depend on a moral valuation of human life and wholeness and not on the merely natural physical world. How then, one
may ask, is it possible to say that the use of contraceptives within
married life is illegitimate if, in fact, the moral aims of married life
are assisted by their use? It may reasonably be held that it is in-
advisable to depart from the normal use of a human act unless
there are positive gains to be achieved in the moral field, but that
is a far less certain and demanding attitude than prohibition.

The quotation earlier taken from Fr Davis's book exhibits not
only the faults which we have been criticizing in exalting what he
terms 'the primary intentions of nature', but he identifies these, as

defined by himself on merely physical grounds, with the will of God by adding 'that is of God'. If we take the phrase 'natural law' to mean the whole of God's purpose, then there is not the same difficulty, since God's purpose must in the case of man take into consideration all those moral and spiritual considerations which differentiate man from the rest of the animal world. In this sense there is indeed a truth of great depth, and one particularly important for moral theology, namely the need for following God's laws in order that man may fulfil his own personality. But that is to take the whole of man—physical, mental, spiritual—as one whole, in which the demands of each aspect of his personality can only be met in a fruitful and growing relationship with one another within an integrated life.

Natural Law and Revelation

W. Lillie[1] draws attention to the recognition of the natural law by Jesus when answering a question as to whether divorce was permissible. Referring to the permission under the law of Moses for a man to divorce his wife by a note of dismissal, Jesus said (NEB Mark 10.5):

It was because you were so unteachable that he made this rule for you; but in the beginning, at the creation, God made them male and female. For this reason a man shall leave his father and mother, and be made one with his wife; and the two shall become one flesh. It follows that they are no longer two individuals; they are one flesh. What God has joined together, man must not separate.

Too much weight must not be put on one extract, but according to this account, repeated by St Matthew, Jesus returned to the original form of the natural law, condemning, to some extent at least, the exceptions allowed by Moses. But it is unlikely that Jesus is here merely enunciating a law which must be obeyed in the spirit of legal exactness, for that goes against the whole tenor of his teaching, especially noticeable in the Sermon on the Mount. The true meaning of this passage is almost certainly an emphasis on not departing from the order of creation, and on the truth that it is only when man lives in accord with God's creative work that he can fulfil God's will. In other words Jesus is saying that, although Moses found it temporarily necessary to permit divorce because of the shortcomings of the people, in the long run it does

[1] *Studies in New Testament Ethics*, Oliver and Boyd 1961, pp. 16ff.

not prove satisfactory, because it is not in full accord with the mind of God when he made mankind. If this is the true sense, Jesus would once again be reinterpreting the Jewish law, as he did in the Sermon on the Mount, and pointing his hearers to the underlying principles on which alone fulfilment can be based. It is such an attitude which ought to inform the Christian's approach to natural law and the problems of moral theology, whether concerned with marriage or with other moral issues. Jesus, as he so often does, puts his finger on the tension which has to be faced, lived with, and creatively used by man. On the one hand we see the need for Christians and the Church to witness to the true principles of morality, and on the other the need, springing from Christian love, to minister pastorally to the people whom Jesus came to save.

Lutheran theology does not have much to say about moral theology as such, but Bishop Gustaf Aulén, one of the greatest modern Lutheran theologians, has some interesting remarks about the natural law in his book *The Faith of the Christian Church*.[1]

Christian faith in God as Creator is inseparably connected with the idea of God's law. In the combination, Creator-creation, there is implicit the ideal of law and a definite order. For faith it is a fundamental and essential point of view that creation stands in contrast to and implies a victory over chaos. Creation in and by itself is subject to the Creator, under his dominion, and under obligation to obey that order which is contained and given in the act of creation. The law which is thus connected with creation is a universal law and is unconditionally valid.

The idea *lex naturae* has often appeared as a substitute for the *lex creationis*, or *lex creatoris*, of Christian faith. *Lex naturae*, the law of nature, could be described as a rationalized and secularized variety of *lex creationis*. The foundation of both is a universal law. The difference between them can be defined in this way, that *lex naturae* is a metaphysical conception, while *lex creationis* is a religious concept, originating in the relation to God and inseparably connected with faith in God as Creator. The idea *lex naturae* or law of nature rests on the false assumption that in a purely rational way a reasonable system of law and justice could be deduced which would be both universally applicable and definite in content. In reality there is no such fixed natural law. A rational analysis can only demonstrate the existence of various and competing systems. Christian faith has no reason whatever to attach itself to the idea of *lex naturae*, especially since it has in the concept of *lex creationis* that universal and unconditionally valid law which men try in vain to reach by a purely rational method.

[1] Muhlenburg Press, Philadelphia 1948, p. 188.

The school of Lund theology, of which Bishop Aulén is one of the foremost exponents, is well known for its abhorrence of anything metaphysical being allowed to mix itself up with the theological. Aulén in the paragraphs just quoted makes a strong and valid point in maintaining that it is in fact impossible to deduce one natural and binding law from metaphysical presuppositions. Nevertheless he draws the line a little too sharply, for there is surely something in common between the man who is attempting to find such a law metaphysically and the Christian who has found such a law from his faith in God as Creator. The metaphysical seeker has made a kind of act of faith in postulating the existence of such a law, for otherwise he would not be trying to find it. It is true that the act of faith is misplaced and his search is doomed to frustration. Nevertheless he can be told that his apprehension of a universally valid law is a dim knowledge of the truth, which can be satisfied only in the Christian faith. Here is a point where Christian and metaphysical seeker have a small area in common, and, if this is the case, it is a point where Christian and non-Christian can speak to one another.

The impossibility of relying on the reason for any final conclusions about the natural law is stressed in the Anglican tradition too. The seventeenth century saw a considerable revival of moral theology in England and Jeremy Taylor was perhaps its greatest exponent. 'Reason', he wrote,[1] 'is such a box of quicksilver that it abides nowhere; it dwells in no settled mansion; it is like a dove's neck, or a changeable taffeta; it looks to me otherwise than to you who do not stand in the same light that I do; and if we enquire after the law of nature by the rules of our reason, we shall be as uncertain as the discourse of the people, or the dreams of disturbed fancies.' He thinks reason by itself to be an insufficient test of what the law of nature is, and that it must be supplemented by revelation.

The truth of Taylor's words is amply demonstrated in the world of today. For whenever a critical case arises which concerns the natural law, there are intelligent and distinguished persons who take diametrically opposite views. The case of the birth of babies deformed as a result of the drug thalidomide is a tragic example of the confusion in men's minds. On one side were those who considered it wrong deliberately to take innocent life, while on the others were those who thought it self-evident that to kill the baby

---

[1] *Ductor Dubitantium*, Bk II, ch. i, Rule i.

out of hand was the only moral course. Both sides appealed to love as the justification for their attitude.

But when all the shortcomings of the idea of natural law are accepted, it must still be maintained that man has by nature a sense of right and wrong, which, when rightly balanced, can and should lead him towards God and urge him on to find what are the true laws of his being and how they can best be observed.

It seems plain, then, that we can use the concept of natural law, and give reason an important place in a subsidiary role, but that throughout our treatment we must insist that their place and importance can only rightly be understood when they are taken with the facts which we have from revelation. They must be checked by reference to the New Testament and the Early Church, by which alone we can truly know what is God's will for us and for the human race in general. If it were not so, we should find ourselves in the position of suggesting that the natural reason of a man is all that is necessary for him to perceive what is the truth about God, whereas in fact all it can do for him is to give some indication of the direction in which he should look.

This means that the establishment of the content of the natural moral law must depend too on what we learn from Christ, and not be based on universal consent. We can say that reason and the wide acceptance of moral law by men indicate the original purpose of God and, where they are confirmed by Christ, unlock the door to the true understanding of human nature.

St Thomas Aquinas himself recognized the limitations of reason when he wrote, 'No one can know the eternal law, as it is in itself, except the blessed who see God in his essence' (I-II q.93, a.2). And he went on to say that what men see is only a reflection of the truth, which varies from man to man according to his circumstances and capabilities. Kirk in writing of the same subject summed up St Thomas's attitude as meaning that 'Natural law, in fact, means simply the satisfaction in harmony one with another, of the natural human instincts, as much on their intellectual as on their physical sides. A modern psychologist could scarcely better this statement.'[1]

The End of Man

A discussion of the end of man, i.e. the purpose for which he

---

[1] *Some Principles of Moral Theology*, p. 182.

has been made, has always formed part of moral theology. Traditionally the end of man has been divided into two parts for the purpose of discussion, though the two parts are merely theoretical distinctions and cannot be separated in practice. They are the objective and the subjective ends of man. The objective end of man is the purpose of man viewed, so to say, from the point of view of the plan of God. Man's objective end is God's plan for him, the purpose for which God has made him. The subjective end of man is the fulfilment of man, looked at from the point of view of his own interests. The two ends are in fact two aspects of the same thing, and therefore the answer to the question What is the objective end of man? is the same as the answer to What is the subjective end of man? For man clearly cannot be fulfilled unless he develops in accordance with the laws of his own nature, which are those laws implanted by God for the purpose which he intended.

In the past the main stress in considering the end of man has been on the objective end of man. The main thought has been of the purpose of God, his creative act and redemptive aim, and one result has been to encourage an attitude of mind which sees the whole moral problem chiefly as God acting upon man *from without*. A prominent feature of the mental picture has been that of an omnipotent God decreeing what shall be the future of man. This has easily passed into a picture of the divine Lawgiver imposing laws on his creatures to which they have to respond, with various penalties awarded for failures to obey the laws which are laid down. There is truth in this conception, but it is only part of the truth. Too much emphasis on the idea of God as Lawgiver can and does easily conceal or disguise his character as Love.

If God is seen mainly as Lawgiver, it is difficult to escape from the categories of the Old Testament law into the freedom of the Gospel. In the Anglican tradition there has been perhaps an over-emphasis on the Old Testament. Too much of the Old Testament is read too often in church with the result that many church-goers absorb more of the ideas of the Old Testament than they do of the New. When, added to this, there is a Sunday school system which often spends the first years of the child's Sunday school experience in telling it Old Testament stories, the imbalance becomes dangerous.

Theoretically the balance of the Church's teaching can be put

right in Confirmation classes, but far more children go to Sunday
school than ever reach Confirmation. They are left with a very
lopsided view of what the Christian religion is, and this view is
reflected in the image of the Church which is popularly prevalent.
From many points of view the reading of the Ten Commandments
at every Communion Service is a dangerous practice. It is something to be devoutly thankful for that the Ten Commandments
may be dropped in favour of the Summary of the Law. Without
them the Holy Communion service is better balanced, and at least
avoids misleading the people by suggesting that the Ten Commandments are binding on Christians in the same form as they
were given in the Old Testament.

Mattins and Evensong also seem to have too much of the Old
Testament in them. The Old Testament lesson is given the same
prominence as the message of the Gospel. Another substantial
part of the service is taken up with the singing of psalms, which
need to be interpreted in the light of the Gospel if they are to be
properly understood, even in their beautiful and positive passages.
For Christians who are intelligent and have advanced a certain
distance in their faith the Old Testament and the Psalms can be
and are fruitful sources of devotion. But to those who are simple
and unlearned they may easily become a trap to conceal the true
message of the Gospel.

No one would suggest that the transcendence of God should be
played down: that is not the point. The transcendence of God is
a vital part of understanding the Gospel, but his transcendence
has nothing to do with an approach to religion which puts all the
emphasis on God as lawgiver, punishing those who disobey him
and rewarding those who follow his instructions. The truth which
is contained in this attitude is a sort of parable, which has to be
worked out and related to other truths before it can be of usefulness to a Christian.

The understanding of the subjective end of man, i.e. the way in
which he can find fulfilment, is necessary to counter-balance over-
emphasis on the objective end. But, as so often happens, the
pendulum has swung too far, so that today interest is focused on
man's subjective end without the balance given by the other
realization. Modern psychology has had a great influence in
encouraging this tendency, for it is of its nature concerned with
fulfilment and with the removal of obstacles to man's growth and

development, at least in the practical branch of psychiatry. Many psychologists do not believe in God, and as a consequence they do not take into consideration the ultimate purpose of fulfilment, as Christians understand it. But for all psychologists, whether Christians or not, it is necessary for the purpose of their work to abstract the conduct of their science from ultimate ends which might prejudice a strictly scientific attitude in their work. It is axiomatic that modern science works within the strict limits of verifiable experiment in the science concerned, and rigidly excludes *a priori* or external influences as far as possible. This is right and Christian, for in terms of the technique of scientific research this is an indispensable means of seeking and finding the truth. Such methods of research do not of course rule out a Christian explanation of the meaning and destiny of man. Indeed in psychology and psychiatry they tend more and more to confirm it in various ways.

But the inevitable result of scientific method in psychological research is that the attention becomes focused exclusively upon the mind and personality of man, and this inevitably throws out of balance a true understanding of man's subjective end in relation to his objective end. This is the danger from which not even Christians always escape. These dangers must be guarded against. Nevertheless the subjective emphasis in itself is useful and helps to put right the lack of balance springing from the lawgiver concept. It is probable that it is more Christian to err on the side of concern with the subjective end than the objective end, merely on the ground of the incarnation of Jesus Christ and his identification with the problems and difficulties of fulfilment of human nature which it entailed.

The objective end of man is to do what God has created him to do. It is not the business of moral theology to justify or demonstrate the truth of Christian faith on this point, but merely to state it. Its justification belongs to other theological disciplines. Man has been created to glorify God and to love him and live with him for ever. This is the message of the Bible and the constant affirmation of the Christian Church. The objective ultimate end of man differs from that of other creatures in that he has a free choice whether or not to pursue it, whereas the other parts of creation do not have such a choice. Foxes have holes in which to live and breed their young: in digging such holes and making their nests they are not exercising a free choice in the human sense but instinctively fulfilling their end. A man has the choice whether to build a house or not, what kind of house it shall be, what it shall be made of, whether it shall be sold or rented to another. He likewise has free choice whether or not to pursue his ultimate objective end as God has planned. It is important to bear in mind man's objective last end when thinking about his moral and spiritual problems and aspirations.

But it is not enough to leave the matter there. Christianity does not stop short at a position which might be derived solely from the first chapter of Genesis. Genesis for a Christian cannot be understood without Christ. The whole understanding of man depends on the knowledge that God was incarnate in Christ, become man for our benefit to bring us to him. In everything therefore in which man and his interest and duties are concerned the Gospel of Jesus Christ is to be found, and all will be coloured by its message. It is important to stress this because too often moral theology has been made to appear a slightly tinted version of non-Christian moral codes. This is put by Professor J. Arthur Boorman of McGill University as follows:[1]

> The ethical system of St Thomas is a two-storey structure which is largely Aristotelian on the first level and Biblical on the second. Accordingly, the cardinal virtues are separated from the theological, and moral precepts distinguished from evangelical counsels. And although the Greek virtues and precepts are 'baptized', that is, they are 'infused together with charity', the whole scheme is a highly organized system of prudential ethics which bears little fundamental resemblance to the ethics of the New Testament.

While not ready to admit that Professor Boorman is quite fair in his criticism, we cannot deny that the followers of St Thomas Aquinas have not infrequently given an impression which justifies his strictures. But Roman Catholic moral theology is moving away from its emphasis on the natural law and its tendency to discuss the subject in terms which are difficult to distinguish from those of Aristotle. Moral theology cannot be content with such an approach just because it is concerned with the Christian life, with the communion of life and love between a Christian and God in Jesus Christ. The Christian is not therefore merely engaged in trying to calculate his own interests from a spiritual point of view, but he is caught up in the life, death and resurrection of Christ

[1] *Canadian Journal of Theology*, vol. VI, No. 3 (1960).

his Saviour, and partakes of the love of God which in Christ and through Christ lifts him up into itself.

His morality therefore is a morality of the love of Christ.

> Commandment and law also retain their place and their validity in the imitation of Christ. But for those who follow Christ, they cease to be mere impersonal forces intervening between God and the soul. They are the living words of Christ addressed to us. They are an ever new appeal of Christ through His grace to us, holding us responsible for fulfillment of His 'great command' according to the measure and standard of the grace He has given us.[1]

For the same reason a Christian morality is religious and of the nature of a dialogue.

> Christian moral teaching, it is evident, is not anthropocentric. It does not center in man. Nor is it theocentric in a sense alien to man and foreign to his world. It centers in grace-endowed fellowship of man with God, in the dialogue of word and response, in 'responsibility'. Only if it is centered in Christ does our moral life possess the worth of response made to God, for Christ is the Word in whom the Father seeks and calls us. Our loving obedience in the imitation of Christ is the echo, the image, the participation in the triune eternal life of God, in the Word and the response of love.
> It is possible for us to follow Christ, to imitate Him, because He is the 'Word' in whom our likeness to God rests and through whom it has been wonderfully restored by the Redemption.[2]

The sort of approach illustrated by these quotations from a Roman Catholic scholar is far from the attitude which Dr Boorman criticizes, and closer to that of many Protestant writers. It denies by implication a treatment which separates God and man in considering man's last end, and shows that from a Christian point of view no moral question can be adequately considered except in conjunction with the new hope and new life which we have in Christ.

In making Christ central to the moral issue we see also how it is that the objective and subjective end of man are really one thing. For if we ask what is the aim of man, we must reply that it is to find fulfilment of human potentialities, as found in human nature and discovered in a particular combination in each individual person. In such fulfilment, and only in such fulfilment, can a man find true happiness, for happiness is the absence of frustration and the flowering of man's capabilities. Such flowering can only come

---

[1] B. Häring, *op. cit.*, I, p. 52. [2] *Ibid.*, I, pp. 52.

about when the laws of growth and health for man are complied with, and the only way in which such compliance can be achieved is by the redeemed life of union with God in Christ, the perfectly fulfilled man.

But if such statements are true, it must also follow that the absence of such unity with Christ must be a failure causing unhappiness and sickness. Such failure may come in two ways: it may be caused by circumstances and be no fault of the person concerned; or it may come from a deliberate rejection of Christ when he is presented as a choice, so that a man hears the voice saying 'Follow me', but chooses not to obey. This may occur in many different ways, and when it does occur it is called sin.

Man's clarity of vision and capacity for choosing aright is partly vitiated by sin, both his own and that of others. Moreover he lives in a world where evil is rampant so that the choices before him are often complicated versions of imperfect alternatives. Yet we must maintain that man is still capable of choosing the right, unless he is psychologically ill to such an extent as to be no longer capable of exercising his reason. It is an academic question as to whether man is totally depraved and has the power of choice by an immediate act of God's grace, or whether he still retains some power of discerning truth from a lie: the effect is the same. Man can choose, as we shall see more fully later, for, if he cannot, it makes complete nonsense of the life of Christ and of his teaching, which clearly rest upon the assumption that man can hear the message, and if he chooses, can respond to it.

4

CONSCIENCE

Conscience and Freud

THERE ARE TWO aspects of conscience which should be distinguished for the sake of clear thinking. The first is the general sense of right and wrong, and the second the application of that sense of right and wrong to particular moral problems. The first is known by the Greek word synteresis (συντηρήσις), and the second by the Latin word *conscientia. Synteresis* does not appear in the New Testament,[1] but it is a useful word for the purpose of the distinction just made. We must give some consideration to it first.

Earlier we maintained that there is in fact a universal sense of right and wrong in men and women, and that this suggested, though it did not prove, that the sense corresponded to a permanent reality in the world and a permanent part of human nature itself. (The word 'sense' here is meant in a general way and is not intended to refer to a separate faculty, perhaps 'general consciousness' would be the best description of it.) In recent years, however, there has been a new view, propagated mainly by certain psychologists, that this sense of right and wrong has no objective validity, but that it is merely the reflection within the human personality of opinions and outlooks which have been acquired from the environment and influences to which it has been exposed. This point of view needs to be examined, especially as there are some Christian theologians who seem to support it by the approach which they take to moral problems.

Before discussing the origin of a sense of right and wrong it is again necessary to emphasize the distinction between the conviction that *there are* some things which are right and some which are wrong on the one hand, and, on the other, an agreement as to *which* things are to be put into each category. As regards the latter

[1] See p. 81.

there can be no doubt that a man's moral attitudes are very much affected by his background and environment. Of course, the fact that a man derives his moral standards from his environment does not help in the least to say whether such standards are to be approved or not: that will depend on whether the environment is itself soundly balanced in its moral principles. But it does warn us not to accept without examination the customary moral attitudes of a group without asking basic questions about their justification.

The question first to be examined is whether the general conviction that there are some things which are right (whatever they may be) and some things which are wrong is inherent in man or whether it is something which has been acquired from elsewhere. In a matter of this kind it is impossible to do more than weigh probabilities from evidence which must inevitably be inconclusive. But the studies of anthropologists seem to show that the sense of right and wrong exists in the most primitive societies, and their discoveries are quite consistent with the view that such a sense is inherent in human nature. If this is the case, the burden of proof would seem to be on those who wish to abandon a universally held conviction rather than on those who want to uphold it. For this conviction has in practice been found to provide a satisfactory foundation for the moral life and for moral understanding of human nature. It should therefore not be abandoned unless it is quite definitely disproved, and this has certainly not yet occurred.

The modern tendency which criticizes these basic convictions is mainly connected with the development of Freudian methods of psychiatry, and in particular of the technique of psycho-analysis. Freud himself was anti-Christian and evidently approached his whole subject with the desire to show Christianity to be both false and harmful. This to a certain extent has affected his explanations of the facts which he discovered. In his case, as in that of all those engaged in research in any subject, the facts which have been found must always be clearly distinguished from the theories which are put upon them. Whereas no one will want to deny the value of the new discoveries which Freud[1] made in the constituents of the mind and methods of dealing with psychological tension, his own presuppositions in the philosophical field have evidently affected

[1] Freud does not use the word 'Conscience' in the same sense as Christians. For him there is no independent sense of right and wrong.

the metaphysical conclusions which he has built upon these discoveries. It is perfectly possible, as can be seen from the attitudes
and actions of many distinguished psychiatrists, to accept the basic
findings of Freud and to be totally opposed to his theories about
their cause and about the best way of dealing with psychological
problems.

Freud, if we may attempt a short summary, took the view that
psychological difficulties and everything which stemmed from them
have the nature of sickness, and that once the sickness is exposed
and cured, the tensions disappear. In this approach no place is
found for moral standards outside the person concerned. Trouble
lies in the tensions of the mind, mainly caused by repressed
natural urges, which have been forced down into the unconscious
by a mistaken sense of guilt. This led Freud to hold that moral
ideas which produce the sense of guilt have no independent
validity but are merely causes of sickness and failure. Therefore,
his teaching runs, if the mistaken cause of the repression can be
exposed and the hidden causes of tension be released, the person
concerned will be well and healthy, and the less moral sense he
has, the better it is likely to be for him and for those whom he
influences.

Since Freud there has been a vigorous dispute among psychiatrists and psychologists as to whether there are two kinds of guilt,
the false guilt which alone Freud recognizes, and a true guilt
which can and does exist side by side with false guilt. For no one
intends to dispute Freud's finding that many guilty feelings are
connected with false guilt which ought to be dissipated. But in and
around the false guilt their exists a true guilt in relation to God.
Freudian hypotheses have turned out to be inadequate even to
some of his followers who call themselves Freudians.[1] Theologians
therefore would be ill advised to swallow Freud without careful
examination of what they are eating.

But it must be freely recognized that Freud has been the main-
spring for important new understandings of the human character,
and that, as a result of his findings, new light has been shed on the
meaning of the Christian Gospel. This is what many people find
difficult to accept. They want to think in hard-and-fast categories
and to pigeon-hole everything in neat packets. But much truth
will be missed if this is done. Freud has, for example, brought

[1] P. Tournier, *Guilt and Grace*, Hodder and Stoughton 1962, p. 91.

home the importance of the idea and fact of 'acceptance' in moral recovery: the Church has to accept men as they are, and to love them as they are, before God's healing love can take effect as it ought. But when such acceptance is present, it must not be associated with an impression that sin does not matter to God. This is the danger. One suggestion which often comes is that sin only matters because it upsets the person who is the sinner, and that it must be judged wholly within the personality of the person concerned. But it is not the teaching of Christianity nor of the New Testament, and in recent years it is being found inadequate even as a method of psychological treatment. It ignores the deepest level of the human personality, namely, its living relationship with a living God.

For side by side with the theory that an unintegrated personality is caused by mental and emotional sickness is an equally important theory, which has centuries of experience behind it, that mental and emotional sickness is often caused by guilt feelings which are justified, and which cannot be exorcized except by the forgiveness of God, quite irrespective of psychiatric treatment of a Freudian or other kind.

The situation is put vividly by Dr O. H. Mowrer[1]:

In reconsidering the possibility that sin must, after all, be taken seriously, many psychologists seem perplexed as to what attitude one should take *toward the sinner*. 'Nonjudgmental', 'nonpunitive', 'non-directive', 'warm', 'accepting', 'ethically neutral': these words have been so very generally used to form the supposedly proper therapeutic imago that reintroduction of the concept of sin throws us badly off balance. *Our* attitudes, as would-be therapists or helping persons, towards the neurotic (sinner) are apparently less important than his attitude *toward himself*; and, as we know, it is usually—in the most general sense—a rejecting one. Therefore, we have reasoned, the way to get the neurotic to accept and love himself is for us to love and accept *him*, an inference which flows equally from the Freudian assumption that the patient is not really guilty or sinful but only fancies himself so and from the view of Rogers that we are all inherently good and are corrupted by our experiences with the external, everyday world.

But what is here generally overlooked, it seems, is that recovery (constructive change, redemption) is most assuredly attained, not by helping a person reject and rise above his sins, but by helping him *accept them*.

[1] *The Crisis in Psychiatry and Religion*, Van Norstrand, New York 1961, p. 53. Author's italics.

Dr Mowrer goes on to point out that there was a 'fundamental fallacy of Freudian psychoanalysis' in that it avoided the key to the whole matter, which consists in a recognition of the reality of sin and the means of forgiveness and of overcoming it. Moreover Dr Mowrer points out that in actual psychiatric practice for many years in the United States Freudian methods and theories have not in fact shown the results which would justify them, and it is urgent that they be corrected.

A lengthy quotation has been given from Dr Mowrer's book because it is necessary from the point of view of moral theology to establish the fact that Freud is not to be taken as an infallible oracle even in his own highly specialized field, in spite of the immense services which he has done for psychology. Still less is he to be accepted in the religious field where his own prejudices and wrong-headedness frequently led him astray.

Those Christians who are engaged in a campaign to bring Freud's insights to bear on Christian attitudes do not, of course, accept Freud's anti-Christian attitudes: that would be absurd. We have already upheld the importance of Freud's insights for a fuller understanding of the Christian message. But there is a danger in some of Freud's friends that they will undermine in the minds of Christians principles and convictions which are just as important as Freud's insights, and thus leave them worse off than they were before. It is in this aspect that exception must be taken to some statements recently made by the Rev. H. A. Williams, Fellow and Dean of Trinity College, Cambridge, in spite of the illuminating character of other parts of his writing.

H. A. Williams and 'Self-Awareness'

Mr Williams's essay on 'Theology and Self-Awareness' in the Cambridge theologians' volume *Soundings*[1] is unfortunately not wholly rational. He claims that Freud cannot be fully understood unless one has shared the experience of undergoing the system of analysis which he propounds. Indeed he compares this experience with the Christian's deepest apprehension of God (p. 71):

> For Augustine the reality was God: for Freud, the unknown self. For Augustine the way was prayer: for Freud, analysis. And just as you cannot come to know God simply by making an academic study

[1] Ed. A. R. Vidler, Cambridge University Press 1962.

of prayer, so you cannot get to know your unknown self just by
studying books about psycho-analysis.

This is really a deplorable parallel. It would be wrong to say that
there is no parallel in the two things Mr Williams puts into harness,
but it is the sort of parallel which is far more harmful than helpful.

In the first place Mr Williams assumes that the only way in
which the unknown self can be thoroughly known is through
analysis. This is, at the very least, an unproven and unprovable
hypothesis, and it would be most strongly controverted by many
who have come to this same knowledge by other means. Mr
Williams here, and in other parts of his essay, falls into the trap
which many evangelists fall into: he assumes that his own experience is the measure to which everyone else must conform. He takes
it for granted that the kind of experience which he has had can
only be known by the same methods which he has used. Such a
claim is almost always false, especially in the religious life and the
things of the spirit. Every man is different and God deals with
each, not according to some theory, or by one method, but by
what that person needs. The knowledge of the unknown self comes
by other ways than analysis, and indeed Mr Williams himself
admits this by implication when in his essay he pays tribute to the
insight of St John of the Cross.

But in spite of aberrations Mr Williams has much of value to
say. Many of his strictures, though often exaggerated and wildly
flung about, have some substance which Christians ought to note.
But he seems inclined to think that most which is below the surface
of consciousness is bad. Why he should do so is not quite clear.
His general attitude is that many people's attitude to God, though
superficially right, is in fact motivated by the dark forces beneath
consciousness and therefore, while superficially right, is basically
wrong. He never seems to give adequate weight to good things in
the unconscious, which might make some contribution to the
whole personality, even though he says that God may act
through it.

Thus he writes (p. 77), 'We could sum this up by saying that our
attitude to God, evoked by the way in which alone we can conceive him, is like an iceberg. A small amount appears above the
surface of consciousness. Below is the vast submerged mass we do
not see.' This submerged mass consists, it seems, mainly of 'a
great amount of irrational reactions to him (*sc.* God) on which I

have continuously to sit very hard. And the diabolical thing is that I seldom know it.' This is true in a limited way, but it does not take into account brighter aspects of human nature, and it generalizes in a way which many will think overdone.

Mr Williams devotes a page or more (pp. 79-80) to a hard-hitting attack on the terms which Cranmer uses for the general confession in the Communion Service of the 1662 Book of Common Prayer. His interpretation of this and of the subsequent absolution and Comfortable Words is both irrational and unreasonable. Mr Williams maintains that Cranmer uses in the Holy Communion service exaggerated language about our sinfulness, and that he adds (in the Comfortable Words) unnecessary assurances about forgiveness. This indicates, he thinks, that Cranmer did not really believe in God's forgiveness and that these two elements show (*a*) that Cranmer is trying to manoeuvre God's mercy by exaggerated beating on the breast, and (*b*) that he is trying to reassure himself (against what he *really* believes) that God is going to forgive him. He interprets every assurance of God's forgiveness as evidence that Cranmer did not really believe it. This is Alice through the Looking Glass with a vengeance. It is only because Mr Williams is so absurdly touchy on the subject that the criticized passages appear to him strange. The most that could be properly said is that the words of the general confession are perhaps somewhat overcoloured for most people's taste in the twentieth century, but that is not necessarily a very weighty criticism. It may be significant that the revisions of the Book of Common Prayer in other parts of the Anglican Communion in recent years have for the most part retained the *ipsissima verba* of Cranmer. The 1959 Canadian revision did tone down the general confession (partly on historical grounds) but it retained all the rest, on which Mr Williams wishes to hang his theory that Cranmer did not believe in the forgiveness of God.

He includes among the objectionable matter the Prayer of Humble Access, described by the liturgical scholar Archbishop Yngve Brilioth of the Church of Sweden as one of the most beautiful prayers in existence, and he ends by asking how many of the little ones 'have been caused to stumble by our incomparably unchristian liturgy?' One can only comment on such a question as this by saying that Mr Williams, though percipient in some things, is strangely blind in others.

There are two main comments to be made about his remarks, apart from the regret, which one must express, that he should have allowed himself to speak in terms which cannot but give deep hurt and offence to many devout members of his own Church. The first point is this. Mr Williams in objecting to what he considers to be exaggerated language about our sinfulness and unworthiness stands on the other side of the fence from all the great Christian saints. One of their most noticeable characteristics is the way they constantly persist in averring that they are the worst of sinners and totally unworthy to receive God's love and favour. In choosing his words Cranmer was echoing this authentic note of the saints. St Francis of Assisi, for example, provides several examples of this attitude. He said, very characteristically, that, if he were to arrive at 'St Mary of the Angels, soaked with rain, stiff with cold, covered with mud and exhausted with hunger' and be badly treated as a ruffian by the porter, and kept standing outside all night in the snow and rain, it must be borne without complaint 'thinking that the porter recognizes us for what we are'.[1] Mr Williams's attempt to isolate Cranmer and to treat him as a psychopath is not substantiated from the passages to which he objects.

The second point is perhaps more fundamental. In complaining in this way Mr Williams misses the whole point of the language which he is criticizing. It is the very sense of unworthiness that makes the forgiveness and love of God so marvellous and redeeming. Without this sense it would not and could not appear to be such a striking manifestation of God's love. And the fact is, as we have just seen in the saints, that as Christians grow in the life of the spirit and in union with God their sense of unworthiness becomes greater, not less. 'What is being suggested', writes Mr Williams, 'is that there lurked within him (*sc.* Cranmer), along with his belief in the Christian gospel, belief in a celestial Mr Pontifex, unloving and incapable of being loved, who must thus be manoeuvred into giving his children what they need.' In fact the sense of unworthiness which Mr Williams criticizes so severely is for many people the very means of opening themselves to the healing influence of God's love, just the opposite of what Mr Williams suggests. Moreover he does not go far in understanding the genius of the best Protestants, if he does not appreciate that

[1] *The Little Flowers of St Francis VII*, tr. Leo Sherley-Price: *Lent with St Francis*, Mowbrays 1958, p. 21.

it was their deepest conviction that God cannot 'be manoeuvred into giving his children what they need' and that it is the worst blasphemy to think that he could. This was at the heart of their protest against the corruptions of Rome.

Mr Williams then goes on to speak of Christian morals, of good and evil. He writes (p. 80):

> Christians have always everywhere agreed that God is love, and that therefore generous self-giving love is the ultimate moral value. Where the reassessment is necessary is in our understanding of how and when we give ourselves and how and when we refuse to do so. This makes it impossible to describe certain actions as wicked and others as good.

The moral theologian can only utter a sigh of sadness and frustration when he reads this, for these sentences show a complete failure to think out the terms which are being used, and the essential distinctions. Let us spend a short time in another kind of analysis, namely the analysis of these sentences.

First, a statement is made which is not accurate. The first half-sentence is quite all right—'Christians have always everywhere agreed that God is love'. There need be no quarrel about this, but the second half of the same sentence is most misleading: 'and that therefore generous self-giving love is the ultimate moral value'. It is misleading because it suggests, whenever there is a sign of self-giving love in a human person, that it has ultimate value, irrespective of any other considerations. Self-giving love is only an *ultimate* moral value in the case of God himself, than whom there can be nothing greater. In the case of human beings, however, the moral value of self-giving love depends on its object, that is, on what it is directed to. It is not, and cannot be, evaluated solely on a subjective measure of giving. Self-giving love may be lavished on unworthy objects. There are many examples of such love being given to a cat to the neglect of the misery of human beings who needed it. There is no ultimate moral value there, for the potential of human love, given by God for his purposes, has been improperly used.

It is necessary to be conscious of the distinction between an action in itself, and the motives of the person who acts. Christians believe in God: so far as external actions are concerned God provides an absolute standard to which actions ought to conform. So far as they conform to the will of God and his plan for the world, they are right actions: so far as they do not, they are wrong. This has nothing to do with the motive or aim of the person who is acting. A simple example would be the destruction of human life. It is God's will that a human being should live and fulfil himself in his life on earth, and an action which violently interferes with this possibility by taking away a man's life is not in accordance with God's will, and is therefore wrong. It does not make any difference whether it was accidental, or whether it was the result of something done with the best intentions, *the actual thing done is wrong.*

But there are many cases where the person who is the cause of a wrong action is quite blameless. It may be that a surgeon has diagnosed a disease and the need for an operation, and that the man dies because of an unknown weakness (an illustration used elsewhere). In such a case, assuming that the surgeon has taken every possible precaution to do his best, his behaviour is not only blameless, it is praiseworthy, because his motive is good. But nevertheless the loss of the man's life is bad.

Another example may be taken. War is wrong, irrespective of the need or cause of any particular war. It is an external moral fact which stands clearly seen and admitted. But some wars can be justified in certain circumstances because they are morally to be preferred to the conditions which would be inevitable in the absence of war. Men often find themselves in a situation of such all-pervading evil that there is no course of action open to them which is free from evil. Nevertheless this does not affect the existence of standards of right and wrong, good and evil, which are measured not in relation to man's condition, but ultimately in relation to God's goodness and his will.

There are therefore two sides to every action—the action considered in itself with its effects, and the praiseworthiness or blameworthiness of the person who commits it. 'Generous self-giving love is the ultimate moral value' only in the case of God, whose every gift is perfect from every point of view. Human beings have to try to approximate to this love of God, through his help, but in doing so they must have regard not only to their own inner needs and motives, but also to the effect of any action they propose on other people not immediately involved in it.

'It is impossible', avers Mr Williams, 'to describe certain actions as wicked and others as good.' Most people hearing such a statement would not credit their hearing. Moreover in the form in which it is given it confuses the issue, because the words 'wicked' and 'good' do not clearly express the distinctions which have to be made. 'Wicked' could either mean that an action is wrong, or that a person is blameworthy: and equally 'good' can either mean an action which is externally right, or it can refer to the motives of the person who does it. It is necessary to dispute the statement we have quoted and to say that it *is* often possible both to say whether an action is right or wrong, and to say whether the person doing the action is to be blamed or praised.

Mr Williams proceeds further to confuse the matter by imagining a situation before the days of social security when 'one of the unemployed, having appealed in vain to all quarters, might have stolen money from a rich man in order to feed his starving family'. This could, he says, be a greater virtue than not to steal. It would be absurd to deny that stealing might be necessary in certain circumstances. But if we ask why it could be morally acceptable, we find that it has nothing to do with the rightness or wrongness of stealing in itself. To steal is wrong. But the man in question is faced with a situation where the only alternative is morally worse than stealing, namely the starvation of his wife and family. And so, in the circumstances, to steal was the lesser of two evils with which he was faced. But that does not make stealing right: it merely makes it necessary at that time in those particular circumstances. There are a great many ancillary moral issues raised by such a situation, for example, the evil social conditions which have caused him to find himself in this dilemma. Then Mr Williams goes on to show how such a man might picture himself in his own mind as moral for not stealing, when in fact he had failed to steal because he had not enough courage. But what does that prove? Certainly that men have a great power of deluding themselves and hiding the facts. But the conclusion of the tale is not that there are no moral principles, but that men are often wicked, which we knew already. And if it was truly the moral duty of the man to steal in order to avoid a worse evil, then the man who did not steal was morally to blame, and the man who did steal was morally to be praised. But stealing is still wrong as a normal standard.

Mr Williams then passes on to sexual ethics, on which he has some astonishing views. 'If I am to give myself away to another person', he writes, 'I cannot, in any circumstances exploit her or him. To exploit is to withhold. It is totally incompatible with giving. But this is not at all the same thing as saying that in certain specifiable circumstances I must always be exploiting and always giving. Yet this is what the Church says about sexual intercourse outside marriage.' This is sheer nonsense: the Church says nothing of the kind. Mr Williams has done a sort of conjuring trick by turning the thing upside down. The Church says that sexual intercourse outside marriage is wrong: that is certainly true. The Church says nothing whatever about the giving and exploiting that Mr Williams fancies to explain what sex relations mean. There is no doubt that in some cases of sexual intercourse outside marriage there is a genuine desire on the part of one or both of the people involved to give to the other. But that does not make the action right. The motives of the persons concerned may very well be twisted and/or unenlightened and/or clouded by emotions which have overcome their judgement.

The Church is not interested in inventing prohibitions in order to stop people enjoying or fulfilling themselves, which is what Mr Williams implies. Indeed the Church is only interested in helping people truly to fufil themselves, and that is the very reason why it says that sexual intercourse outside marriage is wrong. It knows that there are deep needs, both mental and physical, in men and women which can only be truly fulfilled in marriage. Any action therefore which tends to break down this truth in practice, in the first place does damage to the two people concerned, because they are not in conditions where it can be fully experienced, and, secondly, does a great deal of harm to other people who know about it, and to society in general.

In the examples which Mr Williams gives us to bear out his theory he first of all tells how in the film *Never on Sunday* a prostitute by sexual intercourse enables a sailor to acquire confidence and self-respect by overcoming his suspicion that he is not capable of physical union. Mr Williams adds: 'He goes away a deeper, fuller person than he came in. What is seen is an act of charity which proclaims the glory of God' (p. 81). Here again he has completely confused the issue. The act of physical union was wrong. This does not necessarily mean that the prostitute was personally to blame in the first place for being a prostitute or the sailor for having no moral sense: the rightness or the wrongness of the action considered in itself depends on a standard settled in the light of the will of God and the teaching of Christ about marriage. This standard is a proclamation by the Church of the glory of marriage and of its essential nature for the full maturing of the human personality.

There are some people who don't know anything about the Church's teaching through no fault of their own. From the way in which Mr Williams tells the story we must assume that in it neither the prostitute nor the sailor had any moral awareness that sexual intercourse was ever wrong, and that neither of them had come into contact with opportunities for discovering the truth. When there is ignorance of this kind which neither of them could have overcome, their behaviour inevitably moves within the limited boundaries of their understanding. Within those boundaries the prostitute may have behaved well according to her lights to the sailor, and, if she did so, that was *relatively* a good thing to do. But it is entirely relative to her ignorance and lack of moral principle or knowledge. To say that it is 'an act of charity which proclaims the glory of God' is to use words which can only cause misunderstanding. It could be said that *any* movement of good in *any* human being, however depraved, proclaims the glory of God— and so it does in one sense. But to use the phrase *tout court* in such a context as this can do nothing but befog the issues.

His second example is essentially the same. A man is given confidence because a woman of his own age sleeps with him and thus exorcizes his attraction to small girls. When he summons up enough courage 'and they sleep together, he has been made whole. And where there is healing, there is Christ, whatever the Church may say about fornication. And the appropriate response is— Glory to God in the Highest.' Here again Mr Williams uses words which cloud the issue and give a false impression. Looking at the matter from a strictly relative point of view it can be said that every good thing in some partial way reflects Christ, but there are some large gaps in the writer's treatment.

In the first place the whole question is begged by the use of the phrase 'he has been made whole'. This is quite obviously untrue. What the man has received is some temporary relief to one side of his character. But to say that a man has been made *whole*, who does not recognize God and has no knowledge of the Christian faith, is a misuse of language which is inexcusable, especially in a theologian. Moreover there is no reason why we should not suppose that when he later had a fuller understanding of God this particular sexual experience might produce a guilt tension worse than the original trouble which it is supposed to have cured.

But the greatest objection to Mr Williams's treatment is simple. It is that his whole approach assumes that there is no other way in which these particular problems could be solved except by the means which he describes. This is of course plainly false and is contradicted every day by the experience of Christians. Although in the circumstances described by Mr Williams the actions *may* have been *blameless*, they cannot by any stretch of the imagination be regarded as examples of the glory of God, when in fact the news of the Gospel and the possibilities of redemption through Christ have never been experienced. To maintain or imply that such tensions as those described can only be cured by casual sexual intercourse is to maintain that God has no means of bringing people to wholeness except in that way. Such an attitude is the rejection of belief in any God in whom any Christian has ever believed. Mr Williams finds in his theories a method of dealing with part of people's personality problems, and he then goes on to assume that it must be the only method and therefore the right one. But human experience is against him, as well as the psychologists.

'Freud showed us that evil consists of refusing to give through fear masquerading as morality' (p. 82). As a matter of fact Freud showed nothing of the sort. He found that in some cases this was the situation and he went on to build a theory that it was the same in all cases. This has been disproved, not merely by other theories, but by the fact that the theory does not work adequately in practice.

The rest of Mr Williams's essay provides a number of insights from the point of view which he has adopted. His power to convince is limited by the assumption which we have already noticed, namely that this approach is the whole explanation and applies to everybody. But if we keep in mind that it is valid as a description of *some*, it is often both illuminating and helpful. There is more than one obscurity. His discussion of lust in his own sense is not without insight, though the statement that 'the practice of religion can be a form of lust' is not one which it is easy to accept without changing the meaning of the word as generally used.

The opposite of sin, says Mr Williams, is faith (p. 90), and can never be virtue. He is right, but he does not go far enough to

give us help. The opposite of sin is faith or love: that is true
enough. But the opposite of sins are virtues, and virtues are of
course the fruit of the quality of faith or love. It is also curious to
see how Mr Williams writes of the need to accept the 'scandal of
our absolute dependence on him (*sc.* God)', and in doing so he
seems to undo the case which he has earlier built up against Cranmer
by agreeing with what Cranmer actually said.

The new insights which Freud originated pose problems to the
theologian, Mr Williams writes in his last paragraph. They do,
but not quite in the way which he imagines. In his own insights
he shows truly where more knowledge may bring us closer to God,
but most of what he says is vitiated by the assumption that what
he knows in the experience of a few must necessarily apply to all,
and also by the acceptance of some Freudian theories which are
not substantiated and are found wanting in practice. There is
wisdom in the Church as well as in Freud. Freud is not the first
person to have studied the human mind and spirit. There is a
wealth of knowledge and experience in the Church throughout the
ages which is not made less factual by Freudian theories. Freud
made his own contribution mainly in revealing the power of the
unconscious and in working out a technique of exploring it, which
to some people can be a great help. It is for the Church to accept
such assured and agreed knowledge and to integrate it into its own
knowledge of what is required for personal fulfilment. It will be
found that many of the essential principles have already been
applied in spiritual direction for many centuries.

Mr Williams's favourite argument, when analysed, seems to go
like this: Health is always good and therefore in accordance with
the will of God; absence of psychological tension is the same thing
as mental health; therefore anything that gets rid of such tension
is the will of God. It is on some such argument as this that he says
that fornication is an illustration of the glory of God, and that
where there is healing there is Christ. There are, however, some
obvious *lacunae* in this point of view. It may be fully agreed that
health is in accordance with the will of God, but it is totally wrong
to equate the absence of any particular psychological tension with
health in this sense. In a fully integrated personality, integrated
not only in itself but in its relationship with God, which are
aspects of the same thing, complete health comes when tensions
are set in the perspective of a life related to God. But the resolu-

tion of partial tensions may or may not be steps on the way to
this integration: if they are, they are good; if they are not, they
are bad. The examples which Mr Williams gives in his essay in
Soundings are quite inadequate to bear his conclusions that they
should cause us to sing the *Gloria*.

In considering them we take only what Mr Williams has related
of the facts. A prostitute is commended because, by having sexual
intercourse with a sailor, she gives him confidence and thus overcomes his distrust of 'his capacity for physical union'. 'He goes
away a deeper, fuller person than he came in.' The adjectives
'deeper', 'fuller' are value-adjectives which don't help us much.
But supposing it was the will of God that that sailor, who had no
moral scruples or moral background apparently, should meet a
Christian girl of purity and convinced moral principles, and should
fall in love with her, after having this experience with the prostitute.
Both girl and sailor are deeply in love with one another, and
through this experience the sailor learns of the Christian ideals of
love and sexual relationship in marriage. What Mr Williams has
just proclaimed as something which 'proclaims the glory of God'
now becomes far worse than the original distrust of 'his capacity
for physical union'. He sees himself to have betrayed all that he
now considers most pure and beautiful in the very act which Mr
Williams commends so heartily. And this brings us full circle back
to the point where we began, namely that it is only in the observance of the moral law and the principles which that law reveals
in Christ that God can be glorified, or fulness be achieved. Had
the moral prohibition of fornication restrained the sailor from
fornication until he met the girl who was to redeem him, it would
have been a useful contribution to his wholeness, far more
valuable than that commended in the story.

Both the stories which Mr Williams tells shock Christians, and
shock them rightly, because they implicitly deny the power of God
to heal the tensions of the persons concerned in other ways than
those he describes. In his public correspondence with those who
disagreed with him Mr Williams suggested[1] that his opponents
somehow denied that our material instincts and affections flow
from God. He accused them of a hidden dualism 'in which Christ
is considered to have come in order to teach us how to do the least
harm with our instincts which are the product of another creator

[1] *Church Times*, 7th Dec., 1962.

such as, for instance, the devil'. This is not the language of rational discussion, but of propaganda. Christ came in order to teach us how to use our instincts as God meant them to be used, and that does of course include the avoidance of doing harm with them. It has nothing whatever to do with dualism, but a lot to do with free will. Man has the power to use everything in the world, including his own instincts, either for or against the will of God. Christ came to teach us how to use them in accordance with the will of God. They are created good, but they are twisted by sin; they remain potentially either good or bad according to the choice of man, who is made in the image of God and has been given freedom to love or reject him.

Mr Williams tells us that 'to equate our own understanding of truth (including moral truth) with the Truth which is God alone is one of the most dangerous forms of idolatry'.[1] He is right, but we may suppose that he does not therefore conclude that nothing of truth has been revealed to us. If so, we are indeed wallowing in the mire. If there is some truth revealed, it seems to be just as deplorable for Mr Williams to claim that he is wholly right as for his opponents to do so. One gets nowhere by this sort of exchange. But we might say with some show of reason that the moral knowledge of the Christian world, which is an empiric fact, must not be undermined by attitudes which have within them the suggestion that external moral standards do not exist or need not be observed. And whether Mr Williams means to suggest such an attitude or not, that is in fact what he does and what is implied in some of the things which he has written.

It is not because Mr Williams himself is influential that he has been examined so carefully, but because he is probably as competent an exponent as can at present be found of a point of view within the Church which tends to suggest that moral values are relative and subjective. He states,[2] 'The only absolute standard I find in the New Testament is *Agape*.' He goes on, 'It was the Pharisees who objectively stated their standards of right and wrong with a certainty which led them in the end to crucify the Righteous One.' The implication in this sentence seems to be that those who maintain and state an objective standard of right and wrong are to be classed with the Pharisees. St Paul would, I suppose, be one of them.

[1] *Theology*, Dec. 1962, p. 504. [2] *Art. cit.*, *Theology*, Dec. 1962, *passim*.

In one sense it is true that the only absolute standard in the New Testament is *Agape*, but it is not the subjective *Agape* of the individual, but the *Agape* of God which alone sets the standard for all men. The *Agape* of God includes within it the order of creation, and the order of creation includes the order of man's nature, to which he must conform if he is to be fulfilled. It is in this realm that external standards of right and wrong take their place. '*Agape* converts people by accepting them as they are' says Williams, and he is right. But this acceptance is not tantamount to approval of what they are, it is acceptance in love which alone has the power to raise up the person loved to a new life, both moral and spiritual. People can only be accepted as they are because, in themselves accepting that acceptance, they turn from themselves to God and to the standards which he approves.

It is most important that we should get our spiritual priorities right. It is not healing first and after that forgiveness; nor does forgiveness necessarily result in complete healing. The right priority is shown again and again by Jesus himself in his own ministry, when his first word is one of forgiveness, sometimes his only word. The case of the paralytic man is a good example. He said, 'Your sins are forgiven.' This remark caused murmurs of 'blasphemy!' and it was only then that he went on to deal with the physical healing, saying that he did it so that they could know that the Son of Man had power to forgive sins. The whole incident revolves round the importance of the forgiveness of sins, not round the concept of physical healing. Why could not Jesus have said to the man that his tensions were relieved, or told him not to worry so that they were in fact relieved? He could clearly have done so, but he didn't.

It might be replied that Jesus moved within the limits of the beliefs of his time, and that in taking this attitude he was merely reflecting the superstitions of his age that illness was due to some sin which the man had committed, and that it was the judgement of God on him. To such an argument we must reply that Jesus does not at any time give the impression that he did in fact accept such crude views. Indeed there is distinct evidence that he took a different line altogether. But much more important is the fact that Jesus had the unique power of seeing into people's personalities, of making the correct diagnosis, and of providing the appropriate treatment. If we cannot rely on Jesus for this, then he no longer remains a person whom we can call Lord and Saviour. And if he is not Lord and Saviour, then Christianity is altogether a dead letter and the discussion of it a waste of time.

If we go to the New Testament it is impossible to remove from it the assumption throughout that there are standards of right and wrong which are quite independent of the subjective condition of man. The story of the woman caught in the act of adultery ends with the injunction that she should not again commit sin. Jesus continually attacks the Pharisees for what they do. St Paul calls the Corinthian Church to account, not for a lack of *Agape*, but for sexual immorality (I Cor. 5.1). He does not ask whether their motives were good, or whether they were trying to cure each other's doubts of their capacity for physical union. 'A man who has done such a deed should have been rooted out of your company' St Paul writes. It is not really necessary to establish the point in more detail, for it cannot be gainsaid. It is illustrated by a number of parables as well as contained in the assumed background of the whole New Testament story.

We may therefore legitimately come to the conclusion not only that the sense of right and wrong is found in all men, but that it does in fact correspond to outward moral standards to which men must conform, if they are to fulfil the will of God for themselves and for others.

Conscience: its Liberty and Knowledge

We come then to the second main meaning of the word conscience, that is, the application of the general sense of right and wrong to the actual problems of everyday life. But before pursuing this in detail there are one or two general points to be considered. The meaning of the word translated conscience in the Greek New Testament ought to be examined a little. The word used is *syneidesis* (συνείδησις) which appears to carry the meaning of the general sense of right and wrong especially as it affects the outlook of the person on his past deeds or misdeeds. It has in fact a meaning very close to that which we have just seen the word *synteresis* bears. Indeed B. Häring has suggested that the word *synteresis* came into use originally merely as the result of a copying error for *syneidesis*.[1]

C. A. Pierce states in his study of *Conscience in the New Testa-*

[1] *Op. cit.*, I, p. 139.

ment[1] that *syneidesis* meant in ordinary Greek speech 'the pain
suffered by man, as man . . . when, by his acts completed or
initiated, he transgresses the moral limits of his nature', though
its general meaning in classical Greek seems to have been consciousness. W. A. Lillie says that the New Testament emphasizes the
painfulness of conscience, 'rather than the pronouncing of judgement or the providing of guidance for the future'.[2] But while
extremely diffident about differing from a New Testament scholar,
one must say that an examination of the passages in which the
word *syneidesis* occurs does not give the impression that it is used
mainly in a negative sense. On the contrary at least half of the
passages seem to have a positive meaning of having a good conscience towards God, a positive rather than a negative conception,
though the two aspects cannot be altogether separated. It certainly
seems true that the New Testament shows a high regard for the
importance of a clear conscience, though there is not much evidence
to indicate any attempt to define the word. It was probably used
merely in the general sense of having a sense of guilt in the case
of a bad conscience, or being free from such a sense in that of a
good conscience. That indeed corresponds to the general use
which we still have today.

When the general sense of right and wrong, the 'conscience' as
used in the New Testament, is applied to actual problems of life,
we are led to ask, What is the nature of the conscience when acting
in this capacity of deciding whether a particular action is right or
wrong? The conscience has been given various descriptions: it has
been called the voice of God, or a special faculty of the personality.
Lillie gives a list of definitions from great writers of the past.
We should be on unsafe ground if we were to try to treat the
conscience as if it were a separate faculty of the mind or soul,
rather in the same way as sight is a separate faculty of our physical
nature. The interior activities of a man can only be separated for
purposes of theoretical examination; in reality they all form integral
parts of the whole man himself. The conscience therefore is not
so much a separate faculty as the action of a man in relation to one
particular part of his life, namely the moral part where questions
of right and wrong arise.

Jeremy Taylor wrote that 'conscience is the mind of man
governed by a rule', clearly echoing in slightly different form the

---

[1] SCM Press 1955.   [2] *Studies in NT Ethics*, p. 46.

definition of St Thomas Aquinas that 'conscience is the mind of man passing moral judgement.' These definitions, which do contain much truth, are not quite satisfactory, for they are too intellectual, and put too much stress exclusively on the mind. It is certainly true that the mind of man plays a predominant part, or ought to do so, in passing moral judgement, whether on his own actions or on those of others. But the conscience is affected by deep emotional elements of the personality, many of them often hidden. This emotional side of conscience has been brought out very clearly by modern psychological research. Indeed in some people conscience can become almost entirely a reaction of the emotions in which the mind plays almost no independent part. If the emotions predominate to such a degree as this, the personality is unbalanced and the conscience is not functioning as it should, but there is no doubt that many people are in some such condition. It is therefore somewhat unreal to define conscience solely or mainly in terms of the mind. Conscience, we might say, is the personality—mind, emotions, will—passing judgement on what is right and what is wrong. It sometimes does this in reference to an outside code of moral law, but if it does so, it is not fully Christian. What is right and what is wrong for a Christian is what is in accordance or what is not in accordance with the will of God. The mind ought to play a leading part in discovering the truth of any moral problem, but it is not alone.

It is obvious that different people come to different conclusions as to what is right and what is wrong in particular cases, and it will be necessary to examine the elements which affect the reliability of a man's judgement and conscience when he faces a choice of action. But before doing so we must observe that there are two axioms which must be accepted if any discussion of conscience is to have meaning. The first of these axioms is the truth that a man has liberty of choice and that his belief in such liberty is not merely an illusion. The second is that he has moral knowledge, i.e. that he has a sufficient knowledge of right and wrong to make the exercise of his liberty useful and meaningful. Both these axioms have been under attack in modern times from various schools of psychologists and philosophers.

Human liberty is a fact which is attested by human experience and by mankind's attitude, both in individual and in social matters. Every man does in fact order his life on the basis that he has freedom of choice within the possibilities of his human lot, and he speaks, works and thinks on this assumption. He could not indeed live otherwise. It is only necessary to try to see how one could live, believing that there was no such thing as free choice, to realize that it is impossible. It is part of our nature that we have to act as free men. Those who deny this freedom do so on philosophical or behaviourist psychological grounds and say that every reaction of a man is predetermined by what is already past and that the idea of freedom is an illusion. A discussion of moral theology is not the place to argue philosophical or psychological theories of this sort. It is worth noting that the men who put forward these theories do themselves order their lives in contradiction of them. No one has yet met a philosopher or psychologist who does not in fact live his life as if he had freedom, and who does not behave accordingly. There is therefore an inherent contradiction in holding these views.

The view that all is determined and that freedom is an illusion becomes quite valueless, for the theory undermines itself and is self-destroying. For, if freedom is an illusion, then the determinists had no freedom to choose the views which they put forward, they are merely the outcome of their own past history, and therefore such views have no claim on anyone else, for they have no independent validity. And, if in fact we are ourselves determined in our choice, not only of actions but also of the opinions which we hold, what can be the point of putting forward theories which have the aim of persuading us to accept them? For persuasion is nonsense unless there is freedom to choose to be persuaded.

For a Christian the New Testament is decisive on the subject of human freedom, for it is clear that Jesus himself assumed that his hearers had power to choose to follow him or to ignore him. Some heard his message and tried to respond to the Gospel, others went away and left him. Moreover the whole trend of his teaching is such as to presuppose that men have freedom and that they ought to exercise it responsibly. The way in which Jesus used parables for teaching is surely clear evidence that men not only had the freedom to hear or forbear, but that they also were required to use their freedom to wrestle individually with the spiritual problems which the parables illustrated. So we find Jesus often declining to give plain answers to plain questions with the implication that men must themselves work out the spiritual meaning of life, if it is to come home to them. The first clarion cry, 'Repent ye, for the kingdom of heaven is at hand', is meaningless unless men have freedom to respond to it.

But *full* liberty is only found in full response to the Gospel of Jesus. Men have liberty, but it has been eroded and diminished by all kinds of influence, mainly by the sin in which they have indulged and the bad habits which they have allowed to grip them. The liberty with which Christ has made us free is an immense expansion of the liberty known by those who have not found Christ. Right use of liberty leads to a greater liberty, to the glorious liberty of the sons of God. There is only an apparent contradiction between the statement that all men are free and the belief that full liberty is known only in life with God through Christ. In the liberty which is common to all men is to be found the seed which when watered, tended and drawn out by the sun of God's love becomes a flower which only grows in that way. So long as the seed chooses to lie in a sack with lots of other dry seeds it never will find what its liberty can finally mean.

Socially all groups are organized on the assumption that liberty is a reality. Men and women in society have to live on the basis of a certain responsibility. If they deny the responsibility in their lives, they are incarcerated either in a prison or in a lunatic asylum. The prison theoretically is for those who insist on using their liberty of choice wrongly, to the detriment or danger of society, and the mental hospital is for those who have lost the use of their liberty and are no longer able to exercise their choice. Such arrangements are merely the reflection in society of the basic belief that every man and woman has free choice and ought to exercise it without damage to those with whom he lives.

Here again secular society is a shadowy reflection of what man ought to enjoy in the divine society, the Church, which is meant to be a fellowship in which liberty is exercised exclusively in love of other members of the fellowship and of God, and which should, and one day will, show how liberty becomes fully grown only in the fellowship of the sons of God where, without external constraint or regulation, all will contribute fully to the happiness and fulfilment of their fellows. This is expressed in the Prayer Book Collect in the phrase 'whose service is perfect freedom'.

The free will of man to choose good or evil is a constant cause of scandal for those who do not understand the love of God. They have a sense of good and evil and they see evil happening on a gigantic scale, humanly speaking. They complain bitterly that God permits this, without seeing that it is part of the meaning of love that those who are loved should be really free to love or to reject love in return. To reject is the negative side of the ability to love, and, in rejecting love, man brings upon himself the tragedies with which the twentieth century is only too familiar. The liberty of man cannot be taken away or interfered with without breaking up the intentions of a loving God for the fulfilment of man and for the happiness of all his world.

Knowledge of the good is the second presupposition of a responsible conscience. But knowledge is a word which has many shades of meaning. It may mean intellectual knowledge, knowledge of the head only, and this kind of knowledge is limited. Or it may refer to knowledge of the heart, as it is often termed, i.e. knowledge which comes from an inner assurance and which derives from some sort of personal relationship with another human being or with God. Perhaps there is no knowledge which is exclusively of the mind or exclusively of the heart, but all knowledge partakes of both. Yet apart from these two general classes of knowledge there are levels of knowledge which begin at the most superficial and external and end at the deepest level of unity with God. Even the simple facts of the spiritual life have to be continually known in a deeper and deeper manner as life goes on. Spiritual progress is not a matter of learning more and more things about the spiritual life: it is much more learning at a deeper and deeper level the same things about God and oneself. We know that God loves us, but it takes a lifetime even to know that terrific fact on our own deepest level, which, even when fully known, is so feeble a reflection of the full knowledge of the saints. When, therefore, we speak of knowledge we may be using the word in one of many ways.

But, as in the case of liberty, so in the case of knowledge, there is an irreducible minimum of apprehension of the good which never leaves us and which is imbedded in our nature, and it is this knowledge which makes it possible for us to discern between good and evil. It is true that in some cases this discernment is relative and not absolute. In other words a man's vision can be so darkened or clouded that he can no longer see clearly, but he can see something, and his life spiritually depends on his taking the step towards the good rather than towards the evil. If he insists

on doing the good again and again, his spiritual vision will improve
and he will more and more be able to discern God's will. For we
always have to remember that right is not merely obedience to
external laws, but it is the will of God for a particular person in a
particular situation.

There are cases when a man through no fault of his own cannot
discern what is absolutely right, but can only do what seems to
him to be right. In this case what he thinks to be right is right for
him in those circumstances, even though in an absolute sense it
might be wrong. This distinction we shall meet again in the
difference between formal and material sin. There is, however,
always enough knowledge in man for him to step towards the light
rather than towards the darkness, and he is judged by how he
reacts to the circumstances in which he finds himself. However low
a man has sunk, he has never lost the capacity for moving towards
the higher things which God wills for him. God wills the good for
every man, and he cannot will for a man something which it is
impossible for that man to have, otherwise it would be a contradiction within the character of God himself.

Much discussion of good and evil is carried on merely on an
intellectual plane. This often misleads, because unless a man
apprehends the content of good and evil at a deep level, he cannot
properly discuss it. A merely intellectual discussion can be misleading and thus lead away from the good. We suffer in the
twentieth century from an exaggerated valuation of intellectual
abilities, and until this lack of balance is corrected it is difficult,
if not impossible, to discuss moral issues satisfactorily in public,
especially between Christians and non-Christians. 'The more
love grows in us, the more will God manifest Himself to us, the
more shall we also understand the morally good.'[1] St John puts
it thus: 'A man may say, "I am in the light"; but if he hates his
brother, he is still in the dark. Only the man who loves his brother
dwells in the light' (I John 1.9).

It is only in sharing the love of God, which gives to all created
things their value, that it is possible to know moral good in its right
proportion. When New Testament writers use the word 'love' they
refer to God's love and human love in relation to it. But there is
a tendency now for outsiders to change the phrase 'God is love'
into 'love is God' and to twist its meaning into a statement that

[1] B. Häring, *op. cit.*, I, p. 123.

human love, whatever form it may take, is as good as God, and that is all that we need consider. This is another of the many forms of idolatry which sets up in the place which God alone ought to occupy some human standard or image to replace him.

But in spite of the gap between the Christian who knows the love of God and the non-Christian who does not, there is a spark of knowledge which is common, which can enable the man who does not know God to move towards such knowledge. What is needed is the practical application of the sense of good and evil in the light of the best knowledge that he has. If he uses this knowledge and with an honest conscience tries to act in accordance with it, he will be brought to the haven where God would have him be.

We may say then that moral theology, like ascetic theology, is concerned with what man does with the raw materials of his personality. Men differ widely in their endowments as well as in their difficulties. No blame attaches to them because they have feelings which spring from their unconscious, unless of course they have been blameworthy in the first place in causing them to be there. In many cases unbidden feelings depend on experiences over which the person concerned has no control and for many of which he has had no responsibility. But in considering the personal responses to life moral theology is also concerned with an ideal order in accordance with the will of God which affords for man the only complete hope of fulfilment and happiness. It is therefore a mixture of the objective and subjective throughout its length.

The standards of morality which have to be upheld are two. The objective standard of morality is the will of God: what makes an action good in itself is that it is the will of God. The subjective standard of morality is the conscience; from a personal point of view everything must be done in accordance with conscience, or in its classical form *conscientia semper sequenda*, the conscience is always to be followed. The reason for this is simple. Since the objective standard of morality is the will of God, we are bound to do our utmost to do the will of God. It is our conscience which indicates what the will of God is, and therefore it must always be followed, otherwise we should be deliberately abandoning the will of God, so far as we can see it. It is of course possible that our conscience may be wrong, but since our conscience is the equivalent of an absolute conviction as to the will of God, we are under an obligation to follow it.

It is useful at this stage to look at an important distinction in all questions of moral theology, namely the difference between formal and material sin. Much confusion is often caused because this distinction is not understood, or not made. Formal sin is an act done against the conscience, so that, when it was done, the person doing it was convinced that it was wrong for him to do it, or at least he strongly suspected that it was wrong. Formal sin therefore is a defiance of the conscience. Material sin is something which is wrong in itself. The person doing the sin may or may not have known that the action was wrong. In some cases a man may do something which is evidently bad, but at the time when he did it he may have been convinced that he was doing right. In this case he may be free from blame, if he has taken all possible steps to inform himself of the true facts.

It is possible to think of many examples to illustrate these principles. If a man steals, knowing it to be wrong, he commits both formal and material sin. Formal sin because he did something he knew to be wrong, and material sin because stealing is itself wrong.

A judge who holds it conscientiously to be his duty to send a man to the rack is guilty of material sin because torture and cruelty are wrong. But it is not a formal sin if the judge thought that he was doing the will of God in giving this sentence.

It is in the confusion of these two aspects that some recent writers have misled their readers. The case when a prostitute helps a sailor by having sexual intercourse with him exemplifies what may have been without formal sin, because, within their limited lights, what they did seemed to be right; but the sin was a material sin because fornication is wrong in itself. So a distinction must be made between the fact of the sin and the blameworthiness or otherwise of those who were the agents (agent being used in the sense of person acting).

It is possible then to be blameless when doing a wrong deed, that is, an act which is in itself wrong. But does such an act really exist? In other words, is not the conception of material sin an illusion? This is merely another way of asking the question, which has already been discussed, as to whether there are moral standards which fix right and wrong, irrespective of whether men recognize them as such or not. Previous points need not be repeated. We may perhaps give one more example where a distinction between formal and material sin is apparent, the state of war. There is no dispute at present in any circles, either non-Christian or Christian, that modern war is wrong. Anyone who admits this fact is admitting the basis for objective right and wrong which runs through the whole of life. But it is evident that in recent wars those taking part in them were convinced that it was their duty to do so. They were not guilty of formal sin, but they were engaging in something which was wrong in itself. Similar conditions may be seen in racial discrimination in South Africa and the southern United States of America, where men who are genuinely attached to the Christian Faith think that it is right for them to discriminate against men of a different-coloured skin from their own. Such discrimination is clearly wrong according to the will of God, but some at least of those who practise it may be in a state of invincible ignorance, and may therefore be blameless so far as formal sin is concerned.

Absolute standards of right and wrong form the content of the moral law. But the object of the moral law must be seen in its right proportions, if it is to be understood. It is not a law of qualification for spiritual benefits. Its aim is not to provide a minimum of observance, by which a man may claim benefits from God or from his fellow men. If it is so regarded, it becomes a legalistic code which kills true spontaneous moral life as God would have it lived. The moral law is the law of love as it is shown in God's ordering of the world. When a writer says,[1] 'The only absolute standard I find in the New Testament is *Agape*', he is quite correct. But it is quite wrong to deduce from this fact that there are no absolute moral laws outside the inner personality of the individual—that would be a complete *non sequitur*. The moral law is only understood when it is itself seen to be the very expression of God's *agape* in his creative and redeeming work. The moral law is provided not to make life harder, but to make it easier: not to cause conflicts and tensions in the inner man, but to prevent those very tensions and conflicts from arising. We see a number of psychiatrists discovering, or rather rediscovering, the basic fact that the most devastating and difficult conditions of the personality spring from a sense of unredeemed guilt, where the knowledge of true forgiveness has not penetrated.

[1] H. A. Williams in *Theology*, Dec. 1962.

It is in the diagnosis of the condition of the inner man that mistakes are often made which are difficult to put right. Tension and frustration arise from feelings of guilt. Such feelings may be justified or not according to how they arise. If they are not justified, they can be dispersed by being revealed in their true colours, so that the sense of guilt is dissipated. But if they are justified, it is quite another matter. They can then be dissipated in one of two ways. The first is to persuade the person that all sense of guilt is misplaced, and that in the modern enlightened world it is merely the result of outworn taboos and religious superstition. This is the general attitude of those psychologists and psychiatrists who are not Christians. The second method is to persuade the person concerned that his feelings of guilt are in fact justified, and that they may be dispersed and released because God has provided a way back to him, a way of forgiveness and of release, which alone can make his personality whole.

The trouble about the method which dismisses guilt feelings as unnecessary is that it cures the symptoms without touching the underlying disease, which is a disease of the personality cut off from God. Since God has made man for himself, the conclusion that guilt feelings are false and that there is no such thing as sin will merely leave an aching and unfilled void in the personality. It is only by filling this void with God, and therefore by coming to him through forgiveness, that fulfilment and integration can be found. The teaching of a moral law which ought to be obeyed will in many cases prevent men from indulging in sins, which will produce these fearful tensions of guilt, and in performing this function the moral law is indeed an expression of *agape*, the reality of God's love.

'Healing' is a word which is often very loosely used. Sometimes[1] it is used to mean the removal of some cause of tension. But although such removal may provide a sense of relief, it may in the proper sense not be healing at all. It may be merely the alleviation of a symptom which by its removal, because the symptom is a danger signal, may make the real disease far more dangerous. There are numerous parallels in the physical sphere. A headache which is banished by sedatives may prevent the discovery of a serious disease until it is too late to give it effective treatment, whereas in its early stages it could quite probably have been cured.

[1] E.g. H. A. Williams's essay in *Soundings*.

In the mental sphere the removal of a minor cause of tension and trouble may easily distract attention from some far more deep-seated problem, which will become progressively worse, just because the symptom is no longer there to point to it. Healing means being made whole, and this integrated meaning is especially important when considering tensions and hidden problems of the personality. No man can be made whole, in the full sense of the word, who is estranged from God. Everything therefore which happens to him must be judged in the light of this essential truth. The question as to whether a man is brought nearer to God or not is the only measuring stick of any worth. The moral law has the aim of preventing him from alienating himself from God when he is in a condition of only partial awareness of the meaning of God's love. When he has acquired a fuller knowledge of what the love of God is and what it means, the purpose of the moral law will be largely or completely served by his own awareness of what God's love means, without the need to refer to an outside authority like an external law. But the less a man knows of the true meaning of the love of God, the more he is likely to need the guidance of that love of God as it is expressed in the moral law.

In the process of growth from an elementary and inadequate grasp of God's love to a deepening apprehension of its content there are many occasions, especially in youth, when a man or a woman grapples with fierce temptations to do wrong, especially in the sexual field. At moments like this a firm apprehension of the moral law, e.g. that fornication is always wrong, can be and often is the very influence of the love of God to prevent him or her from being swept away into the engulfing torrent of physical surrender with appalling results on moral and spiritual development. How many thousands have thanked God for such moral stamina later in life, when they see how they have been saved from untold disaster! It is to reflect truly these moral truths that all must constantly endeavour to train their consciences.

5

HUMAN AND CHRISTIAN

Voluntary Actions

MORAL THEOLOGY DEALS with what is distinctively human.
There are many things which men do which are done by all
animals. The normal actions to sustain life are examples of them,
like breathing and eating. There are other actions too which are
common to human beings and to animals, which are not fully
automatic. The constituent factor of a human action as distinct
from that of any animal is that it is voluntary, i.e. it is an act of
the will. This means that it is a deliberate act on the part of the
human being concerned, and to qualify as such an action must be
the result of freedom of both choice and knowledge, as has already
been noted in dealing with the conscience.

In some highly domesticated animals there are characteristics
which in superficial ways approximate to human characteristics.
Affection is strongly marked in many cases of dogs and cats, and
they do seem to have some independent intelligence, though, so
far as one can see, such intelligence falls short of any power of
reasoning in the human sense. When we wish to be particularly
complimentary to an animal of this kind we say that it is 'almost
human', a phrase which suggests that we still recognize a distinct
chasm between the animal's powers and that of a normal human
being. This is not the place to conduct an investigation into the
whole matter, but we could not overlook it altogether. It does seem
possible too that, in the case of domesticated animals, the characteristics which they exhibit may in a number of instances be a kind
of projection of human reactions on to the animal from the owner,
derived from the superior power of human mind over an animal
nature which has been in long and continued contact with it.

A human action is therefore a voluntary action, and knowledge is necessary for the voluntary nature of the action to be established. St Thomas Aquinas puts the point clearly (II-I *q*.6, *a*.1):

> for the word voluntary implies that their movements and acts are from their own inclination. Hence it is that, according to the definitions of Aristotle, Gregory of Nyssa and Damascene, the voluntary is defined not only as having a principle within the agent, but also as implying knowledge. Therefore, since man especially knows the end of his work, and moves himself, in his acts especially is the voluntary to be found.

The difference between human action and that of animals is that 'God moves (that is, influences) man to act . . . by moving the will itself'. It is in this that the conception of voluntariness consists. That is why a purely automatic response to an outside stimulus cannot be considered to be a voluntary action. The reaction of a man in the dark who starts away from an imagined obstacle may be an example of an automatic reaction which is not voluntary.

For full moral responsibility both knowledge and choice are needed. It follows therefore that an action done under compulsion is not voluntary, nor is an action done in ignorance. Compulsion and ignorance can be of varying degrees, either small or great, and it follows that the moral quality of the action will be affected to a greater or less degree in proportion as the compulsion or ignorance is greater or smaller. Some further examination is called for both as regards ignorance and as regards compulsion.

Ignorance

Some degree of knowledge attaches to every conscious action. If it did not, the action would be like that of a sleep walker, of which the agent was completely unconscious, or like that of a man under deep hypnosis or a drug. An action which is performed in complete ignorance cannot be considered blameworthy in any way. The important question must then be faced as to what kind of ignorance is blameworthy and what is not.

At first such a question may sound academic, and it can be treated in an entirely academic fashion. But it has important practical aspects in everyday life, both within and without the Christian Church. It is not at all uncommon to meet people who are plagued by feelings of guilt because of something they have done in ignorance. If they can be assured that their ignorance was such that they are free from blame, it will have a beneficial result on their happiness and peace of mind. In reassuring such persons it is additionally helpful if they can be given not only a rational explanation, but also the knowledge that they are being informed of principles which have always been accepted by the great moral teachers of the world.

There has, however, been a tendency in some Christian moral theology to multiply distinctions and subtleties far beyond the point where they can be of much moral assistance in practical matters, and this is a notable feature of some of the traditional methods of dealing with ignorance. The distinction between vincible and invincible ignorance retains its importance. Vincible ignorance means ignorance which can be overcome, and in most cases it means ignorance which ought to have been overcome, although this is not always the case. Invincible ignorance which, as Jeremy Taylor put it, makes a person 'innocently ignorant' always excuses from blame at the time. But it is sometimes loosely claimed when there is in fact no convincing case to be made on its behalf. The necessary marks of invincible ignorance have often been set out. As good a summary as any is that of Lindsay Dewar.[1] These are the marks of invincible ignorance which must all be taken together to make ignorance truly invincible.

(*i*) The ignorance must be complete, i.e. a person must not have a suspicion that the action which he is performing may be wrong. If he is doubtful in the slightest degree, he must make further investigations and seek advice.
(*ii*) He must have taken trouble to see that his conscience is informed. Jeremy Taylor says that this means using such moral diligence as can (*a*) consist with our other affairs and the requisites of our calling and necessities; (*b*) such as is usual by ourselves in the obtaining things which we value; (*c*) such which is allowed by wise men, such which a spiritual guide will approve; (*d*) such as we ourselves do perceive to be the effects of a real desire.
(*iii*) The ignorance must not be of anything which the person might be expected to know by reason of his calling or his circumstances. Thus, if a doctor poisons a patient, he is not to be excused by saying that he did not know the drug was poisonous.
(*iv*) The ignorance must not relate to any of the principles of the Natural Law, since by definition these can be assumed to be known to everybody. However we may disagree as to the details of the Natural Law, we have to admit that every man *has* a set of moral principles which he assumes, and every society is the same.

[1] *A Short Introduction to Moral Theology*, Mowbrays 1956, p. 31.

If these principles are analysed they are seen to boil down in reality to one broad principle which may be stated thus—ignorance is only invincible, that is, blameless, when it is not in any way the fault of the person concerned that he is ignorant. It thus depends not only on the knowledge or lack of it which he happens to have at any particular moment, but also on what steps he has taken to try to inform himself, or to illuminate his conscience as to the true facts by study and by taking advice from those best qualified to give it. St Thomas Aquinas puts it thus (I-II *q*.76, *a*.2):

> Wherefore through negligence, ignorance of what one is bound to do is a sin; whereas it is not imputed as a sin to man, if he fails to know what he is unable to know. Consequently ignorance of such like things is called invincible, because it cannot be overcome by study. For this reason such like ignorance, not being voluntary, since it is not in our power to be rid of it, is not a sin: wherefore it is evident that no invincible ignorance is a sin.

Vincible ignorance may also be considered blameless if it is about something which we are not bound to know, whereas, if it is about matters one is bound to know, it is a sin. The moral theologians have divided ignorance which is vincible into various categories, such as simple, crass or affected ignorance and antecedent, concomitant or consequent ignorance. These distinctions are not without value for technical analysis, but they are likely to be of more hindrance than help in dealing with practical problems of everyday life. They also have the disadvantage of suggesting that moral responsibility can be entirely analysed by this sort of approach, when in fact the main aspects of personal responsibility can only be dealt with according to the background and psychological condition of the person concerned. The minor variations of ignorance, moreover, are only detailed applications of the overall principle that responsibility varies according to the degree of ignorance of the person acting, and from a pastoral point of view it is almost always better to deal with persons, not according to set categories, but in a way which is adaptable.

The Will

The will is not to be regarded as a separate faculty of the personality, as it has too often been represented. The word 'will' is, however, a necessity for the purpose of discussing the human personality, as it is a shorthand way of saying something like 'the total personality of man, cognitive, emotional and conative, making a choice of action'. Man does in fact choose between one course of action and another; we call the 'will' the personality making this choice. Here again there is some practical value in noting the requirements of moral theology which make an action responsible, for it at least gives the chance of removing or helping to remove false feelings of guilt, though it must be recognized that in most cases such feelings do not depend on intellectual factors in the main, but on emotional elements which cannot be removed by mere reasoning.

Three conditions are necessary to make a man fully responsible for an action and its consequences. He must (*a*) have been able to foresee the result; (*b*) have been free to take or avoid the action in the first place; and (*c*) have had a duty to do or omit something. These represent the application of common sense in the determination of personal responsibility in any particular case.

An important supplementary question now arises, namely what is usually called the question of 'double effect'. This raises the issue as to whether it is permissible to do something good if it inevitably involves something bad. The reverse is the problem as to whether it is permissible to do something which is in normal circumstances wrong in order to do something good. The usual short way of putting this is to ask whether the end justifies the means. Roman Catholics are sometimes accused of holding that the end justifies the means, especially where the good of their own Church is concerned, but it ought to be noted that this is not their official teaching nor the guidance of their leading moralists. Stated in such bald terms it is quite inadmissible as a principle of morals by any Christian. Indeed based on a doctrine of love it would be easier to argue from a Christian point of view that the means justifies the end, i.e. that, if what we do is as perfect an expression of Christian love as we can show, God will look after the results. But the statement of general principles in vague terms does not help much when it comes to dealing with particular problems.

In ordinary life men are constantly faced with the difficulty of having to choose whether to do something they think normally to be wrong in order to attain what seems to them a higher good. The most frequent example is perhaps the concealment of the truth or a deliberate lie to a patient who is suffering from an incurable disease, so as to spare him additional mental strain or to prevent a relapse into hopelessness, or both. It is impossible to lay down a hard-and-fast rule in such cases, but it ought to be noted that there seems to be a spreading tendency to conceal the facts in as many cases as possible, and that such a practice is open to serious objection from a Christian point of view. If Christians have indeed absorbed into their own outlook the great facts of their faith that Christ has overcome death and opened unto them the gate of everlasting life, they should not be afraid to look death in the face and to be ready to prepare with equable minds for their own decease. To withhold from them this opportunity, by pretending that they are not facing death in the near future, is a serious offence against their status as human beings, and it is a decision which no one should take without the most serious thought. Unfortunately some members of the medical profession have adopted the opposite attitude, namely to reveal nothing unless it is absolutely necessary. This is partly caused by professional secrecy, based upon a desire not to make mistakes. But it is far better to err on the side of allowing the patient to prepare for death, rather than to take the risk that he will become incapable of coherent thought and action before he knows of his state.

Another example which is not infrequent is the question whether it is right to destroy the life of an unborn child, if it is thought to be indispensable to save the life of the mother. It is agreed by all that if the life of the unborn child is destroyed in the process of an operation aimed at the saving of the mother's life, this is permissible, but it is not otherwise allowable according to Roman Catholic teaching.

> An operation may be performed which aims at saving the mother and brings about the death of the child as an accompanying but not intended effect.[1]

Questions of abortion will be considered later, but there is a point to make here on the matter of principle. In the case of the mother and the unborn child there is in effect a choice between two evils, for the lack of any action will result in the death of the mother, and perhaps in some cases in the death of the child too. The decision must therefore be taken not on some general rule, e.g. that it is never morally justifiable to do an act whose first effect is bad, in this case the removal and death of the child: it must be

[1] Karl Hörmann, *An Introduction to Moral Theology*, Burns and Oates, 1961, p. 249.

settled by weighing the moral circumstances of the particular case. These must include the duties of the mother to her family, the needs of her other children and her husband and similar matters.

It is often difficult to weigh the good against the bad in such a situation. In the case of the mother and child there seems little doubt that the life of the mother must have moral priority. We do not therefore maintain that we may take any action in which we think the good will outweigh the evil. The case we are discussing is one where we are forced to take one choice or the other—either to 'vote' for the mother's death or for that of the child.

The torturing of men by the Inquisition could not, for example, be justified on the grounds that the good which was done vastly outweighed the evil, though the Inquisitors certainly believed that to be the case. There was no external compulsion on the Inquisitors to make the choice to torture their prisoners: the absence of torture would not have worsened the position of the heretics or put them or the Inquisitors in additional jeopardy.

Sin

The word 'sin' has many disadvantages because it has a number of different meanings and therefore it has to be used with discretion and care. It is commonly very loosely used, and some have suggested that it ought to be dropped from the Christian vocabulary. But in fact this is impossible, for if it were abandoned it would be necessary to find another word to take its place, which would soon have attached to it all the disadvantages of the original word.

Sin, properly speaking, is a condition of the personality alienated from God. The person of man can be so alienated from God that he is no longer capable of finding his way back to that relationship of love for which he was created by God. It was this condition which made it necessary for God to enter into the sinful world of man and to overcome sin, in the sense of ridding it of its power to separate from God. Sin now no longer separates from God except by the free choice of man himself. God loves man too much to force him to do his will; he will only draw him to himself by the power of sacrificing love. We can still by our own choice continue in sin—i.e. we can turn away from God and thus alienate ourselves from him—but there is no longer any excuse for this alienation. Man can no longer say, 'It is not my fault. I have been born into a sinful world which prevents me from knowing the love of God.' God himself in Jesus Christ has overcome the barrier which man made and has united to himself all those who care to take advantage of his act.

Acts of sin are sins—in the plural. A sin can, as we have seen, be either formal or material. It can be a conscious act of defiance of God's will, in which case it is a formal and material sin; or it can be an innocent action which turns out to be wrong, in which case it is a material sin only. The difference between the two is important, but it does not require further treatment here. There is another distinction between different kinds of sins, namely that between mortal and venial sins. This favourite distinction of moral theology is harmful in a great many ways, and it is high time that it was altogether abolished. Of course some sins are more serious than others, and the pastor or theologian must be able to distinguish between them for his own purposes, but sins vary as much in gravity as the persons of the human race vary in temperament and character, and sins cannot be conveniently divided into two clear categories of mortal and venial.

There is a general objection to such classification which has never been adequately answered. To divide sins in this way is bound to give the impression that there are some sins which matter and some which do not. No amount of explanation can avoid this impression. It becomes even more firmly fixed in people's minds if, as is the case in the Roman Church, there is a rule that only mortal sins need be confessed in the sacrament of Penance. There can be no doubt that the general effect of this distinction is unhealthy, and that it introduces into the heart of the Christian life a legalism which can only be harmful.

There is another general objection to the teaching, common at least in the Roman Church, that a mortal sin puts the immortal soul in jeopardy, whereas a venial sin does not. The first difficulty about such teaching is that it is obviously impossible to say whether such a theory is true or not. It cannot at its best be more than inspired guesswork to say what sin has this effect. The second difficulty is that venial sins (so called) can be more spiritually harmful than mortal sins. The distinction is therefore most misleading to those whom, presumably, it is intended to help.

In about 1935 Dr Kenneth Kirk, the most distinguished of modern Anglican moral theologians, delivered some lectures to clergy in London. He upheld the distinction between mortal and

venial sins, and in explaining what constituted a mortal sin he gave
three tests.

(*a*) The first was that the sin caused grave injury either to an
individual or to the Christian community or to God and his
purposes. Such a consideration must of course enter into any
judgement as to the gravity or otherwise of any particular sin. But
the hidden sins which are classed as venial may have a hidden
injurious effect on the Church, or on an individual, or on God and
his purposes, far greater than a sin whose immediate effects seem
to be more glaring. It is not a realistic distinction.

(*b*) Second, the sinner must be fully aware of the evil character
and consequence of his sin. How is such a knowledge to be evaluated
or tested? There are some cases where sins are grave and known
to be grave by the sinner in general terms. But for him to be *fully
aware* of its character and consequences is so unlikely as to make
the test more or less useless.

(*c*) The third test was that in spite of the two foregoing elements
being present the sinner must have sinned with absolute deliberateness and intention. Here again it is a test which is not really useful,
because its conditions are hardly ever or never fulfilled. If they are
never fulfilled it merely means that mortal sins are never committed, which makes the whole affair ridiculous. The discoveries of
psychology in recent years has made it plain that men are affected
by all kinds of influences of which they are not aware. *Absolute
deliberateness* therefore never really exists in a human being. This
does not mean that he is not responsible, but it does mean that this
particular way of categorizing sins is inadequate.

Perhaps an even more powerful objection to the kind of approach
which this division suggests is that it takes men's attention away
from the love of God and focuses it upon the legal requirements of
external actions. This is an ever-present danger in moral theology
which constantly needs correcting. Sin can only have meaning in
relation to the love of God. A man who knows something of the
love of God and is growing towards a closer unity with him wishes
to avoid anything which will hinder such growth or cause sorrow
to God who is loved. Venial and mortal sins cease to have any
relevant meaning to him. If the man commits sins, it is because
he has failed to respond to God's love as he ought, and his penitence
is a reflection of the measure of his love, as God's forgiveness is
the measure of divine love. He cannot discuss sins in legalistic

terms, for such discussion is itself a kind of betrayal of the meaning of God's love for him.

Lesser of Two Evils

It has from the earliest times been the rule of common sense that, if a man has an inescapable choice so that he must choose one of two evil courses, he should choose the lesser evil. According to Kirk,[1] it was first officially stated by the Church at the Council of Toledo in AD 653. The sinful condition of the world is such that it is not infrequent for men to find themselves in situations where no choice before them is good, but all possibilities involve them in evil in some degree. And it is important to remember, when examining such a condition, that absence of action is as much a choice as a decision to do something actively. We have already said something of the same kind in reference to the surgeon who must decide either to let the mother die or to cause the death of an unborn child. It is only possible to deny the reality of such a choice by maintaining the fiction that no action represents no choice.

Failure to act can be just as serious a fault as acting wrongly. We might quote in support the condemnation of such failure by Jesus Christ implied in the parables of the Good Samaritan and of Dives and Lazarus. It was not a wrong action that deserved condemnation, but the failure to exercise the office of love when presented with an opportunity to do so. Even more strikingly is the same lesson driven home in the parable of the sheep and the goats: the condemnation of the goats rests entirely on the fact that they did nothing when there was a chance to do something. The condemnation is severe (Matt. 25.41): 'The curse is upon you; go from my sight to the eternal fire that is ready for the devil and his angels.' However we may interpret such words, they are as severe as any Jesus used, of which we have a record. We must therefore accept the responsibility for doing nothing as quite as serious as that of a positive action.

The Christian Community

The consideration of moral theology, so far as it is casuistry, for the most part means a concern with the individual person and with the moral choices which lie before him, for it is inevitable

---

[1] *Conscience and its Problems*, Longmans 1948, p. 332.

that an analysis of the subject breaks down into this form. But these moral choices cannot be seen in their right perspective unless they are put into the context of the life of the worshipping community, the Church. It is not for us in considerations of moral theology to try to set out the liturgical and spiritual meaning of the Church's life; that is the business of other branches of theology. We are concerned with this life only as it impinges on questions of morals.

A secular society makes moral demands on its members. Restraints are necessary in order to defend and establish the life of the society. Such restraints, expressed in civil laws, make a moral demand on the society's members, even when they do not altogether coincide with the ideal system of morality, as we shall see in our discussion of human justice. But the demands of human society are radically different from those of the divine society, the Church, although there is much superficial resemblance between their aims. For the Christian life, whether in its moral or spiritual aspect, cannot be lived fully except in the fellowship of the Church. Within the Church the moral aspect is not to be thought of as demands on the individual by the Church, for that gives the impression that the Church and the individual are different and separable. The truth is that the Christian life can only mean what it is intended to mean when it is part of the Church, when the individuality of the person is fulfilled and wholly integrated into the life of the People of God.

One of the dangers of the dissection of the Christian moral life is that it tends to weaken the sense which Christians ought to have of the common life in which they partake, which alone makes full sense of the Gospel of Christ. When therefore we consider demands of the Church on the individual we should see them as minimum demands, put forward for the guidance of the Church's members, rather than as regulations which qualify for particular benefits. Basically the rules of the Church serve the same purpose as general moral standards, i.e. they provide a minimum level which must be accepted before any real progress is possible. For those who have advanced any distance at all the rules become minor elements of their whole life which are taken as a matter of course.

Let us consider, for example, the obligation of a Christian to take part in the worship of the Body of Christ on Sunday. We do

not say that in order to qualify for membership an individual must
take part in the Sunday worship of the Church, but that there is
no person who has truly participated in the life of the Body of
Christ who would or could absent himself from the worship of
the Body without serious cause. It is certainly permissible to advise
Christians to observe the rules of the Church on the grounds that
it will help them in their spiritual lives, but the primary objective
of these rules is not individualistic but corporate.

The moral life of a Christian must spring from the love of God
(*agape*). This necessarily involves the conception of the common
life of the Body of Christ, because love cannot be exercised in
isolation, nor can it be merely a relationship between the soul and
God, if it is to be true to the Gospel: it must be love exercised
in the common life of the Church, expressed in its fellowship
(*koinonia*). God himself is a *koinonia* in the deepest sense of the
word—that is the meaning of the doctrine of the Holy Trinity.
The Church is to reflect and express this divine life, which is to
course through its veins and to create in it the true *koinonia* of the
Body of the Son. *Agape* is the character of the life in the *koinonia*.
It could be called the 'law' of life in the *koinonia* in the sense that
without it the life cannot exist.

Because of these basic facts members of the Church who see
the truth will urgently wish to fulfil all the demands which the
Church, as an earthly corporate Body, makes upon them in trying
to express in this world the substance of the life-giving truth
revealed to and in it by its Head, Jesus Christ. As Hooker[1] put it:

> It doth not stand with the duty which we owe our heavenly Father,
> that to the ordinances of our mother the Church we should show
> ourselves disobedient. Let us not say we keep the commandments of
> the one, when we break the law of the other: for unless we obey both,
> we obey neither.

But there is a special danger within the life of the Church itself,
that the demands which it makes in the form of rules may turn
into a form of legalism, which undermines the true spiritual life
of the fellowship. Yet the Church can hardly avoid giving some
sort of answer to those who ask, 'What should be the basis of my
life in the Church?' The Roman and Anglican Churches diverge
at this point in an important manner. From a practical point of
view the Roman attitude has much to commend it. It lays down

[1] *Laws of Ecclesiastical Polity*, Bk III, ch. IX, 3.

laws, which make moral demands on its members, and which tend to give answers to all the details of daily life and religious observance. Thus moral behaviour has in large measure come to be identified with the observance of Canon Law. It can hardly be denied, and it is admitted by some Roman Catholics, as we have already had occasion to observe, that this results in a deplorable legalism in the religious life. It is an attitude which is the result of identifying the moral demands of the Christian Gospel within the *koinonia* with legislation which, from a human point of view, seems to be advantageous to the wordly organization of the Church. If the Church can make any moral demands upon its members, there is an ever-present temptation to its authorities to make such demands, not because they are the inevitable result of the Gospel, but because they seem likely to help to hold the Church together.

An excellent example of this latter kind of regulation is to be found in the Roman regulations designed to prevent Roman Catholics from becoming contaminated by contacts with heretical Christians, i.e. all non-Roman Christians. Fortunately the old attitude is now passing, but it provides a vivid illustration of the particular point we are discussing. Canon Mahoney, a great authority on the subject, felt constrained to change his opinion about what relations were permissible with fellow Christians outside the Roman Church, and to contradict the definite authoritative advice which he had for many years been giving to the Roman clergy through the columns of the *Clergy Review*. His conclusion was[1]:

> It must follow that those amongst us who have held that a united prayer with heretics . . . *is always of its nature wrong*, have been defending a too rigorous interpretation of the law in Canon 1258, an outlook due to our conditions in this country, to the traditions received from our forefathers, and to the necessity, as we conceived it, of discouraging the faithful from any religious contact whatever with non-Catholics.

The whole attitude referred to by Canon Mahoney has been completely reversed by the latest developments in the Church of Rome, which, we are thankful to say, now encourage Roman Catholics to have contacts with Christians of other traditions and to join with them in common prayer under specified conditions.

[1] Quoted by Fr Maurice Bévenot, S.J., in *Christian Unity: a Catholic View*, Sheed and Ward 1962, p. 114.

It is, of course, perfectly possible to hold that for many years it was inopportune for Roman Catholics to have such contacts, and that it was right that they should have been discouraged. But it is clear that the Roman Catholic clergy and laity were misled to suppose that such contacts in themselves were morally sinful. A canonical regulation (whether advisable or not) has for centuries been elevated into a moral principle, which is now shown to be false. It exhibits the tendency of the Roman Church to confuse what are temporary canonical expedients with moral principles, and it is very difficult to escape this confusion if, as is the case with the Romans, there is an accepted practice of laying legal obligations on the clergy and laity and legislating for them in a wide field.

The Anglican approach is a different one. It avoids laying down detailed prescriptions, and contents itself with general moral obligations rather than with detailed laws. This has serious practical disadvantages since it leaves matters too vague, if regarded from a purely practical angle. But the weakness is the reverse side of an important strength. Some general rules are laid down, but in almost all cases it is left to the individual to interpret them. It is not left to the individual to decide *whether* they should be observed, but only *how* they should be put into practice. The one exception is the rule that every member of the Church must receive communion three times a year at the least, of which Easter should be one.

The rules of fasting and abstinence provide an example of the Anglican approach. Fasting and abstinence are both enjoined, but the exact form which they take is left to the individual himself. In England an added complication arises from the relationship with the State, which has prevented any effective revision of the Book of Common Prayer. It is felt, with some justification, that the rules of fasting and abstinence decided in the seventeenth century are not those which would be accepted generally by the Church today.

The practice of religious duties, accepted by the Church to which one belongs, is a clear moral obligation for a Christian and can therefore be considered a part of the moral law. But it is not to be regarded as a legalistic minimum with which a man may be satisfied, for such a view indicates shallowness. He may be a member of the Church by Baptism, but he is not fully united to Christ or living in the Gospel.

Since the worship of the Church in the Eucharist is the life-giving centre of all its existence, the Church assumes that its members shall take part in the Eucharist as a means of safeguarding their own spiritual health, and as an expression of the love which animates the Body. Only in this way can the life of the Body continue to exist, for this is the mystery of the divinely given life, and it can only be fully shared in this way. The Church has both the right and the duty to say what are the indispensable conditions of the Christian life, and to insist that those who claim to be its members should in their lives demonstrate, by fulfilling these conditions, their sincere desire to know God and Jesus Christ whom he has sent.

Anglican demands are not many, and merely reproduce the minimum requirements of the Catholic Church throughout the ages. Besides the rule about communion, already mentioned, they assume the worship of God on Sundays and major Holy Days, the observance of days of fasting, abstinence and special prayer, confession in the case of troubled consciences, lifelong marriage, and forbid marriage within the prohibited degrees.

Unhappily the fact must also be recognized that among Anglicans these obligations are taken very lightly, and sometimes totally ignored. This must certainly reflect in some degree the failure of the clergy to give proper and regular teaching on the subject. The consciences of the people wait to be enlightened though responsible laymen have a clear duty to know and observe the Church's requirements. The absence of a clear legal requirement, such as the Romans have, makes the task more difficult, but also more rewarding when it evokes a response. Anglicans in interpreting these duties to their people have the right to find guidance in the practices of the universal Church. They do not have the right, however, though some of them assume it, of adopting the same line as Roman Catholics and trying to apply Roman rules. As we have seen, the Anglican approach is different in kind from the Roman, and, apart from that, it is quite absurd to adopt a system of rules without at the same time adopting the system of dispensation which goes with them. No such system of dispensation is possible within Anglicanism, since it is part of a legalistic system which Anglicans have rejected. In Anglican practice dispensation is a matter which must finally be decided by the individual conscience with whatever help the person concerned may care to seek in the way of guidance from his priest or bishop. The appeal to the individual must be a moral appeal to his loyalty to the Church, the same appeal to Christ in the Church which was characteristic of the earliest communities of Christians as we find them in the New Testament.

Laws of the Church should so far as possible reflect the *consensus fidelium*, the general consent of the faithful. This is not because of any democratic principles, which can be very misleading if applied to the Church, but for the spiritual reason that the rules of the Body should be the expression of the fellowship of its members, and not be imposed externally or even internally by a legislative authority which is independent of such consensus. But it is not in fact possible by any known method to be sure that any particular rule will meet with general approval. Rules should for this reason be kept to a minimum, but members of the Church should regard it as an obligation upon their consciences to do their best to keep such rules.

In applying the rules of the Church and in considering individual cases a constant preoccupation of priests and other authorities must be the question of scandal. There are two aspects to every case. On the one hand there is the position of the individual and his actions considered in themselves, on the other the effect of the action in public and its consequences for the Church's reputation and discipline. It is here that the question of scandal arises.

A simple example, not at all uncommon, may be given. A member of the Church may have intellectual doubts about certain doctrines of the Creed, or he may even reject one or more of them. If he has made every effort to understand what the teaching of the Church is, and still does not accept it, he will be in invincible ignorance. He is therefore not guilty of any fault, and he should be encouraged to continue to come to church and to live the Christian life.

But if he begins to teach publicly doctrines which are at variance with the teaching of the Church, the matter becomes the subject of scandal, and the Church may have to act for the protection of its own fellowship and integrity. The person may then be excommunicated, or denounced, or other suitable action taken, such as deprivation of office. The result of his action has been to imperil the Church's message to others.

Another common example occurs in the discipline of marriage, a subject which is more fully discussed elsewhere. It sometimes happens that people are divorced and remarried without a full appreciation of the rulings of the Church and the teaching of the Church about the lifelong nature of marriage. *To this extent* they are not blameworthy, if their ignorance is innocent. But the Church has a duty to uphold the sanctity of marriage and its lifelong character: it therefore decrees that no person can be remarried in church if a former partner is living, for to do so would cause scandal. The rule is a necessary witness to the mission of the Church. But, in spite of the prohibition of second marriages of this kind in church, there are provisions for ministering pastorally to those who have been remarried after divorce.[1]

The final authority for drastic action, if it has to be taken, comes from the New Testament. In Matt. 18.15 Jesus himself gives guidance as to how to deal with scandal. There should first be brotherly discussion and correction which is private, and provides the opportunity for re-establishing brotherly love. If that fails, two or three more are to be brought in to give added weight, but it is still to be kept quiet. But in the event of the second step failing, then the matter should be remitted to the church authorities, who have power to act in judgement and penalty in any way that is right, the ultimate step being excommunication, the cutting off of the offending member from the Body.

The letters of St Paul do not hesitate to rebuke those who try to settle their differences in the wrong way (I Cor. 6.1)—in this case by going to law against their fellow Christians before the unbelievers. The reason why it is wrong is clearly that it is an offence against that love (*agape*) without which the fellowship of the Church ceases to be anything but a hollow mockery of what the Body of Christ should be.

[1] See also p. 129 f.

6

VIRTUES AND VICES

THE 'THEOLOGICAL' VIRTUES of faith, hope and love are normally thought to be part of the moral life. They can be studied separately, but it is important always to remember that each is merely one aspect of a whole life and that none of them can exist without the other two. They correspond to different elements in the human personality and are parallel to the three psychological aspects of human personality, the cognitive, the appetitive and the conative, though these divisions too are arbitrary and somewhat unreal. Yet for the purposes of study it is necessary to accept the artificiality involved in analysis.

Faith

The scholastic tradition in dealing with the virtue of faith is inclined to be too intellectual in approach. 'Faith' is one of the great words of Christian life, but it is used with very different meanings by different Christian traditions. It always has an intellectual content, but that intellectual element is by no means the whole of the concept of faith, and in some ways it is not even its most important aspect. Popular misconceptions about what faith means often rest on the mistaken idea that faith is concerned only with the intellectual recognition of facts, or that it is a substitute for intellectual belief. St Thomas Aquinas himself did not confine faith to the intellectual activity of man. He held that faith could exist in a fashion without hope and love, but maintained that it could not be perfect without love (II-I q.65, a.4). This is equivalent to saying that there is an important element of faith which is not mere intellectual assent.

The scholastic method of dealing with faith generally lacks the richness of meaning which the word carries in the New Testament and in many of the historical traditions of Christendom. Some commentators (e.g. Mortimer) put side by side the phrases 'the faith once delivered to the saints' and 'justification by faith' as though the word was used in the same sense in both cases. Jesus himself constantly used the word 'faith' and it is evident that it was far more than intellectual assent, and indeed in many cases conscious intellectual assent seemed to play a very small part in it. Jesus was always trying to draw out faith from those with whom he came into contact. No doubt the kind of faith which he wished to encourage did include intellectual assent, but much more important was the personal relationship which it implied between the person concerned and Jesus, by which the former put his trust in Jesus and yielded himself in surrender to the personality of Christ, throwing all his cares on him. It is this act of trust and surrender which restores the right relationship between the person concerned and God.

Throughout the epistles the same emphasis is put upon faith by St Paul especially in his letter to the Romans, where Abraham is chosen as an example (Rom. 3.19-5.11). In the epistle of St James in the famous passage which maintains that faith without works is dead, he might well be aiming his shafts at those who wished to make faith an intellectual operation rather than commitment of the whole person to Christ. That seems to be the real meaning of what James is saying—it is the deadness of faith that is serious, and the absence of works is merely a sign of the serious lack of faith. When therefore the theological virtue of faith is discussed, the fulness of its meaning must be remembered, and in particular the implications which it carries of full surrender to God without any merit or standing on our part. The Lutheran insistence on this aspect is an essential part of true Christianity. Unhappily Roman and Anglican criticisms of Lutheran views have often misrepresented what they really meant.

There is often a discussion under the heading of faith as to whether the Church can fall into error. Mortimer[1] follows a Roman method of reasoning in holding that the Church exists to mediate to men the knowledge and the grace of God and that it is therefore inconsistent with the character of God that he should permit the Church to err, and that therefore it cannot err. The basic false assumption of this reasoning is that it assumes that what we think is congruent with the character of God must necessarily be so.

[1] *The Elements of Moral Theology*, p. 109 f.

It is not the case, for God's actions can only be judged by one with the same powers as he, and by definition there can be no such person. All human judgements about God must be accompanied by a humility which refuses to impose upon God human views, which are of necessity limited.

A belief in the inerrancy or infallibility of the Church overlooks two serious objections. In the first place it underestimates the power and the effect of sin in man. The Church on earth is composed of sinners, who are always affected by their sin even when they are forgiven. This brings out the second objection, namely that the preservation of the Church on earth from error necessarily implies the limitation of men's freedom and the inhibition of their free will, so that the state of error may be prevented. Moreover this form of argument merely ends up in the Roman conclusion, for, if it is the case that the Church cannot fall into error, it must equally be the case that the Church must have a localized authority which states definitely and unequivocally what the belief of the Church is. But these views are neither necessary nor in accord with the New Testament.

We have no reason to believe that the Church on earth as a corporate body is divinely prevented from sharing in the free will which is the human lot of its members, and which is also the basis of the Christian doctrine of man and of the love of God, so far as man is concerned. Jesus is not recorded as saying that the Church would not fall into error. He did say that his followers would be led into all truth. This is quite a different kind of statement—it is the difference between infallibility and indefectibility. We have the assurance that if we remain loyal to the Church God will bring us and it to the place where he would have us come.

The further conclusion, again supported by Mortimer, that what the Church has taught for a very long time must have been revealed by God is a still more astonishing theory. No doubt anything which the Church has taught for a very long time must carry great weight with Christians, but more cannot be claimed. Moreover one would want to know what a 'very long time' is. In our Christian life we move in the perspectives of eternity, where a thousand years in God's sight are but as yesterday. It would be possible to find beliefs which have prevailed for a majority of the Church's life which are entirely superseded now. To look to the Church for authoritative statements of belief, which can never be wrong, betokens quite the wrong approach. We look to the Church for guidance, and we are loyal to the claims which it makes upon us, but we expect to revise our views as we learn more in different ways of God's truth.

It may be objected that this attitude leaves us with no reliable guide and that we might as well give up the Church altogether. But such a view is only tenable on the assumption that the Church is there for the purpose of making statements, and this is manifestly not the case. The Christian life is not a process of discovering propositions about God, though in certain circumstances these may be and are of importance. The Christian life is a process of men growing together and wrestling with intellectual and moral problems together in loyalty to Christ, the Head of the Church, and to the Church itself, which is the living fellowship of those who are seeking to do God's will in partnership and true membership of one another.

If faith were merely a form of intellectual knowledge, assent to that knowledge would be necessary, whether a man wished to give it or not, and this would be an interference with the freedom of choice, which is an essential element in a personal relationship. If faith were knowledge in the intellectual sense, religion would be primarily a matter of calculation and not of love. Faith, however, is reasonable and gives the only complete satisfaction to the questions which reason asks. Reason and faith are united in Christianity, as O. C. Quick has admirably explained.[1] Faith and reason are not separate faculties each dealing with a different section of truth. Both are needed to supplement one another, in order to enable man to grasp the whole truth, so far as it is within his mental and spiritual comprehension.

People sometimes complain that they do not have faith. But faith is within the grasp of all: there is no man who cannot have faith if he wills, unless he be mentally incompetent. For faith in its barest essentials is the act of the will which takes Jesus as a man's Saviour and Lord. It is the decision which recognizes the truth of the claim of Jesus, 'I am the way, the truth and the life.' 'But', the reply comes, 'how can I take him, if I do not believe what you say?' The answer to that query is that to wait for assurance before choosing is to refuse to choose at all, for the essence of the choice is trust in a person, and trust in a person must have

---

[1] *Doctrines of the Creed*, Nisbet 1958, p. 16.

an element of uncertainty or doubt about it, if it is to be a free
choice. The step must be taken before assurance comes, and final
assurance only comes in living the life of Christ, and then in ways
which are unexpected. W. R. Inge's remark remains profoundly
true: 'Faith begins with an experiment and ends with an
experience.'

Some of the obstacles which prevent people from exercising the
virtue of faith are intellectual. Some do not find it possible to
accept as reasonable the basis on which it rests. This may be due
to a number of causes, some merely subjective and others external.
There are some brought up in an atmosphere hostile to the Christian
religion, especially those influenced by a pseudo-scientific attitude
which has never examined Christian beliefs honestly or adequately,
or which has instilled wrong presuppositions in their minds. There
are some who seek for the wrong kind of intellectual assurances;
others are guilty of an intellectual pride, which makes improper
demands.

But there are also moral difficulties, which pose as intellectual,
as a cloak to conceal the true obstacle, even to the mind of the
person concerned. The word 'moral' in this context bears a wide
connotation, and may be taken to include the difficulty of facing
the demands which the Christian faith makes upon its adherents
in many different ways.

When we make an act of faith, we put our trust in Christ and
submit to him and also to the Church. We do not abrogate our
powers of reason and thought in favour of some ecclesiastical
authority, but we recognize that God has founded the Church
through Christ, in order that it may be the place where the Holy
Spirit leads men into all truth. The corollary of this recognition is
the knowledge that no man can know truth as a solitary, because
it can only be lived and therefore fully known in community, in the
fellowship which Christ founded for that very purpose.

St Augustine wrote: 'If you believe what you like in the Gospel
and reject what you like, it is not the Gospel you believe but
yourselves.' A proper humility should be the mark of a Christian
in intellectual as well as in other matters. It should be shown by a
careful hesitation not to deny the teachings of the Church or of
Christian leaders, if they have been widely and for a long time
accepted, without the strongest possible cause. But on the other
hand not to be afraid to exercise the God-given faculty of reason

within the limits of a proper loyalty to the divine society. '*Quod ubique, quod semper, quod ab omnibus*' (everywhere, always, by all) will be a test of Catholic and Christian authority which the individual Christian will try to apply.

Within the framework of faith doubts can continue. The fulness of Christian truth is something which is not known until a Christian grows to the fullest divine knowledge of which he is capable. The inevitable corollary of this must be that, until that fulness comes, there must always be patches of darkness and uncertainty in our understanding. Every Christian ought to be ready to face the temptation of doubt from time to time. Sometimes the intellectual assurance of faith entirely disappears, even from people who have been well established in the Christian life. The experience of losing assurance, though a sore trial, can be, and is often meant to be, a means of strengthening the inner will to cling to God in pure faith without the buttress of intellectual support.

It is important to realize that doubt is not a sin, as many Christians mistakenly believe; it is an opportunity or, at the worst, a temptation. Like other temptations it only becomes wrong when it is encouraged in its negative aspect. Doubt is a necessary step in the ascertaining of truth. Without doubt there would be no advance in intellectual knowledge, and it must therefore be seen in the first place as something with a positive purpose in finding the truth.

People differ widely in their ability to understand the intellectual side of the Christian religion. A university professor is clearly more able to understand theological propositions than a simple peasant woman, who certainly has as much chance—probably more—of reaching the kingdom of God as the professor. It is not necessary for salvation that everyone should have a full intellectual understanding of the doctrines of the creed, and there are doubtless many excellent Christians who say the creed who have never tried to analyse its contents. There is nothing wrong in this. Every Christian ought to try to understand his faith to the best of his ability, but this does not mean a complete study of every article of the Christian faith.

A Christian may give his attention to other parts of the Christian message, such as its teaching about prayer, which is itself a large enough subject to occupy a lifetime. No moral fault lies with a

Christian because his intellectual abilities, or lack of time, or some other good reason do not give him the chance to become an expert theologian.

Some of those who come to church have reservations about items in the creed, such as the Virgin Birth, and sometimes of even more serious matters such as the Divinity of Christ. In such cases the persons concerned have the duty, where their mind is not satisfied, to do everything possible to enlighten it, by asking guidance from the clergy or from others qualified to give it, and by reading such books as may help them to a fuller understanding of the teaching of the Church. If, after doing everything possible, they are still doubtful, they should not consider themselves to be barred from full participation in the Christian life. They would then technically fall into the category of the invincibly ignorant, to whom no blame attaches. They should continue to attend church and take part in the life of the fellowship. If, however, they were to spread abroad their doubts as to the truth of the Church's teaching, the danger of scandal would arise, and the Church might be forced to take action in defence of other members of the fellowship. There would then be a problem of discipline and pastoral care. The Church cannot regard as a member in good standing one who is publicly denying its own teaching.

Another aspect of faith is the right attitude to those who have fallen into heresy. The moral problem which arises is that on the one hand we have to witness to the truth, and on the other we must witness to Christian love. In God the two are perfectly united, but in our sinful state on earth there is often a real tension. We do not have to assume that we ourselves are without fault, since both we and our ancestors have done much to make the situation worse, but we must not behave as though truth were indifferent. The loosening of the Roman rules about Christians praying together is a welcome step, though it has not yet gone far enough. If the divisions of Christians are ever to be overcome, it will only be done by Christians learning to love one another in Christ. This presupposes contacts and meetings between Christians, but more than this is necessary—there must also be true understanding of one another's spiritual traditions and modes of worship.

In order to show that truth is important, there must be some rules which express this fact. The Anglican tradition has been to draw a line at a certain point. The Lambeth Quadrilateral[1] accepted by successive Lambeth Conferences implies that general intercommunion can only be based on agreement in Faith and Order, and full recognition of Ministries on episcopal and apostolic principles. If the differences are important, then there must be boundary lines somewhere. If they are not important, there is no justification for continuing with separate church organizations.

Within the broad limits already mentioned everything ought to be done to build up co-operation and understanding with other Christians, though in a balanced way which is truly ecumenical in scope. So far as Anglicans are concerned, their opportunities lie with Orthodox and Roman Catholics on the one side and with Protestants on the other. This is a moral obligation on every Christian arising out of his faith. It is likely to be best discharged when he has a deep sense of the richness of his own spiritual tradition, for this will bring him closer to all other spiritual traditions which are centred on unity with Christ.

Hope

The concept of hope in the New Testament is developed only in the Epistles and is hardly found in the Gospels, though in actual time of writing the Epistles were earlier than the Gospels. The idea of hope which is found in St Paul's writings is not connected with earthly rewards and achievements, but is exclusively bound up with the thought of the last things and the triumph which is to come. It is grounded on the resurrection and it looks forward to the final consummation of all things in Christ. It is most clearly expressed in I Peter 1.13, 'Set your hope perfectly

---

[1] The full text of the Lambeth Quadrilateral is as follows:

A. The Holy Scriptures of the Old and New Testaments, as 'containing all things necessary to salvation', and as being the rule and ultimate standard of the Christian Faith.

B. The Apostles' Creed, as the Baptismal Symbol; and the Nicene Creed, as the sufficient statement of the Christian Faith.

C. The two Sacraments ordained by Christ himself—Baptism and the Supper of the Lord—ministered with unfailing use of Christ's Word of Institution, and of the elements ordained by him.

D. The Historic Episcopate, locally adapted in the methods of its administration to the varying needs of the nations and peoples called of God into the Unity of his Church.

on the grace that is to be brought unto you at the revelation of Jesus Christ.'[1]

Like faith and love, hope is called theological because its object is God, and it cannot be separated from them in a balanced Christian life. St Thomas Aquinas maintains the same point in regard to hope as he does in regard to faith, that neither can be complete without love. Hope has sometimes been degraded by being identified with ideas of merit and reward in the Christian life. Such a treatment can throw the whole Christian life out of balance, and indeed it was one of the major conditions which produced the upheaval of the Reformation. While not the same thing as faith, hope is closely allied to it and could not exist without it, just as faith could not exist without hope. By hope we accept the promises of God as regards the future.

Hope must not be interpreted as a merely selfish desire for supernatural rewards, for such an interpretation introduces into the heart of the Christian life a self-regarding element which can undermine the whole act of self-surrender to God. We hope for the glory of God to be manifested. Such a hope does incidentally include a future of eternal happiness for ourselves, and there is a clear element of rewards and punishments in the New Testament, though these are often found to be the rewards of character rather than of external acts. If we make our hope a selfish hope, we automatically prevent ourselves from becoming what God wants us to be, and thus fail to have the true virtue of hope which springs out of a God-centred life.

In the virtue of hope we see at work the same principle which runs all through the spiritual life, that it is only those who lose themselves in submission to God who find true fulfilment of the self. It is another aspect of the well-known fact that those who work hardest to find happiness do not find it, because happiness is a by-product of something else—doing the will of God.

There is an important difference between Christian hope and the common use of the word. 'Hoping for the best' is a good example of the ordinary use. The everyday meaning of hope is far removed from Christian hope, for it often rests on a shallow optimism which has no natural or supernatural basis, whereas Christian hope is part of trust in the person of Jesus Christ and in his heavenly Father.

[1] A. Richardson in *A Theological Word Book of the Bible*, ed. Richardson, SCM Press 1957, p. 109.

One of the attitudes opposed to hope is fear. St Thomas divides fear into four categories. Servile fear which springs from fear of punishment; filial fear which is a fear of offending a parent; initial fear which is a mixture of the two; and wordly fear, arising from fear of worldly loss. The last he characterizes as always evil, but the others have their parts to play. Filial fear is the only proper fear in every respect (II-II *q*.19, *a*.2 and 3). But we are told in the New Testament that perfect love casteth out fear because fear has torment, though there remains a place for 'the fear of the Lord', an expression which is used to express the awe of the creature in the presence of his Creator.

The vices contrary to hope are despair and presumption. There are two kinds of presumption, first for a man to presume on his own power, and second to presume improperly on the power of God. In the former case it is shown in a belief that the good life can be lived fully without the help of God, or that a man can earn his own salvation. The second kind of presumption is to act as though God can be relied upon to come to the rescue without any consideration of the circumstances, such as to presume that God will forgive without repentance on the part of him who is to be forgiven.

Despair is a sin because it may mean the acceptance of a false view of God. In practice it is found that, more often than not, despair is the outcome of psychological and emotional stresses, over which the person who suffers from them has little or no control. Such conditions lessen or remove altogether any blame-worthiness in the attitude of despair.

Despair can spring from various causes. One of the most common is the apparent inability to conquer some habitual sin. It is particularly common when the sin concerned is sexual, and it is often associated with habits of masturbation, especially in boys and young men. The treatment of such cases falls within the bounds of pastoral theology, but it may be noted here that the overcoming of bad habits should not be expected to be complete in a few weeks or months, when they are deep-seated. We must be patient in overcoming our sins and be ready to wait for final victory. And even when we have not succeeded, we must always remember that God's grace is greater than our sin.

A true and living hope will guard against some of the above dangers and if properly integrated into a Christian's life will keep them out altogether.

Love

Love is the subject of the whole of the New Testament, and it is not the task of moral theology to discuss all its various aspects. There are certain elements in the Christian teaching about love which especially concern moral theology and it is to these that we must confine our study. One strain of scholastic theology interprets all love in the light of the true love of self, and intellectually this can be justified. But unhappily its effect is to reverse the proper balance of love and to turn it upside down, for in the Christian Gospel love of self is the main obstacle to finding God. To this it may be retorted that it is only false love of self which makes such an obstacle, and that moral theology is concerned with true love of self, but this does not escape the difficulty. It is true, as we have already noticed more than once, that our real self-interest is to be found only in surrendering to God, but if we approach the matter primarily from the point of view of self-interest, as a self-centred calculation, we shall fail to find the secret. The paradox stated by Jesus remains at the heart of true spiritual life: 'He that will find his life shall lose it, and he that will lose his life for my sake shall find it.'

Moral theologians who begin from the position of looking for the true interest of the self do a serious disservice to the Christian faith by introducing at the heart of it a self-regarding element, which is a form, or can easily become a form, of spiritual selfishness. Mortimer even goes so far as to write:[1] 'For a man to say that he would willingly be damned himself if thereby he could save his neighbour is a meaningless exaggeration.' But when his remark is put side by side with one from St Paul, there is a striking contrast (Rom. 9.3): 'For I could wish that I myself were accursed and cut off from Christ for the sake of my brethren, my kinsmen by race.' St Paul is the safer guide.

The besetting sin of moral theologians is that everything is often reduced to a tidy and logical scheme, which appeals to the human desire to have everything docketed and under control. Unfortunately such an approach just does not work when we come up against the great mysteries of the Christian faith. The analysing and categorizing, which moral theology does, is useful, so long as its limitations are never out of sight. An attitude which maintains

[1] *Elements*, p. 142.

that the first thing we ought to be thinking about is our own spiritual welfare is an example of the damaging influence it can have.

Love works the other way round if it is true love. It comes from a response to someone else's love. We do not love our wives or husbands because we think it is in our own self-interest to do so, but because it arises spontaneously in response to their love for us. Still more is it the case with the love of God. 'We love God because he first loved us.' We must always avoid substituting for this statement one of our own which runs, 'We love God because we know where our real interests lie.' That is a form of spiritual cupboard love.

There are two Greek words apart from *philia* (φιλία), which are commonly translated 'love' in the New Testament—*eros* (ἔρως) and *agape* (ἀγάπη). Each of these words has its own particular meaning, and a leading Swedish theologian Anders Nygren devoted two large volumes to the purpose of showing that *eros* was unchristian and *agape* Christian. The distinctions which he made are important, though he went too far in contrasting them and even opposing them to one another. In human nature, because it is created by God, the *eros* is that element in love which seeks its own satisfaction spiritually in God, whereas *agape* is the element which by God's grace gives itself to him who is loved. *Eros*, in short, is the element which seeks fulfilment, but *agape* is the self-giving part. Both, however, are good in a right relationship to one another within the personality.[1]

Other meanings are sometimes given to *eros*. C. S. Lewis, for example, in *The Four Loves* makes *eros* mean mainly sexual love, which is much narrower than the meaning given it by Nygren. The other three loves in Lewis's quartet are affection, friendship and charity (or *agape*). Care therefore has to be taken in discussing the subject of love in English to make certain of the sense in which words are being used.

'When men love God,' write Quell and Stauffer,[2] 'that is the immediate reflection of the love which streams down from heaven upon the elect. Or rather, it is an act of choice like the original act of love itself.' This short quotation brings out the important

[1] Cf. Gottfried Quell and Ethelbert Stauffer, *Love*, Bible Key Words, trs. from Kittel's *Wörterbuch*, A. and C. Black 1949, p. 28.
[2] *Op. cit.*, p. 56.

fact that love in its true Christian sense is essentially an act of the
will and not of the emotions, though the emotions are often deeply
involved. Here again the warning must be repeated that love must
not be separated from faith and hope with which it alone has
meaning in its full sense in relation to God.

We live in a world where the word 'love' is prostituted in all
kinds of ways, and in which radio, television and the press combine
to mislead the public into a false idea of what love is. It is sometimes regarded as a kind of emotional infectious disease, like
measles, which is 'caught' and must be allowed to run its course.
It is frequently identified with sexual passion and almost always
with some emotional state. Such misunderstandings effectively
prevent people from knowing what Christians are really talking
about when they speak of 'love'.

It is extremely important to understand that love in the Christian
sense is not primarily a matter of the emotions, although the
emotions may be engaged. It is a matter of choice, choosing to
submit to the will of God and to follow his path, and as a matter of
choice its essential nature consists of an act of the will.[1] The
Christian life consists in the growth of a Christian in the consecration of his will to God, and it is a process which continues as
long as life lasts.

From the facts mentioned above the duty of care for ourselves
is derived. Our duty to the love of God for us, which alone gives
us value, is to use our own bodies in his service, and that carries
as a corollary the duty to keep our bodies in such health and condition as will enable us to serve him. Mortification, for example,
is not an end in itself, and some saints have indulged in excessive
self-discipline. God gives us the things of the earth as part of the
bounty of his love, and they are meant to be used for him though
self-sacrifice is an essential part of love.

Love of God must involve love of our fellows. This is plainly
enough set out in the New Testament. St John asks how a man
who does not love his fellow men can possibly claim that he loves
God. If he does so, he is a liar. The principle of love for our
neighbour does not mean that we have to *feel* loving towards him.
Our feelings are not always under our control, and sometimes we
have to love people for whom we have an immediate and hearty
dislike. But we are not prevented from loving them on account of

[1] For further treatment see the author's *Life and fire of love*, SPCK 1964.

adverse feelings, for our love consists in acting in a loving way towards them, both in our personal relations with them and in what we say and do about them when they are not present. Love in its essence is an act of the will. A number of parables and sayings of Jesus make this point.

Almsgiving must thus be part of Christian love. A man's possessions like his own existence are a gift from God to be used for God's glory. He must therefore be ready to part with his money or goods in promoting God's purposes. It does not mean that he must give away all his money to the first good cause which claims his help, and leave his wife and children without adequate sustenance. On the contrary he will know that the proper support of his family is the first demand which the love of God normally makes upon him, but he will all the time be seeking for ways in which any money he can spare, any time he can give, any ability he may possess, can be best used to help forward the will of God. In such ways he will be showing the love of God in practice. They are the works which St James speaks of as showing true faith. They are the practical outcome of loving God and loving his brethren in him.

Of those causes which have a claim on the support of Christians the work of the Church has priority, because the Church is the Body of Christ charged to carry on the work of Christ in the world. Almsgiving does not mean spending all that one wants to spend on personal and family purposes, and seeing what is left over. A man should consider the whole of his income, and then ask in what ways God would want it to be allotted: his family will of course be the first consideration.

Jesus himself is the supreme example of the three theological virtues of faith, hope and charity. For Jesus God was the supreme object of his desires, and his life was consciously directed from day to day with the object of fulfilling perfectly in this life the will of God. We find in the absolute obedience of Jesus the perfect fulfil-ment of man's natural powers and desires, showing how he was and is Perfect Man. In him we find man as God intended him to be, without spot or wrinkle, or any such thing. He came into a world of sin and his actions were done, as ours are, by an act of choice of the possibilities which were before him, limited owing to the sin of the world. That led him to the cross.

The Christian life is a life of following Christ, not of following rules. We cannot live the Christian life by knowing all the rules. The rules are useful adjuncts but no more. Love, which contains faith and hope, is the centre of the Christian life because it reflects and takes its origin from the life of love lived eternally in the Godhead of the Blessed Trinity.

The Cardinal Virtues and Capital Vices

Studies in moral theology commonly take the four 'cardinal' virtues (prudence, temperance, justice, fortitude) and the three 'theological' virtues (faith, hope, love) as a basis for an analysis of the moral life. The cardinal virtues have their origin in pre-Christian times: they were, for example, taken to be the basis of the moral life by the Stoics, but they were already traditional in the time of Plato. They were later taken over by the Church and put side by side with the three so-called theological virtues of I Corinthians 13. The cardinal virtues in their origin were natural virtues in the sense that they were upheld and treated as normal in human life. This point has already been mentioned earlier. There was a tendency, in adopting them into Christianity, to continue to treat them as the natural stage of the virtuous life, as opposed to the supernatural stage, represented by the theological virtues. At a time when the natural law was strongly emphasized in moral theology this tendency was much encouraged. Thus there developed an attitude which saw the Christian life as a two-stage affair, the first of which anyone could attain by his own efforts, but of which the second stage could only be reached through the grace of God.

A two-stage approach to the virtuous life, however, throws the emphasis in the wrong place and upsets the balance of Christian truth. For the overarching and revolutionary fact of the Christian Gospel is that Christ transforms everything by renewing living contact with God. This transformation entirely changes the emphasis on all virtues so that the cardinal virtues to a Christian are just as much supernatural as natural. Moreover for a Christian the supernatural is not the antithesis of the natural, but the bringing of the natural home to God. He therefore sees all life as coming under the command of the Spirit, and as understandable only in the light of the death and resurrection of Jesus Christ.

The cardinal virtues do form a convenient categorization of human virtue for the purpose of study, so long as the previous

warnings are borne in mind. But there are others which might
serve just as well. The seven gifts of the spirit from Isa. 11.2 have
been used, and there is no reason why equally good but different
headings should not be found. In his treatment B. Häring uses
the four cardinal virtues, but adds to them humility, thus counter-
acting the tendency to divide the four cardinal virtues from others
as 'natural', for, when humility is added, they cannot all be
regarded as natural, humility being a virtue which comes exclusively from a Christian understanding of goodness, and which
would have been rejected with scorn by many pre-Christian
moralists who upheld the other four.[1]

On the negative side stand the seven capital vices, or as they are
sometimes misleadingly called, the seven deadly sins (pride,
avarice, lust, envy, gluttony, anger, *accidie*). The fact that they
are seven in number seems to be due more to a desire to maintain
the mystic number than to any logical reason. K. E. Kirk thought
that perhaps fear ought to be included among them. The capital
vices are sources of evil, and they represent basic human instincts
which are turned against God's will, instead of being used in
accordance with it: they have been distorted by original sin. It is
unfortunate that they have had so much publicity, since they cover
the negative side of human morals and put the emphasis there,
rather than on the positive uses of human instincts, which lead
man to fulfilment in accord with the creative love of God.

But it can be useful to take the seven capital vices, and to look
at their positive side, so as to find guidance towards the fulfilment
and integration of the personality in God's plan. If we do this,
we find that there is no need to have an additional scheme for
covering the virtues for such virtues are nothing else but the
finding of fulfilment in Christ of the basic urges, and the consequent restoration of our manhood as God means it to be.

At this point it should be said that the essay by H. A. Williams
in *Soundings*, which has been criticized in other connections, has
a useful section on the seven capital vices, showing how necessary
it is for a man to avoid deceiving himself and parading a formal
morality, which may conceal an inner desertion of all that true
morality ought to mean. Even here his presentation suffers from
exaggerations which may cause readers to overlook his insights.
But he rightly points out that each of the seven capital vices springs

[1] For further consideration of the cardinal virtues, see chs. 8 and 9.

from 'an attempt to find security in the limited me of which I am aware instead of in the unlimited me which issues continuously from the fount of Being, and of which I must be very largely unaware' (p. 84). This seems to be another way of saying that sins issue from an attempt to find satisfaction in temporal instead of in eternal satisfactions.

It is a basic truth of human life, an essential part of our free will, that we should be able either to use or to misuse the gifts which God has given us. These gifts include the gifts of personality just as much as those of the external world with which the personality comes into contact. The gifts of personality are in fact primary, because the way we use them governs our actions and reactions in the external world. As Jesus himself taught so plainly in the Sermon on the Mount (Matt. 5-7), it is the inner things which are decisive to a man; the outward things are secondary. The inner things are the aspects of man's personality which can only be redeemed and integrated, healed or made whole, by a proper relationship of love with the God of love.

In human life there is no neutrality. We cannot do nothing, for a choice is forced upon us. In another parable Jesus radically condemns the attempt to do nothing, when the man who hid his lord's talent in the earth is completely condemned, and he is cast out after losing even the talent which he had (Matt. 25.28). Neutrality in life is the same as negativity. In one way it is worse than doing wrong, for it kills the potentiality of the personality and makes God's gift useless and barren, whereas doing wrong is at least still keeping the gift alive, and there always remains the chance of redirecting it aright.

The basic things of which the capital vices are examples are necessary parts of the human personality. Pride, for example, springs from self-hood. Self-awareness and self-hood are indispensable foundations for human life: without them a human being could not exist. The right development of this inner self-hood is essential for the fulfilment of the personality, and its fulfilment is found in the opposite virtue to the capital vice of pride, namely humility. Humility is not an attitude which denigrates the self improperly; that is a false humility which can be dangerous. Humility is the virtue which we see in Jesus Christ, a true understanding of his own relationship to God and to others, a sure sense of perspective and proportion. In human kind it shows itself in an awareness of the great gap which exists between man and God even when it is bridged by God's love, and in a consequent inner awareness of shortcoming and sin. Humility is the acceptance of the truth that man is dependent on God. It is in fact true wisdom, and contains much that is found in the cardinal virtue of prudence. It is the light of God shining in the human person and doing away with the darkness of self-deceit. From pride spring all other vices in some measure, just as from humility come the other virtues.

Avarice or covetousness, the second of the capital vices, is a disordered desire to possess things. It is one of the most common faults in twentieth-century living. What is called the 'standard of living' has been exalted until it has become a god for vast numbers of people, and the phrase is used to refer exclusively to the amount of material goods which people possess. In modern industrialized society great propaganda pressure is built up to incite people to avarice and covetousness as a means for producers to make more profits. Immense sums are spent on advertising in order to create an artificial demand for what the advertiser wishes to sell. Such a demand can only come from causing people to want more than they have got, even though vast multitudes throughout the world have not even the minimum of food necessary for normal health. Politicians too appeal in the same way to the baser instincts of their public and promise more and better material conditions, even though the level of the voters is already far above what could conceivably be thought necessary. Such an appeal, whether from advertisers or politicians, is clearly unchristian: it is directly opposed to the principles and practices of Jesus as clearly set out in the Gospels. In itself advertising is legitimate, for some publicity is necessary if goods which are needed in a complex society are to become known. A distinction has to be made between advertising which is for the benefit of the consumer and that which is trying to create an artificial demand for the benefit of the producer.

Problems of avarice are endemic in the society of the West and have had far too little attention from the personal moral point of view, or from the point of view of the good of society.[1] In the long run personal and social interests coincide, for no society can be healthy which does not in its life reflect sound moral values. Unfortunately in the largely *laisser faire* economies of the free world it is widely assumed that the interests of producer and

[1] See Vance Packard, *The Waste Makers*, Pocket Books Inc. New York 1963.

consumer are the same, and that, if a producer succeeds in selling his products, this must mean that the consumer wants them, and this in turn means that it is in the consumer's interests. Probably no one would defend these principles in such a bald form as this, yet the actual way in which the economic life of our society is run implicitly reflects these assumptions. The stimulation of avarice and desire for more is an inevitable outcome of these assumptions.

The opposite attitude to avarice is possession with thankfulness and detachment. We need to possess things for our full life on earth, but we should be content with what is necessary, and not yearn after what is merely pleasant and superfluous. The Christian attitude to possession is summed up in the clause of the prayer taught to his disciples by Jesus, 'Give us this day our daily bread', the only phrase in the prayer which deals directly with our relationship to things. In this clause we confine ourselves to praying for what is necessary, and refrain from asking God for what is superfluous to our needs.

Avarice is a sign that we are under the control of things instead of being above them and using them for doing the will of God. Avarice shows that a man has lost his sense of seeing created things as a gift to him from God to be used for his glory, for when they are thus seen they become things to use rather than to own. Human possession is not and can never be possession in any final sense of the word, as is shown by Jesus' parable of the man who planned to pull down his barns and build greater. He was told that his soul would be required of him that very night, and was asked whose all those riches would then be. Avarice is a part of man's nature twisted away from God instead of being in harmony with him, and such is the case with all the other capital vices.

7

MARRIAGE AND SEX

Marriage

THE CHURCH HAS different standards from those of the world
in marriage, a fact which should cause no surprise. Confusion is
caused where the Church is closely linked to the State, for it sometimes becomes difficult to disentangle the Christian principles and
rules from those of the secular community. In England, with the
increase of facilities for divorce in the first half of the twentieth
century, there has been a growing divergence between Christian
standards and those adopted in legislation by the State, though
the latter continues to pay lip service to the ideal of lifelong
marriage. There can be no doubt that the facilities for divorce now
accorded by the English law represent a definite departure from
Christian teaching. But the Church of England is technically tied
to these lower standards, although no clergyman is required to
celebrate a marriage against his conscience. The resolutions of the
Convocations indicate clearly enough that church opinion does not
agree with that of the secular power in this matter.

In countries like Malta another situation prevails, for there the
law of the State is the same as Roman Canon law with the surprising result that no mixed marriage is valid which is not celebrated in a Roman Catholic church, that is, a marriage between a
Roman Catholic and one who does not belong to that Church.
This gives rise to various injustices which need not be examined
here. It also tends to make the distinction between Church and
State difficult to keep clear.

Anglican Churches outside England have their own regulations
about marriage and are in no way linked to the law of the country,
except in so far as their marriages are recognized as valid under
State law. But the discipline of its own members is the affair of
the Church alone. Similarly in many countries the Roman

Catholic Church exercises its own discipline over its members without any official relationship to the law of the land. In some countries ministers of religion are authorized agents of the State in performing marriages, while in others all parties have to be married in civil registry offices and can take part in a religious ceremony afterwards, if they wish. It is in countries where this last practice prevails that it is easiest to distinguish between rules of Church and State, and that this should be so has a number of advantages.

But the Church has something to say to the State about marriage. As in other matters of moral importance the Church has the key to the true development of human life and can inform the State on what principles a stable society can alone be built. The Church has an insight into the deepest needs of human life which can only come from the Gospel, and it has the right and duty to share this knowledge with the civil authorities. It does not follow that the Church ought to try to coerce the civil authorities to enforce the principles which are to be commended, for legislation which does not have the consent of the governed, however good it may be in theory, can have the opposite effect to that desired. Moreover the Church ought not to appear to be willing to take away from individual persons the right of free choice to obey or not to obey the Church's precepts, within the limits of what is not dangerous to the stability of society in a direct way. If the Church tries to use the civil power to promote legislation in its own favour, whether it concerns marriage or some other subject, it inhibits its own preaching of the Gospel, because such legislation appears to be a denial to men of that freedom which is a basic need in a Gospel of love.

There is a strong case to be made for monogamous marriage as part of the natural order. On the sub-human level mating is for the mere propagation of the species and is biological only. As soon as marriage is considered in regard to human beings their own special needs have to be examined, one of which is their need to live in society. Jesus himself seems to encourage a view of marriage as part of the natural law when he said (Mark 10.6, 9) that 'from the beginning of the creation God made them male and female', and implies that it was intended to be permanent—'What God hath joined together let no man put asunder.'

Too much weight must not be put upon one or two texts from

the New Testament, but on the other hand the evidence which is found there must be given proper attention. The New Testament passages on the subject of marriage are a constant source of argument as to their exact meaning. Commentators are too ready to approach the subject with *a priori* theories. It is commonly said, for example, that Jesus did not legislate but merely enunciated general principles. But the matter cannot be put in this either/or form. It must be judged on the evidence, and the New Testament text suggests that Jesus did in fact express himself pretty clearly on some subjects, and on others took a different line. The evidence for the teaching of Jesus comes not only from the Gospels, but also from St Paul's letters, which were earlier in date. All of this evidence, which is considerable if taken together, presents the same picture of monogamous lifelong marriage which cannot be dissolved except by death.

The Christian teaching about the character of marriage, which in its details is not a topic for moral theology, requires lifelong monogamous marriage to give it its meaning. The physical union is to be the expression of the complete self-giving within marriage of one personality to another in love. Lifelong marriage is the prerequisite of any such selfgiving. Moreover the mystical element in marriage, its eternal aspect in signifying God's love and the union between Christ and his Church, has the same requirement of permanence.

In civil law marriage is a contract. It therefore normally becomes subject to the same kind of law as other contracts. If it is broken, it is dissolved. But in Christian life marriage is not a contract but a status, and it is probable that the strength of the contract idea has caused much of the misunderstanding which has arisen.

> The more I examine the marriage service, the less I see of 'contract' and the more I realize that 'status' set up by consent and coitus is at the heart of the whole matter. As this is what Christ taught ('they are no longer twain but one flesh'), we ought not to be surprised that the Prayer Book is so emphatic about it—'Holy Matrimony, which is an honourable *estate*, instituted by God.'[1]

This quotation refers to the English Book of Common Prayer but it does in fact echo the constant teaching of the Church throughout the centuries.

[1] Canon Hugh C. Warner, *Divorce and Remarriage*, George Allen & Unwin 1954, p. 39.

For a Christian marriage to be truly celebrated there are certain essential elements which must be found in it. Or to put it negatively, there are certain things which make a marriage null and void from the start, so that there never can have been a true marriage. Full consent is evidently an indispensable part of a proper marriage, and if it is not present the person concerned cannot do what he or she purports to do in the marriage ceremony. The conditions which nullify a purported marriage from the start are called technically 'diriment impediments'. The following are diriment impediments to a marriage:

(*a*) An error of identity between the parties or a trick. Obviously such an error would invalidate the consent which is indispensable.

(*b*) Abduction or terrorization. There can be no true marriage unless the bride afterwards accepts freely the *fait accompli*.

(*c*) Consanguinity or affinity within the prohibited degrees. It is relevant here to observe that these rules have not been always and everywhere the same. At one time marriages were forbidden on the basis of these rules between those who were notionally 'related' by being godparents to others, e.g. godparents could not marry godchildren. In certain cases the Church would exercise dispensatory powers. The State in England now permits marriages to a deceased wife's sister or deceased husband's brother and the Church of England has accepted this as tolerable.

(*d*) Physical incapability for marriage, such as impotency.

(*e*) Parties—or one of them—under the age of puberty.

(*f*) Partner of a previous marriage still living: this according to church practice.

Considerable difficulties are raised by the rules of Churches for their own members which have the result of suggesting that other Christian marriages are not valid. The Roman Church by the Council of Trent and the '*Ne temere*' decree has laid it down that a marriage between a Roman Catholic and another Christian must be performed in the presence of a Roman priest, if it is to be valid. In some countries the Orthodox Church takes a similar attitude. This is a departure from the older view of Christendom, which held that the Ministers of the sacrament of marriage are the two parties themselves. The Anglican view is that, if there is no diriment impediment, and the parties are baptized, the marriage is a Christian sacramental marriage, whether the priest is there or not. This means that the Church recognizes marriages which take place between Christians in civil marriage offices as the same in essentials as those which take place in a church. This was made clear in the Lambeth Conference Report of 1930 (pp. 94–5):

> In the course of our deliberations on these matters, our attention has been drawn to the anxiety and disturbance of mind which have been caused to some members of our Communion, when the validity of the marriage of a member with a member of another Communion has been called in question on the ground that it has been solemnized in one of our churches. We think it right, therefore, to include the following statement in our report.
>
> 1. The essence of a valid marriage consists in the consent before witnesses of two parties, who are competent to marry, to live permanently one with another as man and wife.
>
> 2. When the conditions precedent to a valid marriage as laid down by the civil authority and such other like conditions as are laid down by the ecclesiastical authority have been complied with, the Church solemnizes the marriage with prayers and blessings. The absence of such religious sanctions does not invalidate the marriage.
>
> 3. The Church of England and those Churches in communion with it recognize the validity of marriages which are celebrated by other Christian bodies than itself in which there is no diriment impediment between the two parties, and where the precedent conditions laid down by the civil authority have been complied with.
>
> 4. The denial of the validity of such marriages by any part of the Christian Church is a departure from the true tradition of the Catholic Church and is much to be deplored.

Nullity is a decision that no marriage has ever taken place in spite of the opinions of all concerned at the time. It can be and sometimes is used in a legalistic way which does not commend itself to Christian conscience. But it is important that marriages improperly entered into should be subject to a decision of nullity. If the grounds are certain and substantial, it makes no difference how long the parties have lived together as man or wife or whether they have children. A decree of nullity is a statement that both parties are free to marry (if there is no diriment impediment) since the purported marriage never in fact existed.

Divorce in the modern sense, however, purports to dissolve the marriage bond. The word is sometimes used to signify what is usually now called 'separation', that is, divorce *a mensa et thoro*, from table and bed. This provides for the parties to live separately but does not claim to state that they are no longer married.

There has at various times been a widespread opinion among Christians that the so-called Matthean exception (Matt. 5.32) permitted divorce for adultery. But the text is not clear since the word used is the Greek word for fornication (*porneia*). But whatever the justification for putting away one's wife (it does not mention the husband) the text goes on to state clearly that anyone who marries another commits adultery, so it is difficult to see how it can possibly be held to justify remarriage after divorce. So far then as there is guidance in the New Testament, it is definitely against any remarriage during the lifetime of a married partner.

It is important, though somewhat elementary, to point out that the Church's opposition is to the claim that the marriage bond can be dissolved. So long as this claim is not put forward, there has always been a readiness to approve of separation, where that is the best resort. In the modern State, however, it is often necessary to go through the procedures for divorce in order to secure justice, especially when children are involved. In England, for example, if a woman leaves her husband with an infant child and deserts him, she can sue for divorce after a certain period on the grounds of what is called 'constructive desertion', thus making him the guilty party, unless he himself sues for divorce during the first five years. Evidently therefore if he is to have his proper influence in the upbringing of the child, he is bound to sue for divorce during these years, otherwise he becomes the offending person in the eyes of the law. There is therefore no necessary stigma from a Christian point of view attaching to the fact of being divorced. The offence against Christian principle is remarriage while the previous partner is still living.

The attitude which we have been describing above is that of the Western Christian Catholic tradition. Western Protestant Churches have been more lax than Roman Catholics or Anglicans, generally speaking, and have tended to follow the State whether the civil law was in accord with Christian principles or not. In this they can appeal to the practice of the Eastern Orthodox Churches. It is not necessary to examine all the differences in detail, but the point of view of the Orthodox is of particular interest, as representing the only large body of traditional Christianity which is unaffected by Western developments. There is no doubt that its present outlook is largely the result of too close an identification with the State over many centuries.

In the Orthodox Churches grounds for divorce are very wide. In a lecture on the subject Professor Hamilcar Alivisatos of the University of Athens has described the position as follows:

Marriage can therefore be dissolved only either by natural or even by moral death, i.e. by causes defeating entirely the very end and scope of marriage. On the other hand, the Church has without any objection or hesitation followed the existing civil order as reformed by the Byzantine emperors. . . .

Of course the Church . . . has followed our Lord's and St Paul's severe position. Fathers and teachers of the Early Church and even later have regarded divorce itself, except in cases of adultery, as a kind of adultery and have ordered rather heavy spiritual penalties for those who were divorced in order to marry again. But the severity of this doctrine was not often followed by the practice. . . .

Alivisatos lists the reasons for divorce, including treachery against the life of one by the other, adultery and bigamy 'and even frivolous conduct giving reason to suspicion of adultery', intentional abortion without the husband's consent, serious shaking of the matrimonial union, impotence, abandonment for two years by the husband, incurable lunacy for four years, prolonged disappearance, and leprosy. It may even cover the entry into a religious Order of one of the parties by mutual consent, or consecration of the husband to be a bishop, under the heading of 'serious shaking'!

In theory the Orthodox use a different marriage service for those who marry after divorce, with a penitential note, but in practice its use is infrequent. Judged by the standards of Western Christendom the Orthodox outlook is extremely lax. Alivisatos justifies the attitude as follows:

Abuses, I am afraid, are inevitable and they seem sometimes to be imposed by nature itself, but as to the abuses in the East, our old and rich tradition has laid the weight to the fact that the harm resulting from a very widely applied clemency is perhaps a lesser one than that of the severe and strict application of discipline.

The most recent expression of opinion by Anglican leaders is that of the Lambeth Conference of 1958, which generally endorsed the standpoint of the 1948 Conference.

Resolution 94. The Conference affirms that the marriage of one whose former partner is still living may not be celebrated according to the rites of the Church, unless it has been established that there exists no marriage bond recognized by the Church.

96. Confirmed members of the Church who marry contrary to the law of the Church, as accepted in the provincial or regional Church to which they belong, should be regarded as subject to the discipline of the Church in respect of admission to Holy Communion. Their

admission to Holy Communion lies within the discretion of the Bishop, due regard being had to their own spiritual good and the avoidance of scandal to others.

This typically Anglican arrangement is hard to justify by strict logic, but it has much to recommend it in practice. It is aimed at making a public witness against second marriages but at the same time continuing to minister to the souls which need pastoral care. Those needs are not adequately met by a logical system which permanently excommunicates the parties concerned (and possibly their children). It is not enough to tell them that God will make up for the sacramental grace which they miss, through his uncovenanted mercies.

Dr Geoffrey Fisher, when Archbishop of Canterbury, held that this compromise was the best that could be devised in an admittedly imperfect and unsatisfactory situation, and he ended an address he once gave on the subject with these words:

> Only if the Church is bearing uncompromisingly its witness to the truth of marriage by refusing to marry divorced persons, can it without damage and without causing confusion use discretion in its pastoral work, whereby it seeks to build up those, who can never again bear a full witness to Christ's conception of marriage, into a lowly, penitent, and really blessed life in the grace of God and the strength of the sacraments of the Church.

The problem of remarriage after divorce is, however, not solved by the provision of church rules. The rules followed in Anglican Churches, though illogical, try to meet the two demands of pastoral need and the requirement of the Gospel that the Church should uphold the standard of lifelong marriage. But they do not solve the moral issues in individual cases. It would be convenient if we were able to say that remarriage after divorce is always wrong and leave it at that. But it is necessary to continue, and to add that, although remarriage after divorce is always wrong for Christians, there are cases where the alternative is morally worse. A common attitude on the part of the rigorist moralists is to say that living alone in continence is always possible after divorce, and is in fact morally to be preferred to any other course.

Unfortunately this simple solution does not adequately deal with the moral problems involved. When face to face with a man or woman who has been divorced, it is necessary to deal with the problem of remarriage as a personal problem, the needs of which may outweigh the obligation to obey the law. To put it baldly, there are many situations in which after divorce *moral* reasons would seem to favour remarriage. The most obvious example is the need to care for young children in the case of a divorced husband who has their custody. It *may* be his moral duty to remarry so that those children may have proper maternal care. This does not mean that the break-up of the original marriage was not morally deplorable and damaging, but it means that in the actual real-life situation there are moral demands which can only be adequately met by remarriage. These moral demands sometimes outweigh the requirements of the Church's law. Other moral reasons for remarriage besides that mentioned also often exist.

But if a remarriage takes place it is both desirable and necessary that those concerned should accept as their contribution to the maintenance of lifelong marriage as an ideal and standard the need to forgo a church wedding. The more deeply Christian they are, the more likely they will be to see the point and to accept the deprivation. The absence of such a wedding does not, of course, mean that God's blessing cannot be sought and received for the remarriage, since they are undertaking it because in the circumstances they think it to be God's will. There is in such a situation a clash between the needs of individuals in a far from perfect society and the requirement for the Church publicly to proclaim the truth of lifelong marriage as the will of God for all men in his Church.

Indiscriminate baptism of infants makes the problem more complicated, as it leads to many cases of people contracting what are technically Christian marriages, although the parties themselves have never been committed Christians. It is not uncommon to find baptized persons who have been divorced and remarried, and who become converted Christians after their second marriage. It is morally intolerable that they should then be told that they are 'living in sin' because of the technicalities of their infant baptism. Such persons should be carefully instructed that God accepts them as they are, forgives them all their sins and wants them to find him through serving him in their present marriage, and offering that to God for him to bless and use. But they should also be brought to understand the obligation upon the Church to press for and witness to lifelong marriage.

Chastity

That the sexual element in man is one of his most important attributes is evident from the large part it plays in the joys, as well as in the tragedies of human life. Its fulfilment is to be found in its use in subordination to the will of God, for it is only in such subordination that its full flowering can take place. Being an integral part of man the sexual instinct, like all God's creation, is itself good. The tradition, not at all times absent from Christianity, that sex is something evil is an aberration and does not accord with the Christian Gospel or the teaching of Christ. In its right setting the sexual element has always been regarded, and rightly so, as an essential part of the highest state of human love in married life.

Lust is the misuse of the sexual instinct, or—perhaps more accurately—its disorder. As one of the seven capital vices it has perhaps had more attention than it deserves, with the result that there is a widespread belief that the Church regards sexual sins as graver than any other kind. This is not only a mistake, but it is a reversal of the actual values of Christian teaching. For spiritual sins, being disorders of the inner man, are more deadly and serious than external sins, as Jesus himself taught in the Sermon on the Mount. Over-attention to the external proprieties results in legalism and in a failure to discern where the root of sin lies.

Monogamy is assumed to be the standard of married life in the New Testament and it has been consistently upheld by the Church throughout the centuries. Its importance is reflected in the opposition to remarriage after divorce which has been commonly exhibited by Christians, for monogamous marriage not only meant one wife at a time, but the exclusive union of one man with one woman during the lifetimes of them both. The subject of valid and invalid marriages and of divorce will be dealt with later at more length. But, whatever temporary exceptions and expedients are permitted by Christian Churches, there are few who do not in theory continue to maintain that monogamous marriage is the Christian standard and ideal.

Sexual intercourse between a man and a woman affects them both deeply, far more deeply indeed than either of them can know. Probably its effects in the psychological field are more lasting in the woman than in the man. For this reason it cannot be regarded as merely a question for the individual, for in the act of sexual union each person is affecting the personality of the other in a way for which he or she must take responsibility. It is not possible to shed responsibility for the other person concerned and to behave as if each was solely responsible for him or herself. Moreover in the sexual act a unity is created which goes deeper than the physical.

The prohibitions which are associated with Christian teaching, e.g. that adultery and fornication are wrong in all circumstances, are merely the negative side of the positive truths which it desires to stress. It is plain that, if sexual intercourse can be fully in accord with the will of God only when it is exercised within monogamous marriage, and, if it creates results which are properly exclusively part of that state, it must follow that acts which make the fulfilment within that condition impossible must be wrong, for they make it impossible once for all for the will of God to be completely done. There are people who know no better, who are perhaps brought up in polygamous societies or who live in conditions in which casual sexual intercourse is the convention. For them the fulness of Christian love as physically expressed in Christian marriage is made impossible, though they can experience many aspects of it, which minister to their happiness and are of lasting value. The prohibitions, then, are seen to be expressions of Christian love, walls thrown up to try to preserve for men and women the full experience which God wills them to have.

The positive virtue of the sexual life is purity or chastity, which is not the same as abstinence. Purity in sexual matters means the use of sexual powers as God wants them to be used, for the benefit of the married couple and of their family. In this context the full enjoyment of sexual relations is an experience given by God to be thankfully received and used.

'Chastity' has borne a number of different meanings in the past, but there can be no serious doubt that its proper meaning is the right use of sex. It has too often been taken to mean abstention from sexual activity altogether, and it is still so used in this meaning when monks and nuns take vows of poverty, chastity and obedience. In their case the proper use of sex is the complete abstention which their life requires, but chastity in itself has nothing necessarily to do with complete abstention from sexual activity, any more than temperance in drink has anything necessarily to do with total abstinence.

Mortimer[1] gives three forms of chastity—married chastity, virginity and widowhood. This classification is not altogether satisfactory, for widowhood cannot in itself be a form of chastity; it is a state of life to which one form of chastity applies. There are really only two forms of chastity—abstention from sexual activity in those states of life to which this belongs, namely the unmarried state and that of widowhood; and second, controlled sexual activity in the married state. (The phrase 'sexual activity' here denotes sexual intercourse and sexual acts immediately connected with it.)

Before going further into attitudes of mind towards chastity it is important to give some thought to the question of 'higher' and 'lower' states of life. There has been much written about 'higher' and 'lower' conditions of life in Christian history and it is not absent today. Virginity has been held to be a higher state than marriage. The terms 'higher' and 'lower' are misleading and have caused much harm to the Church and to the Christian life in general, because they have reflected what is called the 'double standard', i.e. that there is a higher kind of life lived by monks and nuns, and a lower kind of life lived by people in the world. This may be encouraged by the continued use of the word 'religious' to describe monks and nuns, for it inevitably implies that they are more religious than other Christians.

The distinction which we have just described is impossible to sustain. There *are* higher and lower states of life, but they have nothing to do with convents or with virginity as such. 'Higher' and 'lower' in a Christian sense can have meaning only if they are related to God's will for each person, in other words if they refer to the vocation which God gives to each person in the state of life to which he calls him. If he calls a man to be a Christian bank clerk and the man insists on being a monk, he is following a lower path than that which he ought to take, because he is not doing the will of God. The higher path for him is the path God wants him to follow.

If God calls a man and a woman to marry, this is the highest path which they can follow, because by marrying they are fulfilling all the possibilities which God has planned for them. The opposite is also true. If they insist on being celibate, they are evading God's highest calling for them. On the other hand there are men and

[1] *Elements*, p. 168.

women whom God calls to the cloister, and for these to deny this calling would be to accept a lower way. Each case has to be taken on its own, and it is impossible to take the vocation of one individual and apply it to others as though it were universally valid.

St Thomas Aquinas held that virginity is in itself a higher virtue than married chastity, and there are many Christian writers who have taken the same view. But it must be repudiated because it is based on wrong presuppositions. It is an interesting point that if the argument from nature, which is so often applied elsewhere, is taken here, it points to the married state as being more in accord with the law of nature, and therefore *a priori* it would appear to be the higher state for men and women. God would presumably not have endowed all men and women with sexual powers unless he had intended them to be used.

Jeremy Taylor[1] follows St Thomas, at least to some extent. He writes,

> Natural virginity of itself is not a state more acceptable to God: but that which is chosen and voluntary in order to the conveniences of religion and separation from worldly encumbrances, is therefore better than the married life. Not that it is more holy but that it is a freedom from cares, and opportunity to spend more time in spiritual employments.

The fallacy in Taylor's point of view is that he assumes that 'spiritual employments' means prayer and specifically 'religious' activities. Whereas in fact spiritual employments in the proper use of the words must mean the sanctification of that state of life to which God has called a man. It is far more a spiritual employment for a man to wrestle with the application of the Gospel to the problems of marriage, if that is what God has called him to, than to spend half his time on his knees. God sent his Son into the world to redeem the world, to fill the world and the activities of the world with his sanctity and his Holy Spirit, and this can only be done by wrestling in the conditions facing those who are trying to live the Christian life in it.

The same fallacy is exhibited by Mortimer.[2] 'The excellence of virtues', he writes, 'is measured by the ends which they serve. The higher the end, and the more directly it is served, the higher the virtue. The end of virginity is, certainly, freedom to serve God.' But freedom from what? From the duties to which God has called

[1] *Holy Living*, ch. II Sec. 3. [2] *Elements*, p. 170.

him? There is here the same mistaken underlying assumption that spiritual employments must be those which are done apart from the world, whereas a very strong case can be made for the principle that the most spiritual of employments are those which are done in the world, in redeeming it: that would seem to be a reasonable deduction from the doctrine of the Incarnation.

Mortimer goes on to say that 'The exercise of the priesthood, ceaselessly occupied with the worship of God, is a higher way of life than virginity.' How can this be? First, there is not any proper contrast between priesthood and virginity—they are two different sorts of things on two different planes. Second, the exercise of the priesthood is a higher way of life only for those who have been called to be priests, and it does not carry any moral or spiritual superiority over others who have been called to be something else. His attitude seems to reflect a hangover from medieval outlooks, where the separation of the priesthood from the laity had such lamentable results in a number of ways.

There is too in the background of the double standard an echo of the heresy that something which is pleasurable must also in some way be sinful. This has been a curse in the discussion of sex in the past, and it is a principle which seems to deny the goodness of God and to throw back in his face the good things which he has given us. It is surely a sounder approach to hold that if something gives innocent pleasure, it is because God in his goodness has meant it to do so: it is another example of his bounty and love in creation. But man, being sinful, has always to exercise particular care in using things which give him pleasure, so as to make sure that he does so in accordance with the will of God. For there is an obvious temptation to do it merely for the pleasure rather than for its true end. It may be noted that the fulness of pleasure can only be experienced when it is enjoyed in perspective and proportion.

In the realms of sex sensuality is wrong because it is an immoderate indulgence in the pleasures which God has given us to use, and does in fact rapidly lead to the break-up of the proper pattern of sexual life, and often to the complete domination of a man's life by his sensual nature and the resulting break-up of his character.

Fornication, adultery, masturbation, sexual activities between persons of the same sex, are all sins of misdirection or intemperance. They are sins of over-indulgence and in three of the cases they involve more than one person. Fornication denies in its act all those higher mysteries of sex which involve the union of a man and his wife in a permanent relationship of love which affects the whole personality. Apart from damage which is done to the self in the act of fornication, damage for the most part unknown is done to the other party too, sometimes deeply affecting the emotional life and of such a kind as to leave permanent scars on the character. It is also a sin against future marriage.

Adultery is clearly even more serious, as it interferes directly with a marriage and concerns not only the two people who are taking part in the sinful action, but also the wife, or husband, or both if both are married, and possibly the family life of children, which depends on the emotional and hidden relationship of the parents. It is anti-social and horribly destructive in many ways.

Masturbation is a very common fault in the young, especially in boys and young men. It is not in itself a very serious matter, though it must be regarded as undesirable. It is more damaging in its associations than in the act itself, for it is commonly associated with sensual thoughts and imaginary pictures which have a deleterious effect on the personality. The act of masturbation very easily becomes a habit and can quickly acquire a power over the person which is harmful. It also often produces guilt feelings which have serious secondary effects. These guilt feelings sometimes spring from mistaken teaching, but much more commonly they arise from ignorance and self-condemnation. Failure to overcome the habit sometimes induces in young people neuroses and breakdown in other moral questions. From the point of view of moral theology these excessive fears should be set at rest, and most of the habits will be cured in course of time, especially when those concerned are married. In all such matters spirit, mind, body form one unity and a fault in one has bad results on the other two aspects of human personality.

Homosexuality[1]

A homosexual is a person who is sexually attracted to those of the same sex (Greek *homos* = one and the same); those with more normal sexual attractions for those of the other sex are known as

[1] Paederasty = male homosexual acts.
Lesbianism, Sapphism = female homosexual acts.

heterosexuals (Greek *heteros* = the other). There are male and female homosexuals, though the comparative numbers are not accurately known. In some countries homosexual acts are criminal offences, but often only in the case of male homosexuals. Britain gives an example of such differential laws, where homosexual acts between males are a criminal offence, and those between females are not. There has been considerable pressure in Britain to have the law changed so that homosexual acts between consenting male adults in private should no longer be crimes, and in this campaign the Moral Welfare Council of the Church of England has played a leading part.

There seems to be no doubt that some people are born with homosexual tendencies. Public opinion often rejects such persons as in some way unhealthy, and the word 'pervert' carries a note of condemnation. There has been some change in the climate of British opinion, but homosexuals still arouse feelings of revulsion on the grounds that they are 'unnatural'. In one use of the word homosexuality is 'unnatural', and in another it is not. Clearly the sexual powers are by nature designed for the propagation of the species, and this is the only truly natural use of them or of the emotions associated with them. But a born homosexual is 'natural' in the sense that to him or her the homosexuality is not artificial. Homosexuals by nature feel attracted by the same sex just as others feel attracted by the opposite sex.

If, as seems to be the case, there are some homosexuals who are born with this innate characteristic, there can be no moral blame attaching to it as such. They have had no choice in the matter. Indeed many homosexuals bitterly resent their condition and would happily be rid of it if they could. It is therefore necessary to assure them that they are in no way morally to blame for their innate tendencies. But there are others who have resorted to homosexual practices in order to gratify their general sexual desires, who are not truly homosexuals at all. Homosexual practices often begin at school, especially at boys' boarding schools, and are carried on afterwards, perhaps as the easiest way to provide an outlet for sexual urges. For such people, whether women or men, there is moral blame attaching to their homosexual emotions, because they have been deliberately *chosen* and encouraged, and they are therefore a revolt against the natural purposes of God in the world generally and in their own natures particularly.

So far we have been discussing the morality of homosexual inclinations, not of actions. Indulgence in homosexual practices, either those which are only mildly erotic, or still more those that involve the sexual organs, is gravely sinful. It is morally wrong for several reasons. First it is an evident misuse of the sexual element in human nature, compared to the purpose for which God has made it. The encouragement of sexual feelings between persons of the same sex can never fulfil their main purpose, which is the procreation of children and the building up of happy and permanent married relationships. Homosexual relations lead always to some sort of frustration, often to very serious tensions. Those who indulge in homosexual activities are on the same level as those heterosexuals who indulge in fornication or adultery; they commit an offence against God and against society, however much relief they may obtain for their feelings. In the encouragement of deeply emotional homosexual relationships men and women not only do harm to themselves but also to the other person involved. If an older person seduces a younger into homosexual practices, a serious offence is committed, often with lifelong tragic results for the young person concerned.

The attempt to have the law changed, so as to avoid making it a crime for consenting male homosexuals to indulge privately in homosexual actions, has nothing to do with the moral heinousness of the activities. All moral offences are not crimes, and the moral seriousness of the offence remains the same whether it is a crime or not by law. The argument for changing the law in Britain is that, as it at present stands, the law is not in the public interest. A homosexual who takes part in homosexual acts lays himself open to blackmail, and there have been a number of cases where this has proved to be very harmful to the security or well-being of the nation. If the law were changed so that such practices in private were no longer a crime, this harmful aspect would be avoided.

It is important to understand that the moral strain on a homosexual may be greater than that normally undergone by a heterosexual, because society is organized on the assumption that its citizens are heterosexual, and there are a number of conventions and rules to protect women against immoral men, and general behaviour is arranged so as to keep sexual temptations within bounds. But the very methods which act in this way for heterosexuals act in the opposite sense for homosexuals, by throwing them together with those to whom they are most attracted sexually, and by providing opportunities for giving way to temptation which heterosexuals do not normally have. Thus special sympathy for their difficulties ought to be shown.

Homosexuals should understand that, although they cannot physically satisfy their sexual cravings without moral blame, they can play a most useful part in society, for they often have gifts of various kinds in greater measure than the rest of society. Artistic gifts are often found in homosexuals, and it is much to be deplored that in certain artistic circles homosexual practices are rife. In their own interests homosexuals should learn that indulgence in homosexual practices undermines their strength of character and often in the end diminishes their artistic ability. Society needs their particular gifts, but it is only by rising above their selfish physical desires that they can develop to full stature in character.

Contraceptives

The widespread availability of contraceptives has had serious social effects, for it has enabled people to indulge in sexual intercourse outside marriage with little or no fear of having children as a result of it. The pattern of sexual behaviour in the young has been revolutionized by the use of contraceptives before marriage. The general effects have been quite serious, in spite of the views of some psychologists. There can be little doubt that an increase in insecurity and neurosis has been directly due to indiscriminate sexual activity in the young. But though this must be deplored, it is not an argument against the use of contraceptives in all circumstances, any more than the fact that some people get drunk is an argument against the use of all alcoholic liquors.

Of Anglican moral theologians both Kirk and Mortimer have taken a rather negative view about the use of contraceptives except on the smallest possible scale. Discouragement in their use is probably a good thing, since it is a natural tendency in human nature for men to give themselves the benefit of any doubt which they think may exist, and thus to over-indulge their own sensual desires. But the arguments which the two theologians advance are not altogether satisfactory. For example, Mortimer wrote,[1]

> To every human faculty God has ordained its proper end and means. He who acts against what God has prescribed sins. The end of the

[1] *Elements*, p. 178.

sexual act is quite clear—the procreation of children. To use it in such a way as to frustrate that end is therefore 'unnatural'.

This quotation oversimplifies the matter and does not provide an adequate basis for reaching a firm conclusion. In speaking of the end of the sexual act the procreation of children is alone mentioned, but that is only one part of one aspect of the act—the physical. There are other ends of the sexual act for men and women, e.g. the physical expression of married love, the increase of that love through the physical union, the fulfilment of the physical compulsion in sex itself, the complete unity of the personalities in the mystery of human sexual union, which forms a sacramental act, apart from the begetting of children. At the same time we must note that the procreation of children is not a natural necessary end of every sexual act, since God has provided in his natural processes that at certain times and during pregnancy there is no chance of children being procreated from the sexual act, and that it may continue to be used properly for its other purposes during those times.

Mortimer argues that there is a difference here because what interferes with conception is outside the act itself, whereas contraceptives introduce the interference in the act itself. But this objection only applies to certain kinds of contraceptives: oral contraceptives for example do not fall within this objection; nor would there be the same difficulty in sexual intercourse after sterilization, though the morality of sterilization may be questionable in some cases.

Moreover it does not seem that the difference between something external to the act and something internal is a *moral* difference. From a strictly moral point of view there seems to be no difference between using contraceptives or using what is known as the 'safe period', except that the latter suffers from several disadvantages. The 'safe period' is not really safe, and consequently the uncertainty may introduce into the act various unfortunate elements, anxieties which could be allayed by the use of contraceptives, upsetting the emotional balance which is such an important part of the sexual act when rightly performed. It is only by holding a rigid view that the prevention of children is always a sin when the sexual act takes place that the use of contraceptives can be morally condemned.

There are a number of other incidental facts to be taken into consideration. The formation of moral principles in the Roman Church where they affected the family was probably not unconnected with the agricultural economy in which they were first formulated. In such an economy children, especially male children, have always been regarded as a form of wealth, and the provision of adequate labour for the land in such societies has always been a strong social interest before the introduction of machinery. The circumstances need to be kept in mind.

Another factor in the situation in past centuries, which was common everywhere until recent years, was a high infant mortality, so that large numbers of children had to be produced in order to be sure of a reasonably sized family. But God has enabled us to overcome this mortality by the skill and discoveries of doctors and scientists. The population problem has been radically changed. When disease is rampant far more births are needed to keep the population stable. It is not surely to be argued from this that disease and death for the young is a 'natural' condition which accords with God's will! Nor are we to assume that it is God's will that disease should be checked but not the overpopulation which results from medical advance.

The great appeal of the Thomistic theologians is to reason, but just when reason seems to upset some of their preconceived ideas, it is put on one side in favour of an *a priori* argument about ends and means which looks at only half the problem.

We ought also to note that, although the Roman Church absolutely bans the use of contraceptives, they are very widely used by Roman Catholics, and their use is often not thought by the laity to be matter for confession. On 21st June, 1960, the director of the National Catholic Family Life Bureau of the U.S.A. (Mgr Irving A. De Blanc) stated that several recent studies show that Roman Catholic married couples use contraceptive birth control 'in about the same measure' as their Protestant and Jewish neighbours.[1] We find then that the Roman rule is bringing the law into disrespect because Roman Catholics themselves do not obey it, for they are evidently not convinced that they are indulging in immoral practices in such disobedience.

In recent years the problem of contraception in the overpopulated lands of South-east Asia has become a burning question, because with the new health and immunity from disease brought

[1] *New York Times*, 22nd June 1960.

by modern medicine widespread hunger and undernourishment have become a present reality and are likely to become much worse. A full treatment of the problem has been published by Dr Richard Fagley of the Commission of the Churches on International Affairs in a book called *The Population Explosion*. The basic question is whether we are to use the skills and knowledge which God has given us to prevent among these peoples calamity which results from using those very skills and knowledge in the prevention of disease. If we are to appeal to reason there seems to be only one possible answer, and when we find that love and compassion urge us to the same answer, it is difficult to see how there can be any doubt in the matter.

Those who oppose contraceptives often seem to imply that in the absence of contraceptives God is given a free choice as to whether conception shall take place or not, and that he makes up his mind in every case separately, and issues a kind of separate *fiat* or *non fiat* in each case. This seems to reflect a crude idea of God, and an inadequate idea of human freedom, for it is the meaning of human freedom that God has put it into the power of men to make their own decisions in fields which are under their control. There is no *a priori* reason for supposing that God disapproves of men exercising their free choice in the field of conception, any more than he resents their having their appendices or tonsils removed for sufficient reason.

The Lambeth Conferences, which have special authority—though no legislative function—for Anglicans, have gradually changed their views on this subject. Among anti-Anglicans this change is held up as a reason for scorn, but, as Anglicans do not believe in the infallibility of Lambeth Conferences, it can be interpreted as a cause for satisfaction that they are ready to reconsider recommendations, which have earlier been reached on an insufficient study of the facts and perhaps under the influence of former conventional thinking. The committee of the 1958 Lambeth Conference dealing with these matters condemned the unilateral withholding of sexual intercourse and the practice of *coitus interruptus*. It clearly stated that 'it is also wrong to say that such intercourse ought not to be engaged in except with the willing intention to procreate children.'

The resolution of the conference itself (No. 115) is as follows:

The Conference believes that the responsibility for deciding upon the number and frequency of children has been laid by God upon the consciences of parents everywhere: that this planning, in such ways as are mutually acceptable to husband and wife in Christian conscience, is a right and important factor in Christian family life and should be the result of positive choice before God. Such responsible parenthood, built on obedience to all the duties of marriage, requires a wise stewardship of the resources and abilities of the family as well as a thoughtful consideration of the varying population needs and problems of society and the claims of future generations.

It should be noted that the Lambeth resolution puts the whole problem in the context of Christian family life, where it belongs. The moral issues must be settled in the light of God's calling to Christians and their responsibilities before him. Nothing is said about any generally applicable natural law, nor does the resolution deal with contraception among non-Christians except by implication. The inference would seem to be clear that there can be no reason to object to the use of contraceptives, if the people using them think it to be right, always providing that such use takes place within the marriage relationship.

Artificial Insemination

The practice of artificial insemination is of long standing on farms for the breeding of cattle, but it has now begun to be extended to human beings. It consists of the artificial introduction into the womb of a woman of male semen which has been separately obtained by the person conducting the operation. In 1948 the Archbishop of Canterbury received a report from a weighty Commission which he had appointed to consider the subject of artificial human insemination. The Lambeth Conference of 1958 called attention to the Report without taking it into its own purview. The findings of the Commission were that in circumstances where for some reason physical sexual intercourse between husband and wife is impossible or permanently unfruitful, it is permissible morally for the wife to be inseminated with the semen of her husband. This is technically known as A.I.H. (Artificial Insemination—Husband). Insemination by semen from some man other than the husband is called A.I.D. (Artificial Insemination—Donor). A.I.D. was considered immoral, equivalent to adultery, and destructive of the marriage bond.

There are already a number of doctors practising A.I.D. on their own responsibility in various parts of the world, including Britain

and the U.S.A. A substantial part of the medical profession objects
to the practice on moral and religious grounds. There can be no
reasonable doubt that it is opposed to Christian teaching about
marriage and must be condemned as such. It also has serious
drawbacks from personal and social points of view, but that does
not fall within our examination here. For a short and thorough
examination of its various aspects the reader may be referred to a
pamphlet entitled *Artificial Insemination by Donor*, containing a
memorandum submitted in evidence by the Archbishop of
Canterbury to the Departmental Committee on Artificial Insemination, 1959, and published by the Church Information Office. In
dealing with the Christian aspect the memorandum points out that
A.I.D. involves injury to the integrity of husband, wife, doctor,
donor, and resulting child.

Put in its shortest form the objection to A.I.D. is that it treats
human beings as if they were animals, merely concerned either
with the breeding of good stock or with the temporary satisfaction
of an emotional desire on the part of the woman concerned. To
treat men and women merely as animals is to reject God's plan
and to arrogate to individual men the right to change its basic
human principles. A.I.D. is wrong on theological, moral and
social grounds. The words of the Archbishop's Commission sum
up the matter:

> Artificial insemination with donated semen involves a breach of the
> marriage. It violates the exclusive union set up between husband and
> wife. It defrauds the child begotten, and deceives both his putative
> kinsmen and society at large. For both donor and recipient the sexual
> act loses its personal character and becomes a mere transaction. For
> the child there must always be the risk of disclosure, deliberate or
> unintended, of the circumstances of his conception. We therefore
> judge artificial insemination with donated semen to be wrong in
> principle and contrary to Christian standards.

An aspect of the matter which Christians ought always to bear
in mind is that A.I.D. denies the sacramental character of human
life and action, and thus evacuates it of its personal religious
content. It abstracts the physical from the personal, as the above
paragraph says, and in doing so it destroys the whole mental and
physical aspect of sexual intercourse concerned with personal
relationships. Physical sexual powers are provided to be one aspect
of a total act involving the whole personalities of the two persons

taking part in it. It is a denial of this human aspect which reduces A.I.D. to a mere breeding process.

It is commonly argued today that any desire which can be met ought to be met, but such a proposition is evidently false. Life is full of frustrations which have to be accepted, which in the Christian life are necessary means to a deepening of the Christian character and of growth into closer union with God. Those who for no fault of their own find themselves unable to bear children find a constructive and creative life in accepting their disability and turning such acceptance to good account in God's service. The lack of children can, of course, be creatively used by the adoption of children, who would otherwise be deprived of a loving home of their own.

Sterilization

The question as to whether sterilization is morally acceptable or not has become one of urgency in the attempts which are being made to reduce overpopulation in countries like India. The increase of population there is so immense and so rapid that it is constantly overrunning the increasing production of food, and the deterioration of the food position is an ever-present threat. There are already millions of undernourished people, whose lot can hardly be improved unless some check can be devised on the ever-increasing total number of births. Medical skill preserves the lives of millions who in former years would have died in infancy or youth, and they are destined to grow up to suffer disease and deformity because there is not enough food to keep them healthy.

Traditionally sterilization in the only form in which it was known, i.e. castration, was always condemned among Christians, when it occurred voluntarily. The first canon of the Council of Nicaea in 325 dealt with eunuchs and ran:

> If any one be made an eunuch by a physician for any disease, or by the barbarians, or by any one whom he served as a slave, he may continue or be admitted into the clergy; but not if he makes himself an eunuch, when he was a sound man.

There is already in this Canon the distinction between sterilization for medical reasons, which is generally permitted by all Christians, and that which is not medically necessary. The Roman Catholic view is quite clear and was expressed by Pius XI in the Encyclical *Casti Connubii* of 31st December, 1930.

Christian doctrine establishes, and the light of human reason makes it most clear, that private individuals have no power over the members of their bodies than that which pertains to their natural ends; and they are not free to destroy or mutilate their members, or in any other way render themselves unfit for their natural functions, except when no other provision can be made for the good of the whole body.

Anglican opinion, however, does not follow so strictly these traditional views, and in 1961 a report was made by a committee set up by the Board of Social Responsibility of the Church Assembly of the Church of England, entitled *Sterilization; an ethical enquiry* (Church Information Board 1962). Readers who wish to follow the reasoning in detail must be referred to the Report. The most important conclusion which the committee reached is that there are circumstances in which sterilization without medical necessity may be morally acceptable. It expresses its conclusion cautiously (p. 25):

> But faced as we are by a situation in which a responsible government is pursuing, together with other ameliorative measures, a policy of persuasion for voluntary sterilization, and asked by Christian doctors and nurses involved in the carrying out of this policy for help in deciding for themselves how far they can co-operate, we are bound to conclude that we find no grounds on which to reply in terms of an absolute negative.

In spite of the caution this conclusion opens the door to serious possibilities, for there is an evident danger that once it is admitted that there are some circumstances which make voluntary sterilization permissible, an important obstacle to its wide use is removed. The committee seems to have based its conclusion on two or three salient facts, and their reasoning would seem mainly to rest on them. The first of these is the population explosion to which we have already referred, and the pressing need to take effective steps to reduce the birth rate, if the health and lives of millions are to be saved. Side by side with this need is the impossibility of securing the reduction of births by sexual abstinence. However desirable continence might be as the best solution to the problem, living conditions, social habits and other factors make it impossible. The committee presumably also thinks that there are no contraceptive measures which can be taken with an illiterate population, so that this method too cannot be effective. This leaves sterilization as a possibility when it is voluntarily sought.

In declining to dismiss voluntary sterilization as a moral means the committee also seems to have been influenced by the consideration that vasectomy, which is the most common form of male sterilization, is in many cases reversible and, therefore, not inevitably lifelong. But, as the Report itself points out, the likelihood of vasectomy being reversed is very small. Indeed it could be said without much fear of contradiction that, if vasectomy were carried out in large numbers in India, it would be surgically impossible to deal with more than a minute number of men who wished to have their sexual powers restored. It should, however, be noted that vasectomy is not 100 per cent effective and sometimes corrects itself naturally.

For those who are responsible for deciding to initiate a programme of voluntary sterilization in a country where standards of literacy and intelligence are low it must be almost impossible to ensure that the word 'voluntary' has any real content. How can a man who has been brought up in an Indian village, for example, who is illiterate, and who has no knowledge beyond what he has gained from the village tradition—how can he make a decision about permanent sterilization (for it would be permanent in almost all cases) or know what that really implies? And, as the Report points out, there are serious dangers if a reward is offered to those who undergo such sterilization, for the reward itself in a country where dire poverty is common may be a serious interference with the voluntary character of the act.

It must be recognized that voluntary sterilization is not uncommonly performed in the U.S.A., and there are a number of cases of Canadians crossing the border to have the operation, because it is illegal in their own country. The cases which have been reported in the press have been of those who merely wish to avoid having any more children without the trouble of restraining their sexual impulses, or of using contraceptives.

What can the Christian moralist say further about sterilization? He ought first to distinguish between the attitudes of Christians and non-Christians. It is one thing to look at what ought to be the Christian life, and it is quite another to consider what laws ought to be made for the teeming Hindus of India. The latter are no less valuable in the sight of God, but they cannot be expected to live the life of God without the opportunities which the Gospel and its message brings. We want to bring others to the Christian faith, but it would be absurd to expect them to have the same outlook on life as a Christian before they have even heard of Jesus Christ.

For a Christian voluntary sterilization is difficult, if not impossible, to justify. It is an indispensable aspect of Christian truth that in life man finds his growth in God, not only by doing the things which he wants and likes to do, but even more in using his sufferings and the buffets of life to refine his faith, and with his Lord to bring him closer to God. The spiritual power to overcome what is in itself difficult, or a 'diminishment' as Fr Teilhard de Chardin would have said, and to turn it into good is in some ways the key to the whole of Christian spirituality. It springs directly out of the teaching and example of Jesus, that he who would follow him and is not willing to take up his cross cannot be his disciple. It is therefore inconceivable that a true Christian would wish to mutilate his body, itself a gift of God of creation, in order to spare himself the trouble of restraining his sexual impulses, unless indeed he is mentally ill. We must then follow the Christian tradition, so far as those who profess and call themselves Christians are concerned. Sterilization cannot be fitted in with the Gospel of Jesus Christ, except when for other reasons it is the result of necessary medical and surgical treatment.

For those who are not Christians the matter is different. It is desirable that they should also come into the fulness of light which comes from the Gospel, but if they do not, Christians cannot take away the responsibility which belongs to them as men with free will. Nevertheless practical dangers are so great, that men of good will may think that the dangers of a programme of voluntary sterilization may well outweigh its advantages. And whatever happens, the Christian doctor or nurse must never take part in an irreversible act of this nature, if there are any doubts as to the truly voluntary character of the act, both in the sense that the patient knows fully what he is doing, and that no improper pressure, such as rewards, has affected his judgement.

Sterilization is sometimes advocated as a punitive measure for those who have been guilty of sexual crimes, or as a eugenic measure in the case of those whose offspring are likely to be mentally defective. It is not acceptable for such actions to be taken by the civil authority unless there is no other means of safeguarding society and the danger against which it is to be guarded is of paramount importance. In fact such measures are likely to be unsatisfactory, for though they would prevent the men in question from causing children to be born, they would in no way hinder their sexual tendencies and might even encourage them in the knowledge that no woman could conceive by them. This might well have the result of spreading venereal disease, and could have other effects which would be as bad as the condition the sterilization was meant to put right. There is in fact always an alternative to sterilization, namely the care of those unable to care for themselves and the incarceration of those who are dangers to society. Bodily mutilation has long been considered a barbaric punishment in civilized countries, and sterilization is a form of such mutilation.

Breeding Techniques

A British Council of Churches booklet, called *Human Reproduction*, issued in 1962, examined various breeding techniques which are used for the breeding of cattle, and discussed the question of their applicability to human beings. *Prima facie* there seems to be no technical reason why such techniques could not be used for human beings. The question of their morality needs to be examined. Some of the techniques have already been discussed, for example, the forms of artificial insemination.

The general questions raised by the prevention of conception have already been considered, but there are a number of techniques for breeding which have not come under examination. One of these is the use of stored sperms (telegenesis) in which sperms secured by masturbation are stored in a temperature which allows them to be used at a much later date for breeding by insertion into the womb of a woman. If the sperm came from a man other than the woman's husband, the act would be definitely immoral and a form of adultery, just as the usual A.I.D. technique is adultery. It is conceivable that an elderly husband with a young wife might ask for his sperm to be stored, so that his wife could continue to have children after his power to take part in normal coitus had been lost. What is the moral character of such an arrangement?

The first thing to be noted is that the sacramental aspect of sexual relations is of prime moral importance to the Christian. The sexual act is not merely a means of breeding, it is also the expression of mutual love and is intimately and inseparably connected with the full expression of the emotional and spiritual content of married love. Anything therefore that denies this sacramental character cannot be acceptable morally to Christians. It is somewhat ironic that a strong opposition to all forms of contraceptive methods, which is based on the physical aspect of the sexual union as being decisive, may weaken the case against immoral breeding techniques, the aim of which is to produce children for the marriage.

Most of the techniques mentioned in the British Council of Churches pamphlet are methods of treating the female animal so that it can produce more or better offspring. One of them is the grafting of ovaries. This would involve the removal of ovaries from a healthy woman and their grafting on to one who had a fault which prevented her from ovulating. Such an operation would make it possible for the woman who received the graft to bear children as the result of normal sexual intercourse. The genetic characteristics of the child, however, would be those of the woman from whom the graft was transferred. But there would seem to be no serious moral objection to this practice, if it were applied to human beings. It would have the same basic character as the transplantation of a kidney, or the grafting of a cornea. Its aim would be to cure a defect and to make the woman physically whole. The fact that the child born as a result would have the genetic characteristics of another woman is not morally relevant, and is no more objectionable than in the case of adopted children. The child would be born as a consequence of a sexual act of full moral content between the married partners.

Another technique is the transplantation of a fertilized ovum from a woman, where it had already been fertilized as a result of sexual intercourse, to the womb of another woman, where the embryo would develop and eventually be born. It could be used to take the fertilized ovum from the womb of a wife where an ovum had been fertilized as a result of sexual intercourse with her husband for insertion into another woman's womb. The embryo would there be incubated, born, and handed back to the original mother after birth. Although there is no interference in such a practice with the marriage bond, the incubation and birth of the child is so intimately a sacramental part of motherhood and family relationships that the most favourable verdict which could possibly be given is that it is morally neutral. It is, however, morally undesirable and would tend to break up the exclusive relationship between husband and wife in the conception and bearing of children.

The same method could be used for transplanting a fertilized ovum from another woman into the womb of the wife. If the fertilization had been caused by sexual intercourse by the husband with the other woman, that would be an adulterous act and a denial of the marriage bond. If, however, the fertilized ovum came from sexual intercourse with a man not the husband of the woman to whom the ovum was to be transplanted, it would again be an interference with the marriage bond of the same immoral character as A.I.D.

There are practical problems which would result from the afore-mentioned techniques which tell strongly against the application of them to human beings. They would cause very difficult tensions in personal relationships, because the appearance of those relation-ships would in fact be different from what they were in reality.

In the future it might conceivably be possible to conduct the whole business of the growth of a child outside the human bodies of father and mother from the moment of conception. There seems no reason why a technique should not be invented for obtaining sperm by masturbation and an ovum by extraction, for uniting them together in some laboratory construction so that the embryo grew completely outside the mother's body, and then merely returning the child, when sufficiently developed, to its mother, without any of the normal physiological activities of incubation and childbirth. Such methods would be morally unacceptable because they would remove the essential physical aspects of the sacramental act, that is, the expression through physical means of the emotional and spiritual content of marriage.

The induction of multiple births has already become possible, and the determination of the sex of a child may become possible before long. As regards multiple birth great caution should be exercised. If the technique can be regarded merely as a natural and harmless extension of normal health, there would seem to be no moral reason against it, so long as the births come about as a consequence of marital coitus. The same principle would seem to apply to the preselection of the sex of children. So long as the process did not involve any action which maimed the body in any way, but was a mere extension of a natural development, there would seem to be no moral objection *per se*. On the other hand there may be serious practical objections if the possession of such a power were to result in a serious numerical lack of balance between the sexes.

There are two main principles to be borne in mind when considering the moral implications of breeding techniques. The first is that persons must never be treated as things: they are ends in themselves, created to obey and love God. The second is that the physical elements of such techniques must not be detached from the emotional and spiritual values which they are intended to express. The physical is to a Christian the means of serving God, and his physical make-up is part of his spiritual and emotional personality. The various parts cannot be divided, and if they are treated as if they were separate, a moral offence has been committed.

8

THE USE OF FORCE

RELATIONS WITH OTHER people are the stuff of human life and form one of the basic elements of human personality. There is an inescapable need for good relations with others, relationships of love, so that the human person can know fulfilment. Like all human attributes human relations have two sides, the aspect which concerns the self considered in artificial isolation, and the aspect which concerns other persons. It is only in the generous outpouring of genuine love, and the consequent adoption of loving attitudes towards others, that the needs of the true self can be realized. This generosity towards others is more than once stressed in the teaching of Jesus, and forms a basic element in it.

The misuse of this human need for others is represented in the capital vice of envy. Of the seven capital vices this is the only one which exclusively deals with other people, although most of the others do so indirectly. Lust and anger usually directly affect other people, though both can be indulged in privately, without in fact bringing anyone else into them. But envy is always envy of a person, and is the opposite attitude to that generous love which is alone the mark of the true Christian. Envy is a denial of love, for it is basically the desire to gratify one's own selfish wants and to take good away from others, if one cannot have it oneself. It sets up the self-centred desires of the personality as the standard to which others are to be made to conform.

But the positive side of personal relationships is at the heart of human happiness and forms the field in which the love of God and obedience to his will can most fruitfully be shown. The love of God, which is poured out into the hearts of Christians, spills over into their relationships with other people and comes alive in the world, primarily through these contacts of Christians with others. In this context must be seen the various principles of moral theology which concern relations between people, the first and most important of which is justice, one of the four 'cardinal' virtues.

Justice and Punishment

'Justice is the moral principle which regulates the relations of men to one another' is the opening sentence of a most illuminating little book on the subject by O. C. Quick.[1] It is because it is to be seen within the context of God's love for man that justice is of prime importance to Christians, not because it can be set up as a principle apart from the Christian Faith. It is true that there are and have been secular principles of justice outside Christianity of a high moral order. But in moral theology justice must be kept in the perspective of the love of God, if it is to remain true. For without this background justice becomes very easily a matter of human law without any ultimate standard to which it can be referred. If this happens, what is called justice can easily become unjust in reality.

Justice deals with man as the subject of rights and the object of duties, and claims that these rights and duties are inalienable from him as man. This principle is common to all codes of justice which are not frankly relative. In the modern world there have unfortunately been powerful States which have rejected the principle that man in himself has certain rights which cannot be taken away from him except wrongfully. The Nazi régime in Germany rejected this principle, and based its actions on a theory of superiority of what was called the 'Aryan' race and on the supposed inferiority of the Jews. The practical result of this theory was the cold-blooded murder of millions of Jews between 1939 and 1945. The Communist State in practice adopts a theory that the only morally compulsive principle is the good of the Communist Party, an attitude which has also resulted in the death and persecution of millions of innocent persons. If we are to judge from the Declaration of Human Rights, subscribed by all the members of the United Nations, we must believe that the fact that man, as such, has rights is now generally accepted. But unhappily the actual behaviour of governments within their own territories rarely accords with the splendid principles to which they profess allegiance in international bodies.

[1] *Christianity and Justice*, Christian News-Letter Books, Sheldon Press, 1940.

Justice is based on the principle that the individual person has inalienable rights, and this means that man must be treated as an end in himself and not merely as a means to something else. Such treatment includes the consideration of the rights of other men: a man's rights do not exist in isolation from his fellows, and they cannot therefore extend to rights which would harm the rights of other men. Many non-Christians will accept such a basis for justice and morals, even though it is difficult or impossible to justify it except on Christian principles. To accept the truth that man is to be treated as an end in himself means that he is considered in himself as having some ultimate value, which again must presuppose a value which outlasts his temporary life on this earth, otherwise he would have to be placed below other values which do outlast the span of human life, such as artistic achievements or some other end. To treat man as an end in himself therefore implies some lasting or eternal value in man as such. If a man has no future and no eternal life, there is no reason why he should not be treated as a means to all kinds of ends which do not concern him personally, such as the good of unborn generations, to which he might be sacrificed without any moral scruples about his own fate, so long as the betterment of others was thought to be secured. On this basis it would be possible morally to justify the murder of millions of Jews during the war on the grounds that it brought benefit to the German people, and this appears to have been what Hitler believed. The only practical moral obstacle to such doctrine and behaviour is the principle that man in himself has an ultimate value which must not be denied. But if man has this ultimate value, the reason for it can only be found in the eternal fact that God loves him, and that God has created and redeemed man for his own eternal love and life. Justice rests on this basic religious fact and is only fully understood when it is related to it.

With this background the description of justice provided by St Thomas Aquinas has proved to be a good starting-point. Justice as a virtue is, according to him, 'a steady unchanging will to give every man his due'. One aspect of the conception of justice has traditionally been associated with the question of property, springing it is said from the primitive practice of barter, and, although this aspect of the subject is connected with that of personal relationships, it can very easily deteriorate into a mere consideration of weights and measures. Mortimer has a chapter on justice in his book *The Elements of Moral Theology* and gives the greater part of it to dealing with justice in connection with property. He adopts the traditional distinctions and terms of Roman moral theology for the purpose. (These terms are shortly explained in an appendix on technical terms at the end of the present book.) Jeremy Taylor (*Holy Living*, ch. III) bases his treatment of Christian justice on two passages from Scripture. The first is 'Whatsoever you would that men should do to you, even so do to them', and the second 'Render to all their dues: tribute to whom tribute is due; custom to whom custom; fear to whom fear; honour to whom honour. Owe no man anything but to love one another' (Rom. 13.7-8).

Justice is usually divided into three parts. (*a*) *General* justice is the name given to the relationship, duties, etc., of the individual to the community. (*b*) *Distributive* justice is the reverse of general justice and deals with the duties of the community to the individual. The third, (*c*) *Commutative* justice, is concerned with the duties of one individual to other individuals within society. As soon as one begins to look at these aspects in detail it is necessary to examine from the moral point of view the status of human civil law. There is, of course, a clear distinction between human law and the Christian moral law. Sometimes they coincide and sometimes they do not. But in general there is a moral obligation to obey the law of the land, if it is not plainly against Christian moral principles. We shall have occasion to notice some of the difficulties in human law a little later.

Civil law does not pretend to reproduce the moral law exactly, and it cannot be identified with it, but it does enforce the moral law at certain points where it is necessary to do so for the good of society. There is a widespread popular view that no moral blame rests on anyone who defies the law so long as he can 'get away with it'. This, of course, is nonsense, but moral and legal obligations do not always coincide. We may take as an example a bankrupt who has been discharged and has been able to pay his creditors only a proportion of what he owes them. If he finds himself later able to repay his debts, he is morally bound to do so, even though there is no legal obligation.

There is always a moral obligation to put right what has been done wrong, if this is possible, provided that the evil caused by putting a wrong right is not greater than the original evil. No hard-and-fast rules can be made, and each case must be considered on its merits with its circumstances. A simple example would be that of a man who had stolen money from his employer and wished to put the matter right. If he were able to do so without any serious ill results, then he has a clear duty to do it. But if it involved worse evils such as starvation for his wife and family, whereas his employer was in no hardship as a result of his theft, the evil caused would be greater than the original evil, and there would be a moral duty not to pay it back so long as those conditions prevailed. But the general obligation to right the wrong would remain.

Both general and distributive justice deal with the State and the individuals within it. The purpose of the State is to provide conditions in which the individuals within it, in association with one another, are given opportunities for the growth and fulfilment of their own personalities. This must be measured by the end of man, which is growth in the love of God, and therefore the conditions of the community should be such as will best help men to live a life consonant with this end. Such a purpose inevitably implies liberty of the individual, but it also requires safeguards against the depredations of others, which might destroy the possibility of a decent economic existence, and against external pressure, which might inhibit the flowering of his gifts and potentialities. We certainly cannot agree with those who think that the State is something intrinsically evil, for it is a necessary outward expression of the need of man to live together in societies. Nevertheless it must also be recognized that there is no State which approximates to the perfection of the divine community, which should be solely motivated by that love and self-sacrifice which is reflected from the nature of God himself.

There are various elements which make the actual State in practice fall short of perfection. The first is the sinful nature of man himself. So long as man is filled with rapacity and greed, selfishness, and disregard for others, so long will the State's condition reflect these evils. And in addition to the imperfections of the world, other inadequacies spring from the tension between the need for order and the requirements of freedom, for at the best only an uneasy balance is maintained.

Quick[1] points out that there are some inescapable difficulties in

---

[1] *Christianity and Justice*, pp. 9-10.

the just application of human law in the treatment of criminals. The general moral principle applies that a man must be treated as an end in himself. Punishment is often regarded by the uninformed public as a form of injury, but it is not meant to be anything of the kind, but rather an instrument to awaken the wrongdoer's conscience and a means by which he may purge his fault and put himself on the road to moral recovery. Quick makes the point that retribution is an important safeguard for offenders against society. Retribution is very much out of fashion and is often regarded as being a barbaric idea. But this is not the case. Probably the unpopularity of retribution springs from the mistaken notion that it is the same thing as revenge. The prime object of punishment is retribution, which safeguards the individual offender because it contains the principle that the punishment must be proportionate to the offence, and must be governed by what is due to the offender, and not by some outside consideration, which might not take the offender into account. Moreover retribution ought to take into account the guilt of society in the offender's wrong. Thus in a case in which a man, starving from unemployment, stole food for his wife and family, the guilt of society might well be held to be so great as to do away with any punishment for the individual concerned. If punishment is considered merely to have as its object the protection of society, there is no adequate protection for the individual wrongdoer. For the protection of society might be better served by exacting a punishment far in excess of the crime which has been committed. Indeed English law in the past has given many examples of this fault, when men could be hanged for stealing a sheep, or given long prison terms for petty theft. The sad history of the treatment of poor offenders also gives salutary warning against the tendency to exalt the rights of private property, to which we refer later. Russian law exacts disproportionate punishment for offences against the community.

The morality of capital punishment has been much debated in recent years. In normal circumstances it is difficult, if not impossible, to justify morally the practice of capital punishment. With his usual clarity and succinctness Quick puts the essence of the matter:[1]

> If an offender is thought to have no chance of amendment, he must be regarded as no longer responsible for his actions, and it is then

[1] *Op. cit.*, p. 11.

illogical, on the retributive principle, to treat him as a criminal at all. And this argument seems to be decisive against the justice of capital punishment. The penalty *due* to an offender cannot fairly be extended to the taking of his life. For if there is still a chance of his amendment, it is unjust to him to deprive him of it. But if there is no such chance, it is unjust to treat him as though he were still a responsible agent. Human justice may not arrogate to itself the right to pronounce at what point a moral being has become unfit to live.

He goes on to say that summary executions may sometimes be justified in emergencies, and that the use of force by the State in any form logically involves the right to take life in extreme circumstances. This also affects the standpoint of pacifists, for they do in fact continue to live in a society where the right to take life is an integral part of the maintenance of order. But in referring to the retributive principle in connection with capital punishment, it is important to note that retribution is not the same thing as the 'eye for an eye' teaching of the Old Testament—it is not an equivalence of punishment, but is founded on the rights of the human personality as such.

It is necessary to face the fact that the administration of justice in a State must always fall short of the ideal moral principles which the Christian religion maintains. This does not mean, however, that it is therefore to be regarded lightly. On the contrary the upholding of just laws is indispensable for the creation of conditions in which man has the best chance of living as the child of God. But because justice in human affairs is relative to the conditions in which men live, it never completely corresponds to the ideal. The following points may be noted:

(*a*) The law of the State must be enforced, a point which we have just mentioned. This enforcement must carry the inevitable consequence that in an emergency even human life must be forfeit in the course of putting it into practice, since resistance has to be overcome. If it were not overcome, then the law would not be able to be enforced and would become of no effect. This happens in the United States of America when commercial concerns are forced by gangsters to pay bribes under threat of death if they do not, where it is only by the death of the criminals involved that the threat can be removed. But the right to kill contradicts one of the moral principles of justice that each citizen must be considered as an end in himself.

(*b*) It is generally recognized that the laws of a country cannot

be far ahead of public opinion, and that if they are not supported
by public opinion they had better not be made. But public opinion
is always a noticeable distance behind the maximum moral
standards of the best men, and even further behind those of God.
A just law which cannot be enforced without creating a greater
evil than its breaking had better not be made at all, since the effect
of making it is to worsen moral conditions.

(*c*) In meting out punishment to a criminal the authorities of
the State must take into consideration the needs of safeguarding
public order in society, as well as what ought to be done about the
offender. Laws and punishments of a general nature cannot in their
general form take account of each individual need of each individual offender. So far therefore as the order of society is decisive
in framing the law, the individual is punished as a means to an
end and not as an end in himself.

(*d*) The character of human justice itself creates a difficulty
which springs out of a good side of its nature. In fact it has to
hold together two principles which are not compatible with one
another. The first is that every person must be treated as an end
in himself, and the second that justice should be impersonal and
treat all persons alike. The principle of equality before the law is
a basic principle of human justice, and yet it is incompatible with
the individual treatment of each offender. Yet equality before the
law is a principle which must be maintained in order to defend
the individual against unjust and arbitrary treatment.

The Right to Rebel

In the sixteenth and seventeenth centuries English moral
teachers were so afraid of sedition, or so afraid of the powers that
be, that for the most part they exaggerated the duty of citizens to
obey the king without question, and the divine right of kings was
a doctrine which buttressed such views. It is quite impossible to
maintain such an outlook in the twentieth century, and the growth
of democratic liberalism has removed its political sanctions. But
there are difficult moral choices to be made in considering if and
when rebellion is justified morally against the ruling power. Since
the end of the Second World War Egypt, Cyprus, Asia and Africa
have provided such problems in an acute form.

It is a certain fact that justice cannot be maintained without
order, but there is a strong tendency on the part of those who are

satisfied with the *status quo* to argue that order is all-important.
The result is that those who are groaning under injustices which
demand political remedies are prevented from gaining redress, or
what they conceive to be their rights. Cyprus provided a good
example. The vast majority of Cypriots wanted, or appeared to
want, union with Greece. The British Government refused to
grant it to them, and also refused self-government of a sufficiently
independent kind to satisfy the desires of the people of Cyprus.
The Cypriots therefore rebelled, and by armed rebellion they
secured most of the aims for which they were hoping. The British
attitude held that it was all-important to maintain order, and it
was on this ground that they resisted the rebellion. But by granting
independence to the Cypriots under pressure they have implicitly
admitted that in this they were justified. Yet to any outside
observer, and certainly to the Cypriots before their rebellion, it
appeared hopeless to expect the British Government to grant such
requests unless they were forced to do so. Is it possible to say that
the Cypriots had no right to rebel? They cannot be condemned
for rebelling. We must then ask what moral principle is involved.

It would seem that where an appeal to order is used by those in
control to deny changes which are indispensable for justice,
resistance may be justified. The injustice which is being imposed is
being imposed by force. If there is no other remedy, it seems that
an appeal to force is justified, so long as the evil created by the
use of force is not disproportionate to the evil which it is desired
to put right. Yet in practice this principle is almost impossible to
apply, since there is no measuring stick between the evils, which
may be guessed at as the result of rebellion, and the oppression,
which is suffered beforehand. Quick draws a distinction between
insurrection which is an open revolt, and assassination which is
clandestine, and concludes that the former is morally tolerable
and the latter is not.

There seems to be no definite standard which can be used in
such affairs. It is certainly morally intolerable that a whole people,
or the majority of a people, should be condemned to permanent
tyranny merely on the grounds that order must be maintained.
On the other hand rebellion causes great evils and suffering. Who
is to measure, say, the evil of apartheid now against the possible
evils resulting from an armed insurrection against the Government
of the Republic of South Africa? A cynical view might be that

rebellion is only justified when it succeeds, or when it has a good chance of succeeding, in the spirit of the couplet:

> Treason doth never prosper: what's the reason?
> For if it prosper, none dare call it treason.
>
> (John Harington 1561-1612.)

It is more difficult to answer the question how far a Christian ought to support a movement which aims to achieve its end by violence, which will probably involve the death of innocent people. If it is permissible for a Christian to bear arms in a just war, which is certainly the traditional teaching of the Christian Church, is he not permitted to bear arms in a just rebellion? If it is morally acceptable to resist aggression by force, is it not equally acceptable to resist tyranny by force? In trying to answer these questions can a distinction be drawn between what is permissible in theory for a non-Christian group fighting against a tyrannical government and what a Christian may do? The problem resolves itself into something very like the pacifist question when faced with war. There is a difference, however, since in the pacifist problem the persons concerned have been and are deriving benefits from a society, whose claims they decline to meet. In the case of rebellion this is not the case. On the other hand it might be retorted that the Christians who stood aside would be benefiting from a rebellion, to which they refused to give help in the critical hour.

There seems to be little doubt in the case of a rebellion that a Christian would not often be morally justified in identifying himself with a plan of violence to overthrow the régime, though he would certainly be justified in trying by non-violent means to replace tyranny by freedom, and wrong by right. In practice the line between the two might be very difficult to draw, since the logical consequence of political agitation is often armed revolt. In the case of rebellion against an oppressor, there is a closer parallel with the New Testament situation than is the case with the general question of war. Jesus was the member of an occupied country, where the duty of patriotic Jews was to get rid of the Roman yoke, and where there were from time to time rebellions against the occupying power. But it is clear that he would not have anything to do with political agitation. His witness was of quite a different kind. Nevertheless it is not without significance that he was condemned to death on political charges, and the authorities responsible for government and authority can easily mistake Christian witness for something political, because the influence of that witness undermines the basis on which their rule rests. Jesus was executed on a political charge of which he was innocent, though his influence and witness were far more revolutionary than those who condemned him ever imagined. Christians should give their non-violent witness uncompromisingly, and not be surprised if the result of such witness, even when it is not directly concerned with political issues, is condemnation unjustly. For it is in the acceptance of this consequence that the witness of the cross consists.

If we take a practical example, we may say that it would not be morally right for a Christian to be in any way concerned with plots against the lives of people in a multi-racial State, but that they must be ready to witness without fear in favour of a truly creative and constructive brotherly relation between the races, for that is *the* way in which the truth of the Gospel can be shown. But in doing this they are likely to meet with the opposition and displeasure of the government, as indeed happened at the inter-racial settlement of St Faith, whose members were dispersed and some of them imprisoned, not for being concerned with violence, but for teaching the Christian Faith, the principles of which had become for the government identified with subversion. The excuse of a government is always that the teaching and practice of such principles encourage the elements which want to overthrow the government by force. But when a government reaches the stage of saying this, it has ceased to have any moral authority to govern. This is of course the situation in the Republic of South Africa where men are haled before the magistrate and subjected to penalties for teaching that the Fatherhood of God is a reality for all men, and that it is only in equality and brotherly unity that their happiness and fulfilment can be found.

There is another difference between the call to fight in a war and taking part in a rebellion. However distasteful the tyranny may be under which one is living, there are benefits of order which we derive from it. In rebelling therefore we should be renouncing the moral obligation which the reception and use of those benefits puts upon us. It may not be a great obligation, and it may be an obligation which is outweighed by other considerations, yet there remains some obligation even in the worst conditions. In a call to serve the State in war it has always been recognized that the community through the State has a right to call for sacrifices from its members in defence of its existence, and that the obligation of the individual to the community to respond to this call is implicitly contained in the acceptance by the individual of the benefits which the State provides for him in his normal life.

Christians and War

The question of whether war in modern conditions is acceptable to a Christian has become more acute since the Second World War. There is a strong chance that in modern times war on a large scale will result in the total destruction of the combatant nations, and possibly in the destruction of the rest of the world as well. Destruction beyond a certain point obviously cannot be justified on the grounds of defence, since it involves the destruction of the very thing which is supposed to be defended. In small quarrels between small powers destruction is not inevitable, but as soon as the big powers become involved the risk of extensive destruction is very great.

Nevertheless[1] if we admit that force is ever morally justified in order to support what is right in society, it seems illogical to hold that there can never be a just war. The absence of any independent authority which can decide whether a war is just or not does not affect the facts of the case. Moreover to maintain that there can never be a just war may mean that Christians would encourage those with less scruples to use violent methods with the knowledge that Christian influence will be thrown on the side of non-resistance in the country attacked. It is also necessary to bear in mind that, if war is not justified morally because it contains so many evils, the same is true of peace, which may and often does perpetuate conditions of injustice which cannot morally be defended on any grounds. It ought to be possible to change conditions in the world without military upheavals and rebellions, but in fact it is often not possible to do so, and to condemn all force is to give moral support to the *status quo*, which is morally indefensible, since it would have the effect of confirming those who are in power, and condemning the unfortunate and under-privileged to permanent inferiority.

If, however, wars are still to be justified morally, those who wish to take this view are bound to follow the Christian teaching about

[1] Quick, *op. cit.*, p. 19.

the just war, and to observe the conditions of restraint which that doctrine imposes upon them.

> The amount of force must not be more than is strictly necessary;
> the evils which the war creates must not be greater than the evils which it is designed to correct;
> force must be discriminatory, and must not be aimed at innocent persons who are not combatants or directly engaged in the war effort;
> the war must be defensive in character;
> the aim of the war must be to re-establish creative and friendly relations with the enemy as soon as he has come to his right mind.

This rules out several courses of action which were adopted by the victorious allies in the Second World War. A policy of unconditional surrender is not morally compatible with the aims of a just war, nor is a method of attack like pattern bombing, or the dropping of atomic bombs aiming at wiping out a large area, with the consequent killing or wounding of thousands of women and children who are not combatants.

> When once a war has become simply the attempt of one State to vanquish another by any and every means, it has become by that very fact utterly unjust and wrong.[1]

If the dangers of war are to be avoided, it is necessary, as the Churches have clearly seen, that the underlying causes of international tension be attacked, and one of the chief causes of tension can be a sense of injustice which has not been corrected. The Western nations are open to serious moral criticism in some of their policies, for in order to resist the spread of Communist influence they not infrequently ally themselves to régimes of rotten moral fibre and record. Not only is this a wrong policy, it is also in the long run a self-defeating policy, for it merely strengthens the invisible power of Communism, which will reap its harvest in due course. Justice is prior to peace, and many Christian thinkers and spokesmen in recent years may be criticized because they have spoken too much of peace, giving the impression that they, like the rest of mankind, are chiefly motivated by fright. But this is a fatally dangerous approach, for it is only by approaching the whole question from the point of view of morals and justice that any long-term improvement can be hoped for. A continual reiteration of the fact that war is contrary to the will of God, though true, does not advance the cause of peace very far.

[1] Quick, *op. cit.*

It is also not uncommon to hear leading churchmen state that war is not inevitable. This statement is open to misunderstanding, and can bear a meaning which is essentially immoral. In one sense Christian spokesmen, if they are to be true to the prophetic tradition, ought to be proclaiming that war *is* inevitable unless men turn themselves from their evil ways. Otherwise it is crying 'Peace, Peace' where there is no peace.

Lambeth Conferences and meetings of the World Council of Churches have given close attention to matters of war and peace and have spoken constantly of the need to ameliorate the causes of tension and to produce a new ethos. In the Commission of the Churches on International Affairs the Churches have an instrument which is engaged in the difficult and delicate task of trying to bring Christian influence to bear on the day-to-day problems of international tension, and to encourage the governments concerned to move towards solutions which will reflect the principles of justice which alone can provide a firm basis for peace, order and happiness. They have done notable work in this field. In a small book entitled *Christians and Power Politics*[1] the secretary of the Commission, Alan Booth, has written with discernment about these questions from a Christian point of view.

In the whole matter of peace between the nations moral issues are mixed up with questions of calculation which do not have any moral content. Many of the decisions which have to be taken are chosen from alternatives which from a moral point of view are all on the same footing. A very serious crisis faced the world towards the end of 1962 over Cuba, and the world was on the brink of war because the Russians were building missile bases in Cuba. The U.S.A. first imposed a naval blockade, and then said they would destroy the bases by military action if they were not dismantled. Any ship going to Cuba which refused to be searched would be sunk. After several days of acute tension the Russians agreed to dismantle the bases under United Nations supervision, if the Americans would undertake not to invade Cuba. War was thereby averted, and the Caribbean was made free of the direct missile threat to the U.S.A.

The success of the U.S. President's action (though there have also been some gains for the U.S.S.R.) has been widely acclaimed as proof that it was right. But on abstract grounds there are a good

[1] SCM Press 1961.

many objections to what he did. He failed to consult his allies, or the United Nations, before taking action. The decision of timing and of the character of the action was taken by the U.S.A. alone. There is doubt as to whether the action was objectively necessary to the security of the U.S.A., whatever may have been the mental condition of American citizens. Such unilateral action is a direct repudiation of its own publicly avowed principles by the U.S.A., and is in startling contrast to its attitude to others who have done similar things in the past—notably the U.S.S.R. in Hungary, and Britain and France at Suez. The long-term effect may have some bad consequences, though this cannot be known except in the event.

But the interesting moral problem is brought clearly to the front by this sequence of events, namely the connection if any between success and moral right. Is it true in any sense to say that because the action succeeded, therefore it was right? There seems no doubt that the answer is at least partly 'yes', and this brings out the tremendously important part that calculation plays in decisions in international affairs. The particular moral distinctions which apply usefully to the Cuba affair are those which (*a*) connect the morality of an action with its consequences, and (*b*) distinguish between formal and material sin.

The relation between the morality of an action and its probable consequences seems often to be overlooked by those who campaign for various causes such as unilateral disarmament, and it is important to realize that the morality of a course of action can change from one year to another, simply because the probable consequences have changed. This is a distasteful doctrine to many who would like to purge their feelings of guilt by upholding what they think are absolute moral principles without regarding consequences. There are in fact very few absolute principles of this sort, except in the vaguest form, and these have little relevance until they have been applied to a concrete human situation. The question of possessing H bombs is different from that of their use, which must be wrong in any circumstances conceivable at present. Both those who wish to renounce nuclear arms unilaterally and those who don't are at one in wishing to promote peace. It is the promotion of peace which is the overwhelming moral objective. Those who wish to abolish nuclear armaments think that this is the best way of achieving peace: those who oppose them think otherwise, though all are agreed that it would be better if the world were without nuclear weapons.

This is all plain sailing. But circumstances change, and whereas nuclear armaments might have made an important contribution to peace in, say, 1947 they may no longer make this contribution in, say, 1965. In the latter case they should, of course, be abolished. The morality of having them depends on their being a contribution to peace. The danger of using them, if they exist, is obviously so serious that they ought to be abolished as soon as they can no longer be plainly justified as contributing to peace.

It is therefore perfectly moral to have nuclear weapons, so long as they are not used, if, and only if, one is conscientiously convinced that they are essential for the avoidance of war, for the avoidance of war is an indispensable preliminary to the establishment of peace.

The general principle then can be stated in relation to international affairs as follows. An action is moral if its conscientious aim is to maintain peace as its overriding objective. There are subsidiary conditions which also ought to be fulfilled, such as faithfulness to proper treaty obligations, full attempts to have the right information, avoidance of nationalistic prejudice, etc., but the principle remains generally true.

But there is a second aspect, namely the difference between formal and material sin. This is the difference between the conscientiousness of the person concerned, and the actual rightness or wrongness of what is done. A simple illustration will make this distinction clear. A surgeon may consent to operate on a patient in order to cure his disorder, but the patient dies under the anaesthetic because he is suffering from a complaint of which there was no means of knowing beforehand. The surgeon has acted conscientiously and is in no way to blame for what occurs. He has therefore not committed any formal sin, no guilt attaches to him. But there can be no doubt that the action was wrong in itself because it resulted in the death of the person concerned. In the language of moral theology the action was materially wrong, but there was no formal sin.

If this principle is imported into international affairs we see that whether an action is materially right or wrong can only be discovered in the event, if we rule out actions which in themselves are always wrong, such as the torturing of prisoners or the slaughter of conquered peoples. Outside the range of the limited actions which are always wrong lies a huge field of actions which are done because, in calculating the result, they are thought to be beneficial. In such cases as these the result which is aimed at must be in itself a moral result, because, if it isn't, then the action is formally wrong from the start. But if we take an ordinary diplomat or statesman, who is genuinely and primarily anxious to promote the peace of the world, we find that the material wrongness or rightness of what he does depends on whether he has calculated correctly.

In the case of Cuba, therefore, it is perfectly proper to hold, and this is the teaching of moral theology, that the U.S. President's action was materially right, and, if we assume him to have been motivated by the right aims, formally right as well. It is, of course, possible that, at a later stage, disadvantages may appear to be consequent on his action in the Cuba crisis.

There are also advantages which may appear in the future, such as a new urgency for disarmament discussions and for a more stable form of international community. So far as we can, we must take all these things into consideration.

But above all we should remember that Christian teaching is that history has been and can be redeemed. This will be done only by scrupulous care in taking risks, and by a genuine and determined search for peace, even at the expense of one's own comfort and standard of living.

Nuclear Weapons

As we have seen, the traditional Christian attitude to war and peace has been that in a just war, of which the conditions were clearly laid down, it was proper for Christians to take part. Nevertheless the conditions in which modern war has been waged, or is likely to be waged, have so increased in frightfulness that many Christians who are not pacifists are anxious about the matter.

Some Christians in these days, not pacifists in the strict sense of the word, hold that war has now become so appalling and destructive that there can never be a 'just' war, and therefore there can never be a war in which Christians can properly engage without moral blame. Their argument is based on the theory that the difference between the wars of the past and those of the present is so great as to have become a difference in kind and not merely a difference in degree.

If we analyse this point of view we find several difficulties in accepting it. The case really rests on the assumption that war is justified up to a certain point of destructiveness, and thereafter is not. But a distinction merely on grounds of numbers killed is difficult to sustain. It might reasonably be held for example that it is less immoral to kill thousands of people with one H bomb, than to kill them over a long period by conventional bombs. It is quite impossible to say that it is more immoral to cause them sudden death than lingering death. Moreover how shall suffering and destruction be measured? We are inclined to see only those things of which we ourselves have had some experience. Many people alive today have lived through two world wars, in both of which there was fearful suffering and loss of life, but it would be uncertain to maintain that the suffering and loss of life was greater, relatively speaking, than that caused by the Thirty-Years War from 1618 to 1648, which caused widespread and prolonged misery. Moreover, if it is wrong to kill many men in resisting the evil, then it must surely be wrong to kill one man. (We are not here dealing with the distinction between combatants and non-combatants which we shall consider later.)

The strength of the Christian tradition in favour of a right use of force may perhaps best be seen from a passage in the *Encyclopaedia of Religion and Ethics*.[1]

> There are . . . besides non-resistance, two other principles, deeply embedded in the teaching of Jesus, which demand to be carefully weighed before a judgment is formed as to the lawfulness of war in the abstract or the sufficiency of a particular occasion of war. The doctrine of retributive justice, to begin with—that wickedness ought to be and will be punished—filled at least as large a space as the doctrine of non-resistance in the circle of Christ's thought. He pronounced upon Jerusalem an inevitable doom because of its obdurate blindness and disobedience (Matt. 23.37), and He drew the picture of a last judgment in which the wicked and impenitent would be punished according to their works (Matt. 25.31ff.). The idea of penal retribution, moreover, is the central and inspiring thought of the apocalyptic sections of the New Testament, represented by the eschatological discourses of Jesus (Matt. 24), the Pauline Apocalypse (II Thess. 2), and the book of Revelation. And if it be a law of the universe that wickedness ought to be restrained and punished, if God

[1] Art. 'War', vol. 12, p. 679.

Himself, while ready to forgive on condition of repentance and submission, and ever taking the initiative towards reconciliation, fights
against the obdurate rebels of His dominions with all the resources
of His providential order, not to speak of the menaces of apocalyptic
prediction, it may well be thought incredible that Christianity has
made it criminal for a nation to be a fellow-worker with God in
restraining the powers of wickedness and in seeing justice done upon
the earth. The ultra-pacifist school thinks it fit to impose upon the
nations a code of morality and a plan of procedure which, if absolutely
binding, would entail grave censure on God Himself and give ground
for an indictment of the methods of His governance of the universe.

The article goes on to point out that war may be an exercise of
true love and that it is absurd to suppose that Christian morality
holds that rulers of nations ought to sacrifice those who look to
them for protection. The quotation makes it clear that it is by no
means self-evident that Christian teaching forbids the use of force
to those with national responsibility. Most Christians continue to
take the view that they have the right and even the duty to engage
in defensive war on behalf of justice and right order. It is on this
basis that we must consider nuclear weapons and the radioactive
fallout which they entail, both in testing and in use.

The first point to be faced is whether large nuclear weapons are
necessary at all. The case for their development rests on their value
as deterrents to war. In other words the possession of large nuclear
weapons by both sides is thought to be the main guarantee that
war will not start, because neither side could risk the consequences.
This brings us into the realm of calculation, where there is no
particular religious or Christian point of view. No Christian
principle enables me to know whether in fact the existence of H
bombs on both sides makes war more or less likely. We are at
liberty to have our private views as citizens, but we are not justified
in claiming for such views any religious sanction.

In a book published in 1959 (*Enigma of Menace*) Air Marshal
Sir Victor Goddard argued forcibly that unless they are blinded
by fear, it is plain to all that only a balance of power and of menace
in fact produces a position in which war is unlikely to occur, for
it makes it too risky. His view is not unreasonable and may be
right. He maintained that the outbreak of war in recent times has
always followed the conviction on one side that it was strong
enough to overcome the other side, and that, unless that conviction
had been encouraged by weakness, the attack would never have
been a worth-while risk. It would seem at first sight that this theory

is implicitly accepted by the nations engaged in disarmament talks, who are all the time trying to preserve equality in relation to the others during any process of disarmament.

We may express an interim moral judgement on Goddard's point of view by saying that its aim is a moral one, namely to prevent war, and that therefore there is no moral objection to it.

We ought to notice that nuclear weapons include a great variety of types, ranging from the most powerful H bombs to what are called tactical nuclear weapons for use in the field. Such tactical weapons are now (1964) widely available for use by the forces of N.A.T.O. (North Atlantic Treaty Organization), which could not fight much of a battle without them, at least in Europe. Goddard's view is that nuclear armaments are necessary right down the scale, so that a threat at any level, even a small-scale action, becomes too risky to be tried.

The reason for this is clear. If the Western forces are armed only with the big nuclear weapons, the use of which would involve the complete devastation of their own countries by reprisal, they will not be an effective deterrent to a small incursion of forces, because no country is going to commit national suicide in order to stop a limited local operation. To stop such an action it is necessary to have properly armed troops on the spot.

This point was strongly made by the Inspector General of the West German armed forces in a memorandum in 1960. It included this extract:

> The armaments of the opponent make graduated deterrence essential. This deterrent requires a balance of atomic and conventional armament for the shield force as a supplement to the strategic air force and navy. If the military capabilities do not allow a differentiation between resistance to local attacks, limited and general war, there remains only the alternative 'all or nothing'. A shield force armed with conventional and atomic weapons, on the other hand, presents a very serious risk to the aggressor even in a limited war. Tactical atomic weapons in the sphere of the shield force are therefore an essential step in deterrence.

This is perhaps as much as need be said on the subject. We have gone into the matter to this extent because it is necessary for those who criticize or examine parts of the military programme to see it in its totality, for otherwise responsible views are impossible to form. Moreover it is of the utmost importance that religious spokesmen should try imaginatively to understand what the problems are with which the military planners are wrestling. It is not enough for Christians to stand on a high place and give voice to admirable sentiments and principles. That may be a very satisfactory action for them by giving them psychological relief, but many of them often seem to think that in this way they have done something useful, whereas too often they have earned disrepute for the name of Christian.

So far we have been considering nuclear weapons as deterrents, but what if they fail to deter and a war does begin? Quite a different problem confronts us then. The Christian doctrine of the just war always limited the amount of force which it was permissible to use. The teaching in short held that the purpose of the war must be good, i.e. morally justified, and that the amount of force expended must not be more than is necessary to achieve that good end. The evil it creates must not be more than the evil it is designed to restrain or correct.

We are therefore at once faced with the subject of indiscriminate force, for the big bombs are of their nature quite indiscriminate. There are some who argue that in modern warfare the distinction between the military and the civilian, between combatant and non-combatant, can no longer be upheld, and that the whole population must be regarded as combatants. But is this really the case? There still is in fact a distinction between what are primarily military objectives and what are attacks on civilian morale. In the Second World War the distinction became so blurred as no longer to have any influence.

The effect of H bombs is so all destructive and would destroy or maim life over such a wide area, that it is impossible to bring them within any formulation of the conditions of a just, that is morally justifiable, act of war. The aim of a just war is to restrain the enemy, not to destroy him, but the aims of an H bomb are to destroy widely and indiscriminately. For this reason the dropping of H bombs on any country could not be morally justified in any circumstances, because such actions could not consist with any moral purpose and would be bound to frustrate any moral purpose.

The same applies to the use of C.B.R. methods, which are indiscriminate. C.B.R. are the initials of chemical, bacteriological and radiological warfare, which is being investigated and developed in conditions of blanket secrecy. It appears that those in charge of the developments are uncertain of the reaction of public opinion, if their activities were known. But there are some chemical experiments with nerve gases, said to have a temporary effect of paralysing the will to fight, which are more humane than any present weapons. The morality of the use of gas depends, of course, on its aim and effects. But the indiscriminate use of bacteria or other C.B.R. weapons on a civil population could never be morally acceptable.

An article in *The Commonweal*, a Roman Catholic paper published in the U.S.A., of 3rd March 1961 was called 'The Technology of War'. It was by Edmund Stillman and William Pfaff. An interesting and well-balanced article, it yet included the following sentence with no apparent awareness of its absurdity: 'Weapons are chosen according to the issue that is at stake. If national survival is the issue, ultimate weapons will be employed; any disaster is preferable to national extinction, and that is as true for the Russians as for us.' The absurdity lies in the fact that the use of ultimate weapons is the only certain method of ensuring national extinction. To speak, therefore, of using them to avoid national extinction is to talk nonsense. Nothing can be gained by the use of such weapons, for if they are used second (after attack by the enemy with similar weapons) national extinction will already have taken place or be on the way to taking place; if they are used first, the retaliation which is inevitable will equally ensure national extinction.

The eminent historian Herbert Butterfield wrote some pregnant words on the same subject in *International Conflict in the Twentieth Century*:[1] 'Let us be clear about one important fact: the destructiveness which some people are now prepared to contemplate is not to be justified for the sake of any conceivable mundane object, any purported religious claim or supramundane purpose, or any virtue that one system of organization can possess as against another.' He went on to point out that probably no one in his right senses would in fact use the H bomb and that the real risk might arise from the reckless leader who knew himself defeated, and was determined to drag the rest of the world with him. 'On these terms we are going to be more afraid of defeating our enemy than of suffering ordinary military defeat ourselves'.

But though the use of such weapons cannot be justified, their possession as a threat seems to be morally justifiable for the purpose

[1] Harpers, New York 1960, p. 92.

of deterrence. But if they are kept for this purpose, then a posture is required which makes it credible that they would or might be dropped if the enemy opened hostilities, for otherwise they could not possibly deter. Such a posture includes an apparent determination to act, the organization of civil defence, and the provision of means of delivery.

The situation at the present time is that the Western nations, and almost certainly the Communist nations, have more than enough weapons to destroy the whole world several times over. As the development of such weapons involves innocent people in various risks, it seems hard, if not impossible, to justify the further development of weapons of the H bomb magnitude. In order to justify the continued expenditure of huge sums of money on these weapons, responsible military figures, especially in the U.S.A., sometimes use language which gives the impression that in certain circumstances the West might launch an attack first, and such talk has a serious effect in heightening international tension. Tension must be lessened if risks are to diminish, but there are powerful interests opposed to a *détente*, which is a moral imperative as well as a political necessity for peace.

The statements of responsible international Christian bodies, like the World Council of Churches and the Commission of the Churches on International Affairs, have often strongly supported the pursuit of general disarmament. There can be few thinking people who would not like to see progress in this aim. But there are divergences of opinion among experts on the subject of disarmament. There is the preliminary question as to whether either side really wants disarmament, in spite of their professed anxiety to achieve it, but this is a question beyond our present examination. But even when disarmament is accepted as desirable, there are differences of opinion about approach and method. Most people have assumed that disarmament should start from the top and work down, in the sense that nuclear weapons should first be abolished, beginning with the largest, or that there should be a general agreement, by which nations would disarm in such a way that the abolition of nuclear arms did not leave one side with a preponderance of conventional forces.

Goddard, however, takes the view that disarmament should start from the bottom up, and that the smaller and conventional weapons should be removed first, leaving the big weapons till last. There is a logic about this view, if his general thesis is granted, although one reviewer of wide experience in international affairs thought the idea laughable. It is interesting to note that the original Soviet proposal to the ten-power disarmament conference at Geneva called 'for completion of conventional disarmament throughout the world before nuclear weapons were touched at all'.[1]

Christians often dislike the notion that there are matters to which moral principles cannot be easily applied to provide straightforward answers. They cling to the outworn superstition that the Christian religion provides solutions to the problems which men face. Such is not the case. The problems to which the Christian religion provides answers are those of the relations of men to God and to each other, and illumination of the principles on which the true interests of mankind can alone be secured. But the detailed problems remain. The Christian religion answers the question as to whether justice is a prerequisite of stability and peace with an unqualified 'Yes'. But it does not give any answer to the question as to how justice is to be secured in any particular situation, except to say that it should not be reached by unjust means.

The practical questions as to how to avoid war are mainly matters of calculation and not of morals, except that means which are themselves immoral must not be used. But when that is stated, the means which face governments are often not choices between right and wrong but choices between courses of action, all of which are more or less wrong. In such a situation of a choice of evils, the positively moral choice is that of the lesser or least evil, which in the circumstances becomes a relative positive good.

Many religious people resist such a conclusion because it seems to them to make moral principles relative. But all moral principles are relative to the will of God, who cannot possibly will for us in an immediate sense what is physically impossible for us to accomplish. Even Jesus Christ himself was limited by the earthly circumstances of his life in his moral circumstances. When he said 'Render unto Caesar the things that are Caesar's', he did not authorize unlimited subjection to the secular power, but he did implicitly and inevitably recognize the need for moral judgements which were relative, and not absolute, for it is quite clear that the support of Caesar could not be considered either then or now as an absolute moral good.

[1] *Survival*, vol. 2 no. 6, p. 259.

The whole problem of nuclear weapons falls within a framework where much has to be based on calculation, though the calculation has still to be made within a still larger picture of eventual moral aims, which must never be lost to sight. Christians can, however, play a part in the general situation. The first thing they can do is to face and not attempt to escape the fearful dilemmas and struggles which the situation produces, and especially to avoid the cheap announcement of moral principles which have not been related to the real problems involved.[1] Ministers of religion in positions of public responsibility in the Churches must avoid statements which have not taken into account the grim decisions which Christians face, who hold positions of trust in the Forces or Defence or Research Departments of governments. It is there that the front line of the Christian religion is at present, and the shouting of platitudes from the religious home-base will merely distract the attention of those who have to conduct the campaign.

Another aspect where moral principles are involved concerns the importance of openness and truth in defence problems, so that men and women may have access to sufficient facts to be able to base on them a considered and reliable judgement. The Christian religion holds that truth is paramount in all moral decisions. But responsible moral decisions cannot be taken if the facts are not available, and the withholding of such facts is a blow against truth.

Moral issues also arise in propaganda in which rival governments are trying to picture their case as all good and their enemies' as all evil. Christians know that such a presentation is a lie, and that there are serious faults on both sides. The attempt to heighten the appearance of evil on the other side and that of righteousness on one's own is a sin against the truth, and contributes to the increase of that tension and misunderstanding, the lessening of which gives the only hope of stability and peace in the future. If Christians cannot see their own faults, it hardly seems reasonable for them to expect others to see theirs, still less to do anything to correct them.

Christians should urge that each side, and especially their own for which they bear some responsibility and with which they are identified, should give a public undertaking never to be the first to use total war weapons. This is an essential moral step, even if

[1] For a useful study of this aspect, see the British Council of Churches Pamphlet *Christians and Atomic War* 1959.

for the sake of deterrence uncertainty has to remain about the use of H bomb methods as reprisal.

Other moral issues too are raised by nuclear weapons. In some countries they have been regarded as a cheap way to escape the need to have adequate conventional forces and armaments. If forces are needed at all, then the sacrificial consequences of such a need ought to be faced by the countries concerned. But conscription is politically unpopular and politicians and their supporters have tried to have their cake and eat it, i.e. to have security with nuclear weapons without having to pay the price in hardship and inconvenience in unpopular conventional forces. These are moral issues with which Christians ought to be seriously concerned, but which for the most part they prefer to avoid.

But as in everything else in life the issues of peace and war, or weapons and disarmament, have to be seen in the light of the love of God, if they are to be seen in their true perspective. There does not at first sight seem to be much connection between H bombs and the love of God, but there is a very close connection between his love and the preservation of peace, the avoidance of destructive war and the maintenance of peace and justice. It is because Christians must be concerned with the positive things, on which alone human happiness can find a secure basis, that they cannot escape the agony of wrestling with the problems which the H bomb poses. For whatever may happen, the H bomb is part of human life and can now never be removed except by total destruction, which removes civilization as we know it today.

But when Christians approach the moral problems of peace and war, they see things in a different perspective from their fellow men. When men and women are worried about their fate in this world, no Christian spokesman can fail to point out that their true interests do not lie here, but in the kingdom of God. This does not mean that the world does not matter: on the contrary the whole Christian message is concerned in saying that it matters very much indeed. But it does mean another perspective about what is ultimately important, and the crises and alarums of our life here, though they sound loudly in our ears, will be a distant tinkle in the light of history and eternal life. 'For here we have no continuing city, but we seek one to come' (Heb. 13.14).

9

THE SANCTITY OF LIFE

Human Laws

HUMAN LAWS ARE necessary for the preservation and life of human society. They are the product of social needs and represent the need for order, if a society is to exist without unbearable strain. Men being what they are, it is evident that in order to live together some order must be imposed to govern their relations, and this in turn implies that there is an authority or force to impose such order, more powerful than any combination of force which can be brought against it.

The need for order in society is a requirement of the natural law in the sense that the concept of order springs from that of constructive and loving relations between men. This is the purpose for which they have been created, if it is seen from the point of view of their relations with other human beings, and therefore it is part of the natural or created law of man's nature, which has the authority of God. Theoretically in a perfect society there would be no need for enforcement of the law by physical force, though there would be no less need of order. But if all men were perfect, they would freely and willingly accept such laws as are necessary for maintaining the minimum of order and the maximum of individual liberty, thus providing a framework in which their personal lives might develop as God wishes.

But men are far from perfect, and every human society of which we have any experience is very imperfect, being made up of men, even the best of whom lack much. The necessary order of society therefore has to be imposed by force on those who would not otherwise submit to it. Because order is a requirement of man's nature, laws which are made by men to uphold this order have a moral claim on the obedience of those members of society for whom they have been made, so long as the laws in question are consonant with the divine principles which govern the proper development of man. This attitude seems to be borne out by St Paul's letters in which he sees the authority of the Roman law as fulfilling a worthy and moral function in the sight of God. 'Whosoever resisteth the power, resisteth the ordinance of God' (Rom. 13.2).

But from a moral point of view men are not bound to obey laws which are unjust. If they were so bound, it would make law an instrument of evil instead of good. In the world at the present time there are many laws which are unjust, which men have perforce to obey because there is at present no practical alternative. In the Republic of South Africa, for example, there are examples of churchmen defying laws which are unjust, which they feel in conscience bound to disobey. There are many other examples of unjust laws in Communist countries, where laws are framed for the perpetuation of the régime rather than for the benefit of the citizens.

We have already had occasion to mention some difficulties in making laws which are wholly satisfactory from the point of view of ideal justice as the expression of love. But apart from these inherent problems there are external tests by which laws may be judged unjust. St Thomas Aquinas considers the matter (II-I *q*.96, *a*.4) from the point of view of the maker of the law—a just law must not exceed the power of its author; and from the point of view of those for whom they are made—a just law must be fair on all members of the community; it must be for the common good and must not be opposed to the divine good. If the whole matter is to be summed up in a sentence, it can be said that laws made properly by human authority must reflect the natural and divine law and, if they do, they are binding upon the consciences of those for whom they are made, and a Christian will think it his duty to obey them fully and promptly.

There are some cases of human law where we may be doubtful whether it is in fact for the common good, and some cases in which the law is morally indifferent. In such cases the benefit of the doubt ought to be given to the law, and disobedience should only be shown where the need for it is indisputable. Moreover in a democratic State where there is an implicit agreement that the majority shall be permitted to govern, there is a moral obligation on the minority to obey the law, and this obligation can only be morally counterbalanced by a clear case of law which is against the principles of truth and right. St Thomas also makes the point that even where the law is not binding in conscience, especially where it concerns private rights, it is often better to obey it 'in order to avoid scandal and disturbance'.

The result is that a decision has to be taken on a balance of arguments when it comes to dealing with individual cases. Even if we have come to the conclusion that a law is unjust and that in conscience we are free to disobey it, we have to weigh against that fact the likely consequences of our disobedience. For rebellion against the law by destroying order may result in a situation which is much worse morally than that which we set out to correct. On the other hand we have to bear in mind that this argument has often prevented men from taking action against unjust laws, when they ought to have done so.

Let us look at the necessities which are required for a just law. It must be a law which is for the common good. We are thrown back on our basic beliefs about the end of man and the purpose for which he has been created by God. A law cannot be just, i.e. in accordance with the love of God, which puts obstacles in the way of man's development as God intended it. A law which defies the purposes of God must be bad without further details being considered. An example of such a law would be a law which prevented a man from growing fully as a child of God in independence and freedom, a law imposing slavery for instance.

From general principles we can derive the truth that the lawgiver is not entitled to make what laws he likes: he is under the authority of God and his purposes as expressed in the creation and redemption of the world. In the case of a lawgiver who is not a Christian, his laws must still be in accordance with the nature of man as created by God, if they are to be just. This applies just as much to the democratic process as to the authoritarian régimes. There is a tendency in democratic countries to exalt the processes of free democracy so as to suggest that a fully democratic decision has a sort of divine authority. It has a moral authority for those concerned within the limits we have seen, but to go further is to give countenance to the ancient blasphemy *Vox populi, vox Dei*, the voice of the people is the voice of God. In the United Kingdom this heresy is represented by the theory that Parliament can do anything it likes. But Parliament, just as much as the individual members of the country it represents, is responsible to God in everything it does.

In North America there is another dangerous tendency, namely to exalt something which is loosely termed 'our way of life' to be a minor or even major God. But democratic societies and assemblies are just as much under the judgement of God as any tyrant, and their actions must be tested by their correspondence to the principles established by God in creation.

A clear example of an unjust law is the deprivation of a man of his natural rights on the grounds of colour or race. This cannot be for the common good because it runs counter to the principle shown by God in creating all men equal in his sight, each loved with a divine love and given status because of that love. The Church in South Africa and elsewhere is fully justified in resisting such laws. Discrimination is quite as serious whether it is practised by white against black, or black against white. In the light of redemption the truth is even clearer, for Christ died for all men and in his love all are bound together in a unity which cannot be broken. Laws which keep apart black and white Christians therefore prevent the expression of these truths in everyday life and form a direct defiance of the truth which God has revealed. No Christian can accept such a condition of affairs without protest.

Another example of an unjust law, very common in Communist countries, is a law which prevents people from knowing the truth. Similar betrayals happen from time to time in other countries too. It is part of the nature of man as created by God that he should seek the truth, for without knowledge of the truth, so far as he is able to know it, a man cannot exercise his reason in any useful or purposeful way. Communist countries have laws which prevent access to the truth on the part of their citizens, by preventing them from listening to foreign radio stations, by preventing them from having free access to information, and by preventing free exchange of visits and travel with other countries. To this negative side is added strong propaganda which seeks to impose one point of view about events, dictated by the government for their own purposes. These laws are unjust because they deny a fundamental need of the nature of man.

St Thomas Aquinas says that to be just a law must be fair and must apply without discrimination to all members of the community. The racial laws of South Africa and elsewhere deny this principle as well as the natural needs of man. Tax laws sometimes raise some difficult questions in this connection. The word 'discrimination' can bear a number of meanings. It can mean that the same treatment must be meted out to everyone, in which case it might be (wrongly) held that everyone ought to be taxed the same amount. That argument obviously leads to absurdity. Lack of discrimination includes the concept of proportionate burdens, and it is not a form of discrimination to tax a rich man much more heavily than a poor man. Indeed if the matter is regarded from the point of view of the burden which is carried, it could well be maintained that the poor carry far heavier burdens in the community than the rich, and that they make much more important contributions to its basic stability than those who reap higher rewards. In a modern community the arrangement of taxation is so highly complex that it is almost impossible to have a tax system which is not open to objection in some at least of its provisions. Sometimes a tax law leaves a strong sense of discrimination and injustice with some who suffer from it. But it is clear that, as society must have taxation and as the general principles of taxation are widely accepted by the community, they must be accepted and their acceptance involves a moral obligation. The fact that they do not perfectly accord with justice cannot be taken as a reason for refusing to obey them. It is important to note that the general readiness to obey the laws of taxation is an important part of making them more just and of helping to secure improvements in them.

Within modern societies the question of the merely penal law has come to play a big part. A 'penal' law means a law which imposes a penalty on disobedience, but which does not claim to enshrine any kind of moral judgement. Some have even held that modern legislation is exclusively penal and that there is therefore no inherent moral obligation to obey it. But when analysed the problem is seen to be the same as it is for any law which is morally indifferent and which does not raise moral principles in itself. Such are laws governing what lights should be carried by cars at night or regulations covering car parking. Laws which deal with such matters are indispensable for order in the State, though there is no moral issue normally involved as to just where a car should be parked. Once the law has been made, however, a moral obligation rests upon the citizen to obey it, since, if he does not, his disobedience, and that of others, will have a bad effect on the order of the society in which he lives.

Some writers suggest that there is no moral fault in disobeying laws which are merely penal, but this opinion cannot be accepted. It encourages the widespread notion that it does not matter if you disobey the law so long as you are not found out, but that, if you are discovered, you need not feel you have done anything wrong, even if you do have to pay the fine. There is a widespread view among otherwise honest people that there is no moral fault in cheating the government, or in stealing things from the army, or in cheating the railway company over the price of a ticket. It is surprising how many normally upright citizens see no fault in smuggling prohibited articles into the country without paying tax, for example. But such actions are clearly morally wrong on at least two counts. First, they involve either direct or indirect lies; second, they deprive the authority concerned of its rightful property. These actions have a bad effect on the general level of morality in the country and also diminish the sense of moral responsibility in the person who is indulging in them.

But on the other hand it is clear that a man has no obligation morally to go beyond the letter of the law in the case of laws which are merely penal. This applies to the payment of taxes. If the legislators who make the law do not succeed in making a law which expresses their intentions, there is no moral obligation on the citizen to pay what they intended he should pay, rather than what the law actually requires. If there are loopholes in the tax law, the citizen has a moral right to take advantage of them, so long as he does not transgress the law in doing so, and so long as he does not indulge in any deceit. What the framers of the law intended can only be judged by the letter of the law itself. If the law is found to be lacking, then it is the duty of the legislators to change it, so that it meets their intentions.

It sometimes happens that there is a clash between a penal law and a moral obligation. A doctor, for example, may be called to an urgent case and find when he arrives that there is nowhere he can park his car which is not against the regulations. He is then morally bound to break the penal law about parking in favour of his moral obligation to give immediate assistance to his patient. Perhaps the problem here is best illustrated by an actual case which occurred in April 1961. A doctor's wife, Mrs C, was summoned for exceeding the speed limit in a Canadian city. She was convicted and fined 25 dollars with the alternative of several days in jail. She admitted the offence, travelling at 46 mph where the speed limit was 35, but said she was hurrying home because her three-month-old baby was outside in a cradle and a rain storm was threatening. 'A sudden and violent storm blew up', she said. 'My baby had been seriously ill and I wanted to get home, as a heavy downpour was starting. . . . I particularly asked the constable who stopped me if he considered my driving in any way dangerous or careless. He said he did not.' She went on to point out that it was a wide road without any side roads or obstacles. She protested strongly against the sentence, and elected to go to prison rather than pay the fine. Among her comments were, 'The law is for the protection of the public. The charge against me violated this concept by doing exactly the reverse.' 'Such charges serve only to antagonize the public against the police and make them regard the law with more bitterness than respect. I have eight children to bring up. How can I teach them that there is justice before the law when they see injustice done?'

Mrs C has muddled a number of things which it may be useful to sort out. *Prima facie* there is a good case for saying that Mrs C was morally free from blame, if her reading of the situation was correct. She had an overriding moral duty to protect her child, and in the circumstances this may have been sufficient justification for her to ignore the speed limit. But there are several points which may be noted:

1. It is necessary to have traffic laws and to enforce them impartially in the public interest. If it was morally necessary for them to be broken, it is also necessary to recognize that there may be a penalty to pay, which ought to be paid in the interest of the community in general. If breaking such a law is to be morally justified, the cause must be sufficient and the breaking of the law must not involve other moral faults, such as danger to others.

2. If the magistrate had no alternative in the law to imposing a fine, no complaint can be made against him for doing it. He does not make the law; he merely administers it. If, however, he had discretion, it is justifiable to maintain that he used it wrongly— that is, without taking into account the fundamental moral considerations in that particular case.

3. There might have been other means of avoiding the danger

to Mrs C's child. She might have stopped and telephoned her home or telephoned to a neighbour to ask her to take the necessary action. There is no evidence to show whether such steps were considered or not.

4. Mrs C refused to pay the fine as a demonstration, so that she as a respectable doctor's wife was sent to prison. Her attitude made an unreal distinction between the fine and the jail sentence, which are strictly equivalent punishments in the eyes of the law.

5. Mrs C did not appreciate the fact that the object of the law is not to achieve perfect justice in every case—that would be impossible. It is to defend the order of society in important matters, where such order is necessary for the benefit of society as a whole. As we have seen earlier, this objective inevitably comes into conflict from time to time with perfect moral justice (as distinct from legal justice) for an individual.

This particular case is not of great importance in itself, but it brings out the kind of moral considerations which must be weighed in conflicts between moral duty and penal laws. On the other hand by implication it brings out another point, namely that the law must accord with the general moral sense of the citizens. A law which does not accord with their moral sense and is merely imposed by outside force will rapidly lose their respect and sooner or later will become unenforceable. As Mortimer rightly points out,[1] it is important to leave people as much moral freedom as possible, so that they may have the chance of training themselves in moral awareness and thus advancing towards moral maturity.

> There will be less crime, only when there are more people who recognize and agree that crime is immoral. Those who believe that crime is only wrong because it is forbidden and punished by law, will break the law whenever they think that they can do so with impunity. It is important to train everybody to understand that if a thing is immoral, it is immoral in itself and not because the law condemns and punishes it. It is important to train people to understand that there are many actions which are immoral, but which are not condemned or punished by the law.

Clear thinking about the relation of the law to moral obligation and the demand made upon men and women by penal law is necessary both to solve moral queries by the individual person, but also for the proper revision of the law and its improvement in

[1] *Parliamentary Affairs*, Spring 1960.

the light of developing understanding of moral issues and social needs.

Kinds of Killing

In the mid-twentieth century a debate centring round the sanctity of human life has been vigorously conducted. The issues it raises are not new, they are old questions in the light of modern conditions. In 1962 a well-known writer in England maintained in an article[1] that there had been a general moral advance in Britain, and he evidently expected it to continue. With some of his conclusions there would be general agreement, especially in the greater sensitivity of public opinion to the hardships and needs of others. But in other matters the advance is not so evident.

There are several problems of public interest which bring up the question of the sanctity of human life in an acute and practical form. We may shortly list them as (a) capital punishment; (b) the prolongation of life in old age; (c) incurable disease; (d) deformed babies; (e) abortion. Before commenting on them in detail we must look into the general principles involved. It is a curious fact that those who are least attached to traditional Christian views in these matters are often not at all consistent in their attitudes. It is noticeable that the type of person who most wants to abolish capital punishment is likely to be keenest on killing deformed babies or permitting abortions freely.

In considering the problems of the sanctity of human life we must distinguish between two quite separate aspects. One is the question of whether we can reach any conclusion which should apply to all cases about the rightness or wrongness of taking human life. The other is the question of the practical results of any proposed attitude on human society and the individual members of it.

The traditional Christian view has been that the deliberate taking of human life is absolutely wrong, except in those cases where it is necessary for the preservation of society itself. The exceptions therefore have been limited to the just war and to the capital punishment of murderers. We have seen however that there is strong reason to suppose that except in dire emergency capital punishment is not morally acceptable on Christian grounds. The taking of life in war is also condemned in itself as an evil, but in

[1] Philip Toynbee, *The Observer*, 23rd Dec., 1962.

the case of a just war is tolerated as the only course open in maintaining justice and freedom, and then only when it is forced upon some nation by an aggressive act.

It is a clear deduction from the Christian faith that human life is sacred, and that man does not have the right to end it as he wills. This attitude is based on the love of God for man, for each person is of ultimate value in God's sight, and the life of each person on earth is the means by which he is to grow into the knowledge and love of God, and to begin his eternal life, which is to continue after his life on earth is ended. There are many who are cut off in youth by external causes such as illness, calamity or accident. Their lives are cut short owing to the faults and imperfections of this world, and God's love surely makes provision for them according to their needs. But it is one thing to believe that God does make such provision when necessary, and quite another for man to say that he will force God to do so by himself taking into his own hands the decision as to when a human life should end. From the Christian point of view the meaning of life is to be found in the way in which man uses the materials, whether easy or difficult, with which he is presented by his nature and by his circumstances. They can be used rightly or wrongly, and in their use is the divinely appointed method of growing into unity with God. The one thing man is not permitted to do is to refuse the gift. Man's moral and spiritual growth, moreover, does not depend on favourable circumstances. On the contrary, it is the man who has the most unfavourable external conditions who often advances furthest in the spiritual life, and there are many deep truths of life which only come through acquaintance with and understanding of suffering.

From the Christian point of view, then, it cannot be said that pain, suffering and difficulty are to be avoided. Indeed if we are to take the New Testament for our guide, they are to be welcomed and embraced as a means of unity with Christ and with his redemptive work. Christians therefore cannot align themselves with a view which holds that physical and mental shortcomings are wholly bad, or that they cannot be the means of great blessing. The man who is condemned in the parable of the talents is he who refused to do anything with the talent with which he was entrusted. We are given life within the merciful providence of God and it is not for us to dispose of it in despite of God's act or an act of an external force over which we have no control. It is a sacred trust from God which must be rendered back to him in due course with an explanation of what we have done with it. It is for this reason that from New Testament times onwards Christians have steadfastly opposed any form of taking of human life, except when justified in self-defence either for the community or for individuals in saving their own lives.

We must say then that the taking of human life is wrong in itself, and that no considerations of convenience can make it right. This forms the basis of a Christian moral outlook on the various problems already mentioned.

But apart from questions of principle, there are powerful practical arguments against permitting the taking of life, and these arguments are relevant, not only for Christians, but for all who have the good of society at heart. The main objection is that once the taking of human lives is sanctioned for purposes other than those we have mentioned, it will be impossible to safeguard the lives of innocent people who are inconvenient to others, or whose demise would be of advantage to others for some reason. As a writer[1] to *The Times* said:

> The law should . . . uphold the principle of the sanctity of life. That principle is vital. Once it is abandoned and its corollary that no individual can evaluate the worth of the life of another person, the security of everyone in society is threatened, because a fundamental assumption which enables civilized life to be carried on, is destroyed.

Any permission by law for the lives of innocent people to be taken might easily be misunderstood as a general permission for suicide or for the killing of aged or infirm people, or of deformed infants. There is already a serious problem of infanticide in cases where mothers do not want a child for some reason. The effect of any such legislation on those whose minds are unbalanced and tend towards suicide might be serious. And once the principle is permitted, it seems difficult to draw a rigid line anywhere. Why should not Hitler be justified in murdering millions of Jews, if it is permissible for man to take life from those whom he is convinced are a menace to the well-being of the community? But, if this is thought a far-fetched example, how is a person to be prevented from murdering anyone thought to be in great pain and incurably ill, if he is already permitted to kill off a deformed

[1] Norman St John Stevas, 23rd Nov. 1962.

infant? Where is the difference in principle? Moreover in the case of aged people, and sometimes of infants, questions of inheritance, personal convenience, temporary insanity, mental breakdown and overstrain in the persons responsible for their welfare may have serious effects on their judgement.

(*a*) The question of capital punishment has already been sufficiently considered. It is impossible to maintain that the taking of life is never permissible by the authorities in dire emergency, but capital punishment as a regular normal part of criminal procedure is impossible to justify from a moral point of view. Punishment, of course, should be deterrent and reformative as well as retributive. Capital punishment cannot be maintained morally on retributive grounds, and obviously not on reformative grounds, as it finally removes any chance of reformation. Its defence on grounds of deterrence has been much weakened by the established fact that, in countries where it has been abolished, there has been no increase in the crimes for which it was formerly a punishment.

(*b*) The prolongation of life in extreme illness and old age has become an increased problem with the advance in medical knowledge and the use of modern drugs. Doctors are rightly anxious to conserve life as long as they can usefully do so. But there is no moral compulsion on them to prolong life beyond the limits of reason. Each case must be decided on its merits, and there must be many borderline cases where decision is difficult. In cases of doubt there can be no question but that the doctor should preserve the life of his patient. But merely keeping people technically alive, that is to say breathing with the heart beating, is no duty of the doctor when the normal processes of age would bring that life to an end. Each case presents its own mixture of circumstances and problems and must be dealt with in the light of reason and duty. Death is an inevitable part of human life and is not to be considered an unrelieved evil.

(*c*) Incurable disease presents slightly different problems, for in reality there is no such thing as incurable disease. What is described by medical men as 'spontaneous remission' happens from time to time in diseases like advanced cancer, which have been carefully diagnosed and pronounced hopeless. The phrase 'spontaneous remission' is merely a medical way of saying that the patient got better without any known cause in spite of the medical prognosis.

There have been many well-authenticated cases of recovery of health from 'incurable' disease through spiritual healing or through such healing centres as Lourdes, though such cases form only a small proportion of those that seek such help. It is important to remember in these cases that doctors know much less than popular opinion thinks they know. To say this is no reflection on the doctors; indeed it should help them by preventing false hopes. It is therefore impossible for anyone to be sure that a disease is absolutely incurable, though moral certainty is available in a great many. But, however slim the chance of recovery, no step should be taken which makes it impossible, and the removal of life certainly does this. It is also possible, especially in the case of neurotic patients, that an individual may have all the symptoms of an incurable disease without the organic disease itself. The symptoms are quite real and possibly indistinguishable from what they purport to be. Moreover illness which is a great physical strain is often the cause of spiritual and moral blessing both to the patient and to those who minister to him. It is an opportunity to grow in stature. It is a chance of deeper spiritual life, which no man has the right to remove from another.

(*d*) Deformed children have been the cause of great discussion since, in 1962, it was discovered that women who had taken the drug thalidomide in pregnancy had in a number of cases given birth to deformed children with misshapen arms or legs, and sometimes without arms or legs at all. In the autumn of 1962 a Belgian woman killed her child, who had been born deformed as a result of this drug, and she acted with the connivance and support of her doctor. She was arraigned before a court in Liège and acquitted of murder. The legal verdict must appear strange, for there was no dispute as to the facts, and the verdict contradicted them. No one attempted to deny that the baby had been killed. The defence was that the woman had taken the right action. But we are not here concerned with the intricacies of the Belgian law, but with the question as to whether such an action was morally justifiable.

The answer must be that in no circumstances would such an action be justifiable morally, for a private individual took upon herself the right to judge whether a human being should live or not. The human being in question was born deformed because of the action of the woman concerned. It was she who caused the child to be deformed, though she did it entirely innocently and in good faith. The deformation of the child was the result of the use of drugs of which there was insufficient knowledge. But to produce a deformed child as a result of human error and then to kill it because it did not measure up to the physical standards of the so-called normal child is morally abhorrent. Such actions are often euphemistically called 'mercy killing', but this is merely a cliché to avoid the moral issue. Is it merciful to take away the life of a child who has committed no offence? The possibilities of development in that child are quite unknown, and there have been many cases of children who are in some way sub-normal being lovingly cared for by their parents, and bringing out of the parents unsuspected depths of love and self-sacrifice. There have also been cases of badly deformed children living full and creative lives. Who is to say that this or that child cannot live a life of usefulness and of moral and spiritual growth?

The action of the mother in Belgium is one of fear and cowardice. She may indeed have much sympathy in the torment of her guilt and anxiety, but that does not affect the nature of the act. Without knowing her inner struggle it is impossible to say to what degree her action was culpable from the standpoint of formal sin, but that it was a sinful action from a material point of view there can be no doubt, and its consequences may be disastrous for many other innocent children who would otherwise have been allowed to live.

Some opinion seems to hold that a doctor is a suitable person to provide the verdict of life or death for a child who is deformed. Doctors are no better arbiters of life and death than any other persons, and it would be neither fair nor desirable to put upon them a responsibility for which they are not qualified. Every child is made for an eternal destiny and his life on this earth is to be used to promote that destiny. No man can rightly deny this opportunity to him.

(*e*) Abortion is a common practice, even where it is illegal, especially among women who are unmarried but pregnant. During the thalidomide case an American woman who had taken thalidomide in pregnancy flew to Sweden, where she had an abortion in accordance with Swedish law. But the same principles apply to abortion as apply to human life generally. The life of a human being starts during pregnancy, after the union of the male and female cells, and no action taken deliberately to end that life is justified, unless it is indispensable for the survival and health of the mother, whose life must itself be in danger before it is justified. Modern psychologists have more than once opined that the character of a person is affected in important respects by what happens during pregnancy. If this is the case, and there is no reason to doubt it, it is impossible to maintain that the person exists only after the birth of the child. Destruction of the living foetus is a form of unlawful and immoral killing, just as the taking of life after birth is.

The fact that a mother has taken thalidomide during pregnancy is no reason why abortion should be allowed. So far as is at present known a large proportion of babies born to mothers who have taken the drug are quite normal physically, perhaps 75 per cent of them. To take the life of the living child in the womb on the off-chance that it may be deformed is an immoral act which cannot be justified.

The false attitude which is so widespread in non-Christian circles in favour of abortion or infanticide seems to be based on a confused appeal to aesthetic and/or sentimental standards, both of which are intensely subjective. In the former case the aesthetic sense is offended by the deformed child and is taken to justify its destruction. In the latter case the people concerned are afraid to face suffering, either for themselves or for the child, and so take away the child's life and forfeit its chance of choosing for itself whether to use the suffering. Christian teaching does not maintain that one should suffer because it is good for the character, as it is sometimes represented. It does teach that suffering cannot be escaped in this world, but that it can be entered into and made into moral and spiritual victory, and that there are some depths and heights of personal development which can be reached in no other way than through suffering. God gives the power to suffer and thus to help redeem the world's evil.

Hunting

In most of the world the word 'hunting' means shooting wild birds or animals, but in England it is used exclusively for the sport of chasing live foxes on horseback with the aid of a pack of hounds, or chasing some other wild animals such as stags or otters. There exists in England a League against Cruel Sports which wages a campaign against sports which involve the hunting and killing of wild animals in the chase. The sport of hunting foxes has been the diversion of well-to-do country people in England for hundreds of years, and it is still popular with many farmers and country folk.

There are many agreeable features of a meet of hounds for foxhunting. It provides healthy out-of-door action and stimulating excitement for those taking part. But the question remains as to whether the sport itself is moral or immoral.

Before examining the essential features it is necessary to deal with two justifications for the sport which are sometimes put forward. The first states that the foxes enjoy the hunt, and that there is therefore no cruelty involved. It is difficult to see how anyone can seriously believe that an animal enjoys being hunted to death, even if it sometimes escapes. The word 'enjoy', moreover, cannot really apply to animals in the same sense as to humans, but every indication goes to show that all animals dislike a position which puts them in danger, and do their best to escape from it. That is surely proof enough that this particular defence cannot be upheld.

A second justification is that the sport is necessary to keep down foxes, that hunting is the most efficient method, and that it is the kindest way of doing it. As to the necessity of the sport to keep down foxes, it is stated on good authority, which has not been denied, that foxes are actually protected in order to make sure that they are available for the sport when needed. This entirely disproves the first of these points. The other two points can hardly be maintained in an age where scientific invention is so successful. It is impossible to believe that for a fox to be torn in pieces by dogs is a 'kind' death, whatever that may mean, and it is impossible to take seriously the plea of efficiency.

Dr Robert Mortimer, Bishop of Exeter, has publicly defended the practice of fox hunting, but the only positive reason he gave in doing so was 'man's high place in the hierarchy of being'. This high place cannot be disputed, but it does not follow that man has the right to do as he likes with the animal creation. There is no general dispute that some actions are cruel, for example the maiming of animals to give sadistic satisfaction. Such sadistic satisfaction is morally wrong, of course, but surely the maiming of animals without some positive good cause to justify it must be wrong too. This is a clear moral issue which ought not to be

obscured. Deliberately to destroy animals, to maim them, or to
cause them unnecessary pain without a positive gain for mankind
which outweighs that pain, is wrong, and even then there must be
the proviso that the gain cannot be procured by any other means.
On these grounds it is morally justifiable to use methods of
vivisection on animals, if such methods are necessary for the health
of the human race, and provided that the health of the human
race cannot be properly safeguarded without them. But vivisection
without such justification is morally wrong, because it is a misuse
of God's creation.

In the case of foxhunting the infliction of pain on the foxes
merely for the purpose of human enjoyment cannot be right,
unless there is a human good which cannot be served in any other
way. It is quite clear that the enjoyment of the chase is only a
minor human good, and that it can in fact be met in a number of
different ways, which do not involve hunting an animal to death.
We must therefore conclude that the hunting of wild animals
merely for sport is something which does not meet the moral
requirements of Christian behaviour.

The question of the blameworthiness or otherwise of those who
take part in the sport is a different question. It is clear that many
who have been brought up to partake in the sport from earliest
years have no sense of wrong in doing so. If they have tried to
examine the matter as well as they can, they are not blameworthy,
though they are in invincible ignorance.

It may then be asked that as foxes have to be killed, why should
it be wrong to kill them in a way which affords pleasure to people
and at the same time does not make it worse for the fox. The reply
to such a question must be what is already implied in our considerations above. Animals should be killed in the most humane
way possible, if they have to be killed, and it is difficult to think
that hunting them to death is in fact the most humane method.
Second, the killing of animals to provide sport is not a moral
purpose when there is no need of it. In earlier days hunting was
the only means by which certain animals could be killed, which
would otherwise have threatened crops or human lives. There was
then no moral reason why as much pleasure as possible should
not be sought in an occupation which was necessary and in some
cases dangerous.

There is another moral consideration, namely, the fact that

blood sports do in fact give hurt and offence to good Christian people. Their feelings ought not to be neglected in any moral examination of the situation, and the Christian attitude is to give no unnecessary offence to Christian brothers, even when their qualms may not be soundly based. St Paul makes this principle clear over the question of eating meat sacrificed to idols. Bishop Hensley Henson of Durham thought it wrong to give offence to the 'growing number of thoughtful and humane persons, who cannot reconcile sports, which inflict suffering and death on animals, with the principles of Christ's religion'.[1]

Temperance

The needs of the body are part of human life and play a role in the total development of the human personality. The capital vice which is associated with them is that of gluttony, while its contrary virtue is that of temperance. The word 'temperance' has a much wider meaning than the abstinence from alcoholic drinks with which it is often associated. Indeed total abstinence is not necessarily temperance at all, and may in certain circumstances be intemperate.

Like all the virtues temperance in its fullest sense means right treatment, in this case of the needs of the body, an attitude governed by the will of God and by the divine intentions for human life. It has sometimes been described as a self-regarding virtue, but in reality it is no more self-regarding than any other. In one sense everything good has a self-regarding aspect, merely because the true interests of the self lie in following what is good and rejecting what is not.

But although temperance deals with physical needs first, it is not confined to them. The body needs to be controlled, but so do the mind and the imagination. Indeed self-control in mental things is often more important than in physical, for the physical faults are almost always a reflection of a wrong mental or spiritual attitude. There are people who give way intemperately to mental pleasures without balancing their particular desire with other calls upon their energy.

There is also an intemperance of the emotions which is dangerous. It is impossible to control the emotions altogether, at least in their initial form, but that does not mean that there is nothing

[1] *Letters of Herbert Hensley Henson*, ed. E. F. Braley, SPCK 1950, p. 61.

204 A New Introduction to Moral Theology

to do about them when they arise. They should be recognized for what they are, and then directed in the most useful way. It is important to notice that the wrong importance should not be placed on the feelings. Too many people mistake their feelings for faults and have an unnecessary and misleading sense of guilt about them. Moral responsibility does not lie in the feelings themselves, which are neither good nor bad but morally neutral, but it lies in the way we deal with them when they arise. In dealing with them we should have a temperate attitude, calm and detached, so that our judgement is not twisted by the turbulence of our feelings. The need for calm temperance in the spiritual and moral life generally is often underrated: it can only come from trust in God and a habitual turning to him in spirit.

Temperance is the virtue of a right balance in managing one's own personality. It does not countenance extremes of any kind, whether of indulgence or of mortification. It is not a heathen but a Christian virtue, though it has some connections with the same virtue as practised by those outside the Christian faith. St Paul compares the Christian life with the preparations and training undertaken by the man who is to take part in the Olympic games. Temperance is this virtue in the Christian life, the habit which keeps the body, mind, and spirit poised and fit to do all that God requires of them.

The good things of life are given to man by God to be enjoyed. Good food and drink are gifts of God meant to be used with pleasure. But their full pleasure can only be savoured when they are in fact received as gifts of God. When they are so much enjoyed as to be pursued for their own sake, paradoxically they begin to give less and less satisfaction. The reason doubtless is that they then are being wrongly used and cannot fulfil their true purpose as provided by God. God intended man to enjoy innocent pleasure, and pleasure is only innocent when it is enjoyed as God meant it. If I am thirsty, I may quench my thirst by drinking a pint of water, but I may have legitimate pleasure by quenching it with a pint of beer, and in doing so I may properly thank God for his bountiful goodness in providing the beer to make glad the heart of man.

The principle of Christian humanism holds the true belief that the Christian religion, far from preventing a Christian from enjoying good things, actually enables him to enjoy them more, just because he finds in them signs of the constant goodness of God. Appetites in man exist for an end, namely the physical sustenance of the body in the case of food and drink. But it is not necessary to hold with some scholastic authorities that they exist only for these ends, though it is clear that they are the primary ends for which they exist. It is part of the peculiar nature of man that in pursuing these primary ends he is able to enjoy secondary pleasures, which are just as much from God as the satisfaction of his appetites in their most elemental form.

Jeremy Taylor gave some principles of temperance in eating. Eat not before the time; eat not hastily and impatiently; eat not delicately or nicely (i.e. don't be fussy); eat not too much.

Over-drinking is more serious than over-eating because its effect is more immediate and serious, and because it suspends the normal controls that a man has over his actions. It also therefore gives encouragement to other appetites which are usually kept under control. Even though we do not agree with the proponents of total abstinence for normal people, we should have a lively sense of the evil results which come from drinking too much. Very common are the dangers, especially sexual temptations, which arise as a result of immoderate drinking, even when the excess is only slight.

Alcoholics ought always to maintain total abstinence. An alcoholic is a person on whom alcohol has a peculiarly destructive effect. This effect is usually a combination of emotional stress and an abnormal physical reaction. It is widely maintained by those who have made a special study of the subject that an alcoholic is a person who by his nature is incapable of moderate drinking. One drink will start him on the downward path to complete alcoholic stupor. It is therefore of the highest moral importance that no one should attempt to persuade an alcoholic to take a drink with any alcohol at all in it. Those who suffer from this debilitating condition should be encouraged to make contact with Alcoholics Anonymous who do a wonderful work of rehabilitation for any alcoholics who will allow them to help. Alcoholics should receive Communion in one kind only, and should not partake of the wine.

On the topic of drinking Jeremy Taylor has practical words of wisdom. He provides eleven rules for obtaining temperance in drink (*Holy Living*, ch. II, section ii). Perhaps two extracts may be quoted from them.

But remember this, whenever you begin to consider whether you may safely take one draught more, it is then high time to give over. Let that be accounted a sign late enough to break off, for every reason to doubt is a sufficient reason to part the company.

And again:

Never urge any man to eat or drink beyond his own limits and his own desires. He that does otherwise is drunk with his brother's surfeit, and reels and falls with his intemperance; that is, the sin of drunkenness is upon both their scores, they both lie wallowing in the guilt.

There are, of course, some situations where it would be the duty of a Christian to adopt total abstinence as his form of temperance, because that is the only satisfactory way in which he can give Christian witness. A missionary or layman might find himself in a lonely outpost where there was no alcoholic liquor except strong spirits, perhaps made from local distilling, and where drink was a raging social evil among the people living there. In these circumstances the only remedy might be to persuade the inhabitants of the desirability and possibility of total abstinence.

Temperance in sex is called chastity, and this subject has been considered elsewhere. Temperance here is the application of the same principle as elsewhere, namely using the bodily functions and meeting their needs as God intended them to be used and met. If God is the guiding will in our lives, then temperance follows. When the pleasures of the body become ends in themselves they become evil, for they have replaced the will of God, and in the long run they cannot of themselves provide the satisfaction which man seeks.

Fortitude

A basic instinct in man is that of self-protection and the protection of those dependent upon him. In this he reproduces the instincts of the lower animal world. When it is wrongly used this instinct becomes the capital vice of anger, and perhaps we may associate with it another root emotion which Kirk thought ought to be included with the other capital vices—that of fear. In their basic nature anger and fear are closely allied, so that in some animals it is impossible to distinguish between the two. The positive virtues associated with these instincts are detachment and fortitude.

In man the exhibition of anger is much extended beyond the

need for self-preservation and protection, and it is constantly evident when his personal pride is hurt, or when he thinks that another person is taking from him what he wishes to keep, whether it be a physical possession or a less material asset such as reputation. It is interesting to note that in many of the early writers on the spiritual life anger is considered to be one of the most disruptive of all faults. There is a righteous anger, it is true, but it must be a detached anger which does not engage the deep emotions too heavily. But anger of the righteous variety must be a reaction against an evil deed. Anger in the wrong sense, aimed at a person, should always be condemned, because it means the loss of self-control and the abandonment of an attitude of love.

Detachment in the right sense is a very important moral and spiritual virtue, for it enables a man to view his feelings realistically and therefore to keep them in their right place. This is well put in a book on moral problems:[1]

> A mutual and genuine respect for individual human differences is the key to the resolution of routine personality clashes. So often a person becomes angry at himself for being angry at others. This is a double dose of anger, which makes the problem twice as difficult to manage. (This may explain why a man with a bad temper can almost never laugh at himself.) If an individual is able to accept, and occasionally even smile at, his own negative and hostile feelings, he will be far better able to make allowances for the similar feelings of others towards himself.

Fortitude, the opposite of fear, or more accurately its conqueror, is primarily the virtue of courage, not necessarily flashy courage, so much as steady readiness to face the difficulties and dangers of life in the service of a high cause. It is the virtue which is translated 'patience' in the Authorized Version of the Bible, which more accurately means patient endurance. But it is not a negative or passive virtue, it is a lively aspect of faith in God and belief in his victory. It is a readiness to sacrifice a life to God and his purposes in the spirit of the life of Jesus.

Fortitude does not mean an absence of fear. A coward is not a person who is assailed by fear, but one who gives way to fear rather than do his duty. There is no normal man who does not suffer fear at some time. True fortitude is shown by those who have real fears, but who go the right way in spite of them.

[1] G. Hagmaier and R. Gleason, *Moral Problems Now*, Sheed and Ward 1960, p. 61.

208 A New Introduction to Moral Theology

The form of courage which a Christian is often asked to show in the world, and in which he most often fails, is moral courage in unsympathetic surroundings. Many of the social standards of the day are flatly opposed to those of Christianity, and the actions of ordinary men and women are often governed by motives which are condemned by Christianity, such as love of riches, power, respectability, social status and such like. Both in youth and adult life Christians are likely to find themselves in circles which jeer at or despise Christian standards. It is here above all that the virtue of Christian fortitude needs to be shown. Fortitude is the virtue by which a Christian witnesses to the Gospel in adverse conditions.

Prudence

Men need rest, and it is right that they should make provision for it in a way which accords with temperance, neither too much nor too little. It is interesting that in the seven capital vices the misuse of this particular instinct has come down to us in a form which most moderns have never heard of—*accidie*. *Accidie* means an attitude expressed in the modern phrase 'I couldn't care less', and it is a spiritual malaise which can have fatal consequences for the Christian life. It exhibits the abandonment of the virtue of persistence and is caused by losing the sense of the realities of God's truth. In this side of its meaning it might be called the opposite to wisdom or prudence.

Prudence, the last of the four cardinal virtues to be considered, can be a merely intellectual virtue, comprising the skill of reaching correct answers to intellectual problems. But it is with the moral virtue that we are concerned, and in its true meaning it corresponds with the wisdom, of which we read in the Bible, which is possessed by a man who knows God and lives his life in accordance with God's will. Christian prudence differs from the pagan virtue, which is self-regarding entirely, in that the Christian use is God-regarding.

It has sometimes been held that the virtue of prudence is foreign to the New Testament, and the command to take no thought for the morrow is quoted in support. There are three answers which can be given to this point of view.

(*a*) The first concerns the meaning of the passages themselves, for they are often misunderstood in translation. The original of 'take no thought for the morrow' is more exactly translated as 'be not anxious'. It is then seen to be an admonition to trust in God, and not to be concerned with lack of planning. Its meaning in fact is a recommendation to true wisdom, to find in each day as it comes the opportunity to serve God in the ways which are given.

(*b*) When Christ taught his followers not to commit themselves to material things, his teaching was always relative to the kingdom of heaven. It was only in comparison with the kingdom of God that meat and drink became unimportant. He did not try to persuade his followers to stop eating and drinking.

(*c*) It must be remembered that the basic truth which Jesus was proclaiming was that men should seek first the kingdom of God, when all these things would be added unto them. When examined, this is found to correspond with the basic truth of moral theology, namely that it is only when man's life is committed to God that he can find the true satisfaction for all his natural needs and desires, implanted in him by God in creation.

Thus what at first sight appears to be an absence of prudence in the recommended attitudes of Jesus turns out to be just the opposite—the recommendation of true prudence or wisdom in following the will of God in all things.

Prudence is a virtue which needs all the equipment, both mental and moral, with which we have been endowed. But brilliance of intellect alone cannot provide true prudence, though it can be of great assistance. More important than any mental endowments in true wisdom is the knowledge of God, that is the experience which a man has of God by living his life in unity with him. There are many brilliant men who are not wise, and there are many humble Christians who are not endowed with outstanding intellectual powers yet who exhibit the truest and deepest form of wisdom— awareness of the will of God for them and for others.

10

PROBLEMS OF WEALTH

Personal Morality and Business

THE DEVELOPMENT OF the modern State has brought with it a number of complicated economic problems many of which have moral aspects which are difficult to isolate. The main difficulty is caused by the fact that economic systems themselves give rise to situations which are morally imperfect, so that the personal moral choice of an individual has to be made within that framework. This is not a problem of any particular firm or industry but arises from the imperfection of society as a whole. There can therefore be no rule of thumb as to what is right and what is wrong for an individual to do over a large field. His moral choices are conditioned by the society in which he lives. A simple example is the problem facing a Christian manager of a firm, who is faced with the distasteful choice of condoning inefficiency or of dismissing a member of the staff, whose dismissal will spell ruin for him. It is, moreover, possible that his inefficiency may be due to causes which are not his fault, such as worry over illness at home. The manager may know this and yet be forced to dismiss him, for his own employment is conditional upon making the firm profitable, and, if it ceases to be profitable, it will be equivalent to dismissing not merely one, but all its employees.

Nevertheless there are other factors. There are firms which may not be making a contribution of moral value to the community, even though they are making a profit. In Western society, unless the activities of a firm are prohibited by law, profit is the only practical measuring stick of its usefulness. The tendency of the managerial staff is to make efficiency (another name for profits) a supreme moral virtue in itself, for this is a relatively easy way to escape the moral tensions. If efficiency has a supreme moral status, then the other moral issues can be made subject to its overriding need, and the personal moral issue (such as that of the worker mentioned above) can be solved by personal kindness, but only so far as efficiency permits.

There are half a million managers, who are key persons in the economic life of Britain, and other highly industrialized nations have proportionate numbers. Lord Franks (then Sir Oliver Franks) has said that the economic programmes undertaken by Britain during the Second World War were 'acts of will' and 'expressions of a purpose'. This, he maintained, is what is required now for proper management. But purpose can only be adequately considered in moral and religious terms. In wartime a temporary urgent purpose overruled everything else, because survival itself was at stake. But in peace time no temporary purpose can be found which can provide the combination of moral and vital urgency, unless it is based on generally accepted moral and religious aims. There seems little chance that such aims will be soon accepted, and, until they are, moral choices within society will be seriously complicated by the immoral conditions which are produced by an inadequate moral purpose.

Nevertheless it is right to emphasize that with the increased power of management should go an increased moral awareness. If the hard work and responsibility of those in managerial positions are needed for economic success and moral stability, it is no less clear that the widespread misuse of such position for personal advantage has sapped the spirit of many workers, and encouraged the spread of moral cynicism. The immoral use of various stratagems by those in responsible positions to give themselves financial advantages which are hidden from shareholders and public alike has been a great weakness in some British industries: in North America some restraint is exercised by the keener edge which competition has there. Unhappily there has been a widespread lowering of moral standards in some circles of British business life, and, until this is corrected, it is hardly realistic to hope for a better moral tone among those in less responsible posts.

There are problems of moral character inherent in all economic systems, but it is a form of escapism to concentrate attention on these before a sustained attempt has been made to raise the standards of personal morals in industry, primarily in management. An essential requirement for this is that all transactions to the benefit of those in responsible office should be publicly reported in full in annual and semi-annual reports and in discussion with labour, so that there are no hidden sources of income (such as subsidized housing, living expenses, cars) which are concealed from any who may be interested, including outside members of the public. The industrial and business health of individual firms is a matter of vital public concern and their details should be subject to public scrutiny.

It is hardly possible to dispute that, whatever be the good or bad points of various economic measures, none of them can serve the public interest unless those engaged in economic life have high moral principles and insist that they be maintained. But moral theology must also be interested in the wider problems of economic life.

The economic and political structures of the twentieth century produce a number of moral problems which have not yet been thoroughly investigated. They cannot be examined adequately here, and no more can be done than to suggest where moral issues arise. The complex nature of modern life makes it very difficult to disentangle one moral issue from another, and to weigh their respective claims is impossible, if one deals only with generalities. An increasing awareness of the nature of the moral claims involved in modern situations will, however, of itself do something to right evils which exist.

Profits

In the economy of the Western nations the present structure puts immense value on profits. In large areas of the West, especially in North America and Western Europe, the impression is given that success in life consists exclusively in making profits or doing well financially. In order to promote profits advertising has run riot, and in many cases has entirely lost its hold on truth, without apparently provoking any widespread objections from the public. Restrictions on advertising by law are for the most part limited to forbidding direct lies in matters which affect the health of the community.

The prevailing atmosphere in advertising turns upside down the real and proper purpose of production. Production is primarily for the sake of the consumer, so that he can have what he needs to live his life to the full. This includes in the Christian view a proper perspective as to what is important and what is not. There is no gain and much loss in an attitude which explicitly or implicitly holds that more consumption is *ipso facto* for the good of the consumer. The increase of consumption is usually euphemistically called an increase in the standard of living, a phrase which misleads by assuming that more consumption is of itself to be desired. The opposite may be and often is the truth.

Archbishop William Temple considered this matter in his book on *Christianity and Social Order*.[1] He pointed out that there is nothing wrong in profits as such, for those who produce for or serve the public are entitled to a just reward for their services. But he went on to say that when the consumer is treated, not as a person whose interests are all-important, but merely as a condition of success, priorities have been improperly reversed. There can be no dispute that we have gone far along this path. Advertising is aimed at stimulating desires which would not otherwise be felt, and at putting ideas into people's heads which are neither necessary nor good. The economic process of capitalism has a technical autonomy of its own which has to be taken into consideration, but when the whole process, or large parts of it, become untied from the true purpose of life, it does harm instead of good to society at large, and must come under moral condemnation.

In a relatively unregulated economic system profit is necessary in order to guarantee production, though there may be services needed for the general good which do not make a profit. Such services have to be subsidized in some way from the general resources of the people. The reward for those services is merely taken from another source than commercial profits, but its moral justification does not differ in principle from that on which profits must be justified.

The conclusion which William Temple reached was:[2]

So we get the general position: for economic production there *must* be profits, there *ought* to be regard for the consumer's interest, and it is wrong to sacrifice that interest to the increase of profits above a reasonable figure.

The consumer's interest must include his moral and spiritual life, and the efforts to sell products and the type of products which are sold should be such as will promote and not hinder those interests.

The high importance which is placed in our society on financial

[1] Now published by Penguin Books.
[2] *Christianity and Social Order*, p. 60.

success much encourages a false idea of the material world. The word 'materialism' is used in various senses. The Communists are materialists in a philosophical sense, for they hold that man's actions and attitudes are determined by material factors over which he has not control. But the Western nations are materialists in another sense, when their people make material success the guiding principle of their lives. Both these kinds of materialism are incompatible with true Christianity.

Christianity is materialist in another sense, the only true sense. It does not maintain that the material does not count or that it is evil—quite the contrary. The Christian tradition holds that the material world is good, made by God for the use of man in God's service and man's own happiness. It is to be transfigured by being the vehicle of moral and spiritual values, all together making one whole. Materialism in the wrong sense is the detachment of the material from the spiritual, so that they no longer have any intrinsic connection with one another, and the material becomes the end of life instead of the instrument for expressing the spiritual. It then becomes an idol set up in the place of God. In such a condition moral and spiritual values have been abandoned and replaced by egotistical self-interest, which finally brings the nemesis of self-destruction as surely as night follows day.

The economic system of the West no doubt has a great many practical advantages. Perhaps it is the best that has so far been devised for modern life: it is not for a moral theologian to make a judgement on this economic question. He does have to say, however, that it is a moral requirement that the men who live in such a system, or any other, should not shut their eyes to the evils which it produces. For Christians the paramount consideration must be the effect of any system on people, for people are men and women whom God loves and towards whom Christians have a responsibility to express that love.

The present system results in a number of men being unemployed. Some are unemployed permanently and others temporarily, against their own desire. This is a serious social evil, and the effects upon those who are unemployed through no fault of their own are often horrible, in the destruction of their morale and sense of manhood. The Christian faith does not claim to be able to say how this can be avoided or remedied, but it is the plain duty of Christians to draw attention to the evils and to promote the good.

No system which treats such calamities as of little account deserves to survive, or will survive in the long run. The inhuman way in which men and women in our society are casually treated, as though they were merely units in profit-making, is often a scandal.

If it is true that the present system cannot be changed without danger to the community, it must be equally true that it is maintained because it is beneficial to the community. If its benefits to the community result in undeserved suffering on the part of members of the community, who are thereby thrown on the scrap heap of unwanted labour, then there can be no doubt that it is a duty of the community as such to counter these effects. Such duty is not morally met by an inadequate dole; there is a moral requirement for constructive plans to make the people concerned feel that they have a place in the life of society as a whole, though their basic physical needs must be cared for. There can be no moral justification for permitting one group of the population to enrich themselves at the expense of another, who through no fault of their own are deprived of the opportunity of earning an honest livelihood.

Strikes

In modern society the welfare of all its members is closely bound together. Yet much of the economic negotiation is conducted on assumptions which belong to a past age, when only employer and employee were mainly concerned. But in modern life the right to withhold labour in the form of strikes ought to take into account other moral issues besides that of the proper wage. The point comes out particularly clearly in the public utility establishments of Britain, like the electricity authority. If workmen strike in the electricity industry, they inevitably impose hardship on the public, who are individually and collectively outside the parties concerned in the dispute, and who are quite innocent of any fault. It is therefore unjust that they should be penalized, and in the case of the absence of electricity it may cause not merely hardship, but danger to life. But less obviously the same principles apply to other strikes in national industries such as shipping, the docks, or motor manufacturing, at least in a country like England whose existence depends on an uninterrupted flow of raw material in and manufactured goods out of the land. The moral facts ought continually to be brought to the attention of employers and employees. But in considering the moral issues of strikes it is important to see them in proportion. If the employers in fact govern their behaviour entirely by the consideration of economic factors, they cannot rightly complain if the employees do the same. The consideration of the public interest is just as much a matter for the employers as for the employed, although much public comment would seem to overlook the fact.

Another moral issue in strikes is the effect of small strikes in key occupations on large bodies of other workers. A minor group may strike in a large factory and put thousands of men out of work who have nothing to do with the dispute. The good of all the men is a moral issue for those who wish to strike, and also for the employers. The evil which is done by a strike, that is, the hardship caused, should not be out of proportion to the hardship which it is designed to put right. There is at present far too little moral sense in both workers and employers in the Western world, and it is hard to escape the conclusion that it is with the employers that a moral consciousness ought first to be shown.

In trying to evaluate the moral issues in an industrial dispute, it is impossible to exclude the historical background on which they take place, for historical experiences have imbedded themselves in the attitudes of those who take part in these disputes, especially in the psychology of the workers. They know, whether consciously or instinctively, that their struggle for higher wages and better working conditions has been resisted tooth and nail by the employers ever since they were first made. There is an inner realization of the frightful conditions under which men, women and children were forced to work for many decades. This historical background has strongly implanted in them the conviction that justice can only come through their own relentless pressure, and that employers will resist demands, whether just or not, as long as they possibly can. Workers who have these presuppositions can hardly be blamed for them, though as much educational effort as possible should be aimed at making them more conscious of the other moral problems which also ought to be taken into purview, such as the need for employers to make their business viable, the duty of all concerned to the community as a whole, and especially to any part of the public which is particularly affected by strike action.

'Working to rule' and 'go slow' tactics raise extra moral problems of their own, since they seem to be a dishonest withholding of work, while continuing to draw full wages from those for whom it is done. There is no doubt that, in the absence of a specific contract limiting work, there is an implicit moral agreement that the worker will do his best work for the employer in return for his wage. If he does not do his best he is guilty of a moral offence against his employer. If he withholds his labour altogether, that is a different matter, since this does not involve him in an action which has dishonest aspects.

Christians when trying to sum up their own moral attitude in industrial disputes should err, if at all, on the side of those who are weakest, rather than on the side of the strong. This will almost always mean a tendency to support the workers, who have less resources to fall back on than the employers. It is the tradition of Christianity to have a special care for the weak and poor, and this should form part of their moral attitude in industrial disputes. But if there is a third party it might well be the weakest, such as the general public in the strike of an essential utility. In this case the workers might be stronger and more prosperous than unwilling parties to the dispute who suffer inconvenience or even danger to their health. All such disputes require a delicate balance of moral responsibilities in which the community, the workers and those engaged in management or ownership all share.

Gambling and Betting

The morality of gambling is a matter of dispute among Christians. It is hardly a subject which can be ignored, since it is such a widely practised social habit: moreover it is used extensively for raising money for charity, and Roman Catholic parishes encourage it widely for this purpose, running football pools and other gambling systems for the purpose of increasing church revenue. Anglicans and other Christian Churches are faced with the question of whether to use gambling methods in the form of raffles and similar small betting practices.

In our consideration of gambling it must be distinguished from other forms of risk to which people are inevitably exposed in everyday life, and which form an inescapable part of human life. 'Gambling' is used here to mean the wagering of money on some chance in the hope of obtaining a proportionately large return on it. In its various forms it includes playing cards for stakes, bingo and various games of chance.

The Church has never held that all gambling is wrong. The traditional attitude has been that in itself gambling is a thing indifferent, and that it must be judged by its effects. It has always been recognized that gambling can be abused, and when it is abused, it is condemned on the grounds that it is a misuse of the gifts of God to us. The moral issue largely depends on the degree in which gambling is indulged. It can hardly be held wrong for a man to play Bridge for a small stake, but it may be a sin to play the same game for high stakes. Apart from horse racing and dog racing many men play golf for high stakes.

There are serious matters associated with gambling which must be taken into account. Even if we agree that gambling is not in itself inherently wrong, there still remains the question as to whether it is ever right for a Christian to take part in it. If we examine this issue, we have to consider various results of gambling in practice and the effect that our action may have on others.

In Britain the amount of money spent on gambling each year is stupendous. Money staked on the football pools runs into hundreds of millions of pounds, and so does the money staked on horses and dogs in racing. Bingo has become almost a national craze. All the money which is spent in this way is unproductive and does no good to the State, except in so far as a tax is levied on certain forms of it. Football pools put immense sums of money into the pockets of promoters, who make no contribution whatever to the public good in the process, and the same applies to bookmakers and totalisators. It is morally unhealthy that such huge sums of money should be used for gambling, when so much misery and under-nourishment remains unrelieved in the world. It can hardly be denied that this is a misuse of resources in the light of human need.

Gambling is also a very serious social evil in personal life, for it is frequently a form of addiction, as powerful as drug or drink addiction. It is an emotional addiction as hard to get rid of as physical addictions. Many people who gamble are quite unable to control themselves, and bring misery and unhappiness to themselves and their families by the practice. So strong is the hold that gambling has over some minds, that men risk their reputations and their liberty by stealing money in order to indulge in it. To act in a way which might encourage such deplorable results is clearly not morally justifiable.

Gambling appeals to one of the lower of the human instincts, namely the desire to get money which has not been earned or deserved. This can and often does have a bad influence on human character, undermining the virtues of self-reliance and responsibility, and encouraging people to depend on a chance which has no relation to human personality and its duties. It saps strength of character.

Many Christians believe gambling to be inherently wrong. They may be mistaken, but, even so, their views ought to be taken into consideration when other Christians, who disagree with them, are trying to see their duty in the whole situation. Christians should not unnecessarily offend their brothers' consciences.

What is there to be said on the other side? The best case that can be put in favour of gambling is that it is a form of innocent pleasure. But, as we have seen, this is only true in a limited number of cases and it is greatly outweighed by the morally undesirable effects both on society and on individuals.

It is sometimes said that, if gambling is to take place, the profits should go to the State, rather than into the private pockets of gambling promoters. From a moral point of view there is much to be said for this proposal, since, if the State is in control of the gambling, it can control it as it thinks desirable for the welfare of the community, it can limit the prizes, and thereby diminish the attractiveness of the gamble, and it can use the proceeds for some constructive and generally beneficial purpose. It could even use the profits to give to those who are undernourished and in need elsewhere in the world.

The conclusion we must reach in view of the facts is that it is highly inexpedient for the Christian to indulge in gambling, so much so that such indulgence is at least morally questionable. It would seem clear that it is morally wrong in these circumstances for gambling to be used for raising church funds, since it puts the Church's *imprimatur* on the practice. The fact that the proceeds are used for the Church does not in any way diminish the evil effects of the habit. Perhaps the decisive thing for the Church is that gambling is a practice which can hardly be associated with the person and life of Jesus Christ, whom the Church is called to bring to the world.

Property

The Roman Church states without qualification that the right
to own private property is an absolute right of the natural law. So
Pius XI in the Encyclical *Quadragesimo Anno* (1931)[1]:

> Their (*sc.* Leo XIII and the theologians) unanimous contention has
> always been that the right to own private property has been given to
> men by nature, or rather by the Creator Himself, not only in order
> that individuals may be able to provide for their own needs and those
> of their families, but also that by means of it, the goods which the
> Creator has destined for the human race may truly serve this purpose.
> Now these ends cannot be secured unless some definite and stable
> order is maintained. There is therefore a double danger to be avoided.
> On the one hand, if the social and public aspect of ownership be
> denied or minimized, the logical consequence is 'individualism', as it
> is called; on the other hand, the rejection or diminution of its private
> and individual character necessarily leads to some form of 'col-
> lectivism.'

It is necessary to distinguish between what is relatively necessary
in human conditions as we have them in an imperfect world, and
what is an absolute principle, for they are not necessarily the same
thing. For example, it is necessary in the world in which we live
that there should be force used for the maintenance of law and
order and for the restraint of those whose actions tend to undermine the law, like thieves and murderers. But it would not be a
necessary consequence that the existence of police forces is part
of the order of Creation, and indeed we do not think that policemen
will be needed in heaven. But for the time being police forces are
absolutely necessary and they therefore meet an indispensable
moral need in our society.

It seems to be rather the same with private property, when
viewed from a Christian point of view, and it is not without
interest to observe that Pope Pius XI, in giving reasons why private
property is necessary, rests his case on arguments which imply that
it is because of man's sin. He begins, certainly, by stating that it
is a right bestowed by the Creator, but he gives no evidence on
which this view may be based. One reason is that individuals 'may
be able to provide for their own needs and those of their families',
and the unspoken assumption is that, unless they owned their
private property, they would not do so. This is tantamount to
saying that men are not unselfish enough to cultivate their land or

[1] Quoted in H. Davis, S.J., *op. cit.*, II, p. 233.

to do other necessary things unless they are given absolute ownership.

Ownership is not the same as use. Men need to have goods to use if they are to survive : that is plain. But it cannot be argued from this that they have to own them, except in the very limited sense of being free to consume them. In a monastery the monks own nothing, yet they live and eat and wear clothes and work for productive ends. A villager living from fruit growing on common land does not own the land or the fruit but enjoys a common right with others, which is freely shared between them according to need. The condition of man before the Fall, as pictured in the opening chapter of Genesis (which would weigh with some Christians at least), does not show Adam and Eve enjoying the Garden of Eden as their private property, but being permitted by God to use it for their own benefit as long as they live lives which are united to him. It hardly bears out the Pope's contention that the right of private property is given by the Creator himself, according to the Old Testament. And so far as we can forecast from the New Testament the condition of things when the Kingdom of God is fully come, we cannot trace the establishment of any right to private property in it.

It is hard to resist the conclusion that there may be a hidden motive in the Church's traditional teaching about private property —a desire to safeguard the property of the Church against the attempts of the State to control or to confiscate it. (In days such as these such teaching is of no avail, if the State in fact intends to take it away.) Church teachers are not deliberately dishonest if they take such a view, for the causes may be hidden from their own consciousness.

The reasons which St Thomas Aquinas gives for the necessity of private property seem to suffer from the same drawbacks as those of Pope Pius XI. He gives three reasons (II-II *q.*66, *a.*2). The first is that man is more ready to get something for himself than for someone else, because man is naturally lazy—a clear appeal to man's fallen nature. The second is that human affairs are better managed when each man has his own particular responsibility, so that everyone is not responsible for everything. But obviously private property is not necessary to establish this state of things. In the modern world responsibility does not go exclusively with ownership, either in the State or in private industry

A New Introduction to Moral Theology

and commerce. This reason therefore is strictly speaking irrelevant to the question of private property. The third reason is that private property promotes peace when every man is content with what he has, and that continual quarrels arise where possessions are held in common. The third reason would seem to be a strong practical argument against the monastic life, but it certainly has nothing to recommend it as a support for private property. For private property often has just the opposite effect, namely to promote strife where it is unequal, as it always has been in the world which has so far existed. And in any case the appeal is to man's fallen nature.

The conclusion can hardly be evaded that it is only because of the sinful character of man that private property is necessary. This makes it a relative moral good and it cannot be held to be part of the natural law. We may justifiably believe that if St Thomas himself was unable to advance better reasons for private property as a natural right, it is almost certain that it is not such a right.

In practice, it might be said, it does not make very much difference. Since we admit private property to be necessary in human society, which is always imperfect, what difference does it make whether it is a natural right or not? To this the answer may be made that it makes a good deal of difference to the readiness of men and women to consider changes. If men already own property, they are reluctant enough to allow changes for the benefit of the common society in which they live, but if they are also able to buttress this reluctance by an appeal to the natural law, it will be a serious obstacle to changes which ought to be made.

The older methods of treating the rights of property as part of justice have not the same relevance today as they had when they were written. There have been such changes in the social structure of modern life that it is artificial to try to apply principles, enunciated several centuries ago, as if they applied directly to the modern world. Archbishop William Temple pointed this out forcibly,[1] reminding his readers that traditional principles were first formulated in a feudal and peasant society and that the forms of that society have vanished. He recognized, however, that important principles were embodied in the earlier outlook 'of which perhaps the chief is the close association of status, and of wealth as conferring status, with social function. . . . There was

[1] *Christianity and Social Order*, p. 59.

no recognition of irresponsible power, such as may now be wielded
by the inheritors of great wealth, either in land or industrial shares.'

K. E. Kirk's treatment of justice[1] gives it a wider connotation
than Mortimer and includes within it the giving to everyone his
due; including God and oneself. Thus it includes truthfulness,
benevolence, forgiveness, compassion as well as the duties of
religion—reverence, devotion, obedience and gratitude to God. It
is possible to stretch justice to include these attitudes, but it seems
a little artificial. All the virtues which he enumerates do have an
element of duty within them, but they are better considered as the
consequence of a living and active love, rather than as falling within
the compass of duty.

There are serious objections to adopting the view, which
Mortimer puts forward, that private property is an absolute natural
right. The conclusions to which it leads stand out all the more
clearly if they are isolated from the argument by which they are
justified, for they then reveal themselves in a starkness which
makes them easier to observe. Two statements[2] may be taken as
examples.

> Private property is thus both a protection against temptation to
> luxury and extravagance and an incitement to thrift.

At first sight this appears to be almost the opposite of the truth.
If examined more closely, however, it seems to turn on the amount
of private property in question. If a man is having a hard time
struggling to conserve his historic acres, it may encourage thrift.
But private property, when it is possessed in large amounts in
modern conditions, often has just the opposite effect, and is an
incitement to luxury and extravagance. It is in fact the means by
which luxury and extravagance are indulged in. There can certainly
be no sort of justification of private property on such grounds.

The second sentence states that in storing what is over in the
present against the needs of the future,

> The possession of private property is beneficial to the growth of
> character and personality.

Here the only comment must be that the experience of everyday
life might lead one to the opposite conclusion. Far more frequently
the acquisitive motive erodes a man's moral standards and exercises

---

[1] *Some Principles of Moral Theology*, p. 35.
[2] *Op. cit.*, p. 192.

a strong pressure upon him to abandon those moral scruples which hinder his acquiring more property and wealth. This temptation is particularly strong in the society of the Western world, where financial success is widely accepted as admirable in every respect. The pressure of life in North America and Great Britain is directed to instilling into the members of society the immoral idea that all that matters is to acquire wealth and the social status that goes with it.

It is impossible to generalize about private property, which in itself is neither good nor bad, but neutral. Private property may be necessary for the stability of society from an economic point of view, but whether it is good or bad depends entirely on the way it is handled. The evils to which it has given rise are uncountable, though no doubt it has been also productive of much good.

The fact that no absolute right to personal property exists does not mean that the State has absolute ownership, merely because it is not the right of an individual. Both personal and State attitudes to property are governed by the same principle, which should guide both in all that they do. The basic principle is that property is given for use according to the will of God and to promote his love among men. If by human laws the individual or the State is given rights over property, whether by temporary or permanent ownership, such rights should be related to the needs of the whole community and to the freedom of persons within it, which freedom is an essential part of their human heritage. We find therefore that it is only God who has absolute permanent rights, except where in his creation he has indisputably conferred them as an integral element in what he has made.

Moral Duties in International Life

The twentieth century has seen more refugees in the world than any previous time in history. Their existence is directly due either to the oppressive character of domestic governments, or to the aftermath of wars between States. Refugees have been a feature of life throughout history—Jesus himself was numbered among them, when he was taken into Egypt to escape the plans of Herod. But the present scale of refugees is a new phenomenon.

For the most part the refugees have fled their own countries to escape conditions which they found unbearable, and which defied the moral law. As we have seen, laws which commit to prison and torture people who disagree with the Government are clearly against the moral law and can rightly be resisted on moral grounds. If they cannot be resisted, they can be evaded, if possible, by escape. The Communist countries give many examples of unjust laws, and those who flee are for the most part morally justified in doing so.

The Christian moral obligation to give help rests on the teaching that we should do to others what we should like them to do to us, and springs from the obligations of Christian love.

As regards refugees caused by war, the Western nations have an additional moral obligation towards them, since in many cases the wars have been fought for the benefit of and by the nations of the West. The Korean war is a good example. The Korean war was a war of the West against the East. It was begun and fought by the U.S.A., Britain, Canada and others. We are not here discussing whether it was a just war or not, though it almost certainly was. The point at issue is that it resulted in thousands of refugees, whose homes were destroyed and who were left penniless, and in many cases starving.

There can be no doubt that in this situation the nations of the West, quite apart from the individuals who make up those nations, have a clear obligation to succour these suffering people, whose hardships are directly due to a decision taken by the Western nations in the United Nations. The general Christian moral obligation to help them if possible would remain without this background, but the actual course of events adds a further moral debt which ought to be discharged by the nations concerned.

Economic assistance to under-developed countries is undertaken for the most part for selfish reasons, rather than from a sense of moral obligation. Most politicians are moved by the thought that this is the best way of preventing the countries concerned from joining the side, or supporting the cause, of their enemies. But even though the motives are not always good, the help itself meets a moral obligation, which stems from the same source as help to refugees, namely the moral duty of the rich to help the unfortunate.

Christians have an obligation to take the matter further and to be ready to set an example in self-sacrifice, so as to assist other people less fortunate than themselves. They could be more energetic than they usually show themselves in educating people to accept what is called a 'lower' standard of living, so that those human beings who lack them may be provided with the basic needs of existence. In acting thus Christians would be fulfilling an important moral duty.

Christians are often thought to be muddle-headed and idealistic, but a Christian ought to see things in a more realistic way than his neighbour and be able to show what might be called Christian cynicism. Christians understand about sin and its power, and ought not to be surprised when they meet it in the world. Christians do in fact understand human nature more deeply and thoroughly than others, and their religion shows this, because at its centre is a Man hanging upon a cross. On the other hand they know that sin is not the whole story, and that it can be and constantly is being redeemed and conquered. These two basic attitudes should be reflected in a Christian's view of the United Nations.

On the one hand the Christian will not see the United Nations through rose-coloured spectacles. He will observe that it is not a democratic assembly in the normal sense of the word, though it follows certain procedures which are common in democratic assemblies. In its structure and constitution the United Nations reflects the actual power situation in the world, and the rights of the great powers are safeguarded in the veto, built in to the procedure of the Security Council.

It would doubtless be excellent if we lived in a world where everyone would happily accept the judgement of the majority, even when it was different from his own. But this is not the case with individuals, still less with nations, and the use of the veto is just as indispensable for the U.S.A. as it is for the U.S.S.R. A change in international opinion might result in the veto being used as much by the U.S.A. as it has hitherto been used by the Soviet Union.

The structure of the United Nations then reflects the actual power situation in the world, and it is one of its virtues that it does so. Had it not done so, it would long ago have collapsed helplessly. A clear understanding of this condition will prevent us from attaching to United Nations resolutions a moral authority which they do not possess, for they do not of themselves carry any moral authority, except so far as the member nations have bound themselves to observe them.

The United Nations is not a democratic assembly and does not have the authority of such an assembly. The delegates are appointed by governments many of whom are the opposite of democratic. Luxembourg or the Ukraine has the same vote as the U.S.S.R. or U.S.A., and China has no vote at all, although it contains six or seven hundred million people. UN representation therefore has no recognizable connection with numbers of people in the world or strengths of States.

Nevertheless the United Nations serves some important moral purposes. It provides a world forum where moral questions can be brought into the open and debated, and there will be few to dispute the fact that the moral influence of the United Nations is considerable and has grown. This is an aspect which ought to be encouraged, for out of it might grow a means of controlling national passions and preventing conflict and war.

But if, as Christians, we do not see the United Nations in an idealized light, we do not go to the other extreme and condemn it out of hand as a mere talking shop, and of no use to anyone. Such a judgement would be a refusal to use an instrument which has been given to the nations, and which can be used to educate world moral opinion. It is imperfect, sinful and irritating, but it has done and is doing many good things, especially through its related agencies. The good ought to be strengthened and the weaknesses progressively eliminated.

Like the United Nations the International Court of Justice is limited in what it can do, and it has no means of enforcing its decisions in the cases which come before it. But it is a beginning, and it introduces into international affairs an instrument, whose very existence is a witness to the fact that there are principles of justice which apply to the nations. Both Britain and the U.S.A. since the Second World War gravely weakened the Court by withdrawing from its jurisdiction anything which seriously inconvenienced them—that was the effect of their reservations: some of them were later withdrawn. There is a moral duty on nations to do everything possible to strengthen the jurisdiction of the Court in support of international principles of law and justice.

Moral Trends Today

In the second half of the twentieth century there are moral trends which can be perceived, though their observation does not lead to any certain results. Some of them are doubtless temporary, and some more permanent; some of them are welcome to Christian people and some unwelcome. There are modern writers who believe that the development of morals is one of progress. Mr Philip Toynbee expressed such a view in an article in *The Observer* towards the end of 1962. But this is to put an *a priori* theory on the facts, and to believe in inevitable moral progress requires an act of faith at least as great as that needed to embrace the Christian Faith. The experiences of the second World War and of events in the Communist countries of Europe and of Asia, the continued use of inhuman and barbaric methods to undermine the human personality, brainwashing and other techniques of torture, the complete submersion of the individual beneath the interests of the Party, do not give much grounds for supposing that man is improving in his morals, unless indeed the traditional moral values are to be regarded as undesirable.

In the Western world of Europe and America there has been a noticeable increase in understanding the needs of other parts of the world. This does not spring exclusively from a heightened moral sense, though in some degree it does so. It is also connected with the world-wide Cold War, and the efforts made by leaders of all nations to win to their side those countries which are uncommitted. For this purpose economic help, as we have noted, has been extended, but alongside this help, there has been a great upsurge of organized assistance, which has relied on individual personal generosity. Both America and Britain have been outstanding examples of the increased sense of responsibility to others less fortunate than themselves. Here a real moral advance can be observed.

In the field of sexual morals there have been significant changes. There can be little doubt that sexual intercourse outside marriage has widely increased among the young, and that immorality among the married has also become more common. The widespread availability of contraceptive devices has helped to remove the risk that sexual intercourse will mean conception. There is also a section of the community, both larger and more vocal than in the past, which advocates abortion and even infanticide in the case of deformed children. These questions are more fully examined elsewhere. It is interesting that the same groups who are in favour of destroying life during pregnancy and infancy are opposed to taking it in cases of capital punishment, and are often near-pacifists and against blood sports. Without a careful investigation it would be impossible finally to identify these attitudes as belonging to the same groups of people, but there is a distinct impression that they do in fact go together in a general way, though doubtless there are many exceptions to such a generalization.

It is quite clear that there is no common Christian moral attitude behind such diverse views about what is permissible. If we ask what common feature would fit these opinions, the only attitude which easily justifies them all is what we might call an 'aesthetic' approach to morals. Everything is morally permissible which gives aesthetic pleasure, and everything is morally reprehensible which does not give aesthetic pleasure. Thus deformed children and foetuses are rather disgusting to the aesthetic senses, and may therefore be abolished. A hanged man is equally distasteful and he should therefore not be hanged; the same principle applies to opposition to war and blood sports. Probably there are few people who would be prepared to defend such a thesis intellectually; nevertheless it seems to be the unspoken assumption of many. Such an aesthetic approach involves the complete abandonment of Christian morals, together with the cessation of the idea that man is an end in himself. It must be entirely subjective in its judgements—but what the English intellectual thinks aesthetically desirable today, the rest of the world may find aesthetically abhorrent tomorrow! There can be no satisfactory morals on such a basis.

Appendix 1

SOME TECHNICAL TERMS OF
MORAL THEOLOGY

TRADITIONAL Catholic moral theology, both Roman and Anglican, uses a number of technical terms, with which a student ought to be familiar if he is to read it with full understanding. Some of the terms have been referred to in the text, but there are others, the use of which in the text would have involved interruption of the treatment. The distinctions which some of these terms involve, though useful for the purposes of detailed analysis, may, if they are given overmuch importance, have the effect of introducing a legalistic atmosphere into the discussion of moral theology. The definitions given below are as short as possible and do not claim to do more than indicate the meaning of the word or phrase in question.

CASUISTRY. The application of the principles of moral theology to individual cases.

CONSANGUINITY. Relationship by blood between two persons which is an impediment to marriage.

CONSCIENCE

Antecedent. The judgement which decides the morality of an action beforehand.

Certain. When the motive for an action is seen to be sound.

Consequent. The state of conscience following upon an act.

Doubting. One where the motive for an action is not certain.

False. A conscience based on something false, whether culpable or not.

Lax. A conscience which is in a general state of error.

Perplexed. A conscience faced with more than one course, all of which appear to be sinful.

Probable. A judgement based on something which is probably true but may more probably be false. (See Probabilism.)

Scrupulous. A conscience tormented by scruples which are unnecessary and imaginary.

Strict. A conscience which imagines obligations where they do not exist.

True. One that is correct and well balanced.

COOPERATION Joining in some way with another in a sinful act.

Immediate. Direct cooperation in another's sinful act.

Mediate. Cooperation in a sinful act in a secondary way, such as providing tools for housebreaking.

Negative. Failing to act to prevent injustice.

Positive. Assisting or encouraging injustice by word or deed.

Proximate. A form of mediate cooperation closely connected with a sinful act, such as holding a ladder to enable someone to steal apples.

Remote. Mediate cooperation not closely connected with the act, such as giving permission for the ladder to be used.

COUNSELS OF PERFECTION Good actions which are not of obligation. The phrase implies that there is a way of life which is better in itself than ordinary Christian life, and the use of the term is therefore unsatisfactory.

DIVORCE

'a vinculo'. The dissolution of the marriage bond, not recognized by Christian tradition in the West.

'a mensa et thoro'. Literally 'from table and bed'. Separation of two married persons.

FEAR

Filial. The fear of offending a parent because of a desire not to hurt him.

Servile. The fear of punishment.

Initial. A combination of filial and servile fear.

Worldly. A fear of losing worldly goods.

IGNORANCE

Affected. Ignorance which is deliberately retained and fostered.

Antecedent. Ignorance which unwittingly precedes an act.

Concomitant. Ignorance which accompanies an act, but is not the cause of the act.

Consequent. Ignorance which is the result of a person wishing to remain ignorant.

Crass or supine. Ignorance, for the dispelling of which little or no effort has been made.

Invincible. Ignorance which cannot be overcome though all reasonable steps have been taken to overcome it.

Simply vincible. Ignorance where some effort, but not enough, has been made to overcome it.

Vincible. Ignorance which could have been dispelled by reasonable effort.

IMPEDIMENT

Diriment impediment. A condition which invalidates a purported marriage so that no marriage in fact takes place.

JUSTICE

Commutative. The duties of individuals towards one another.

Distributive. The duties of society to the individual.

General. The duties of individuals to society.

OCCASIONS OF SIN

Free. An occasion of sin that can easily be avoided.

Necessary. An occasion of sin that cannot be avoided.

Proximate. An occasion of sin when a person almost always sins.

Remote. An occasion where there is less likelihood of sin.

POSSESSION

In bad faith. Retaining property known to belong to another.

In doubtful faith. Possessing property, for which there are good but not conclusive reasons for thinking that it belongs to another.

In good faith. Possession of another's property in innocent ignorance.

PROBABILIORISM. When faced with the question of whether a particular course of action is obligatory probabiliorism holds that it is wrong to take the benefit of the doubt unless freedom from the obligation is more probable than the obligation.

PROBABILISM is the system which holds that in a case of uncertainty the agent may disregard the law, if there is a probable opinion in this sense, even though opinions in favour of the law are more probable. On this basis one reasonably reputable opinion in favour of disregarding the law was considered enough to make that course morally correct.

EQUIPROBABILISM. The system by which in the case of roughly equal arguments as to the *existence* of a law, it may be ignored; in equal arguments as to whether a law is *binding*, it must be followed, and it is in any case unlawful to follow a less probable opinion.

SCANDAL is divided up into various categories—active, diabolical, direct and indirect, passive and pharisaical.

SCRUPLE. An obstacle to the spiritual life consisting of fears and anxieties which are unfounded. It shows itself in imagining things to be sins which are not in fact sins, and in exaggerating the gravity of sins committed. Scruples are often a reflexion of an underlying emotional disorder.

SIN

Actual. An act of sin of an isolated nature.

Formal. An act of sin which is blameworthy, because it was committed in the knowledge that the act was sinful.

Habitual. A sin which has come to be a habit.

Material. An act which is in itself wrong, whether or not the person committing it was blameworthy.

Mortal. A sin which is said to break the link with God and jeopardize the soul. It must be deliberate, committed with full knowledge of its character and consequences, and be a grave matter. The division of sins into mortal and venial has serious drawbacks.

Original. The sinfulness of which every man partakes by reason of his humanity: it has nothing to do with personal acts of sin.

Personal. A sin which we ourselves commit.

Venial. A sin of a less serious character than mortal sin.

TUTIORISM. A moral system which holds that in cases of doubt the safer way should be chosen. While quite unsuitable as a rule for normal moral decisions, it is used sometimes in the Sacraments, when conditional ordination or baptism is administered in cases of doubt.

VIRTUES

Cardinal virtues are justice, temperance, prudence and fortitude.

Theological virtues are faith, hope and love.

WAR

Just. A war to be just must be an act of the State, and must be unavoidable by normal methods of discussion; there must be serious cause for it and it must be waged in accordance with just methods and international law. It must not be extended beyond what is necessary. The force used must not be out of proportion to the end to be achieved, and must be discriminate. The evil produced by the war must not be out of proportion with the evil which the war is designed to prevent.

Appendix 2

SUGGESTIONS FOR FURTHER READING

Anglican Books

RICHARD HOOKER
   Laws of Ecclesiastical Polity (available in Everyman's Library, Dent)
JEREMY TAYLOR
   Holy Living and *Holy Dying* (many editions)
K. E. KIRK

Some Principles of Moral Theology	Longmans	1920
Conscience and its Problems	Longmans	1948
Essay in *The Study of Theology*	Hodder	1939
The Vision of God	Longmans	1934

R. C. MORTIMER

The Elements of Moral Theology	A. & C. Black	1953
Christian Ethics	Hutchinson	1950

234 *A New Introduction to Moral Theology*

L. Dewar
   A Short Introduction to Moral Theology   Mowbray   1956
L. Dewar and C. E. Hudson
   Christian Morals   Hodder   1945
C. S. Lewis
   Mere Christianity   Fontana Books
H. Rashdall
   Conscience and Christ   Duckworth   1916
H. R. McAdoo
   The Structure of Caroline Moral Theology   Longmans   1949
Peter Green
   The Problem of Right Conduct   Longmans   1937
O. C. Quick
   Christianity and Justice   Sheldon   1940
W. Temple
   Christianity and Social Order (available in Penguin Books)
D. L. Munby
   God and the Rich Society   Oxford   1961
G. R. Dunstan
   The Family is Not Broken   SCM   1962
Thomas Wood
   Some Moral Problems   SPCK   1961
H. C. Warner
   Divorce and Remarriage   Allen & Unwin   1954
V. A. Demant
   An Exposition of Christian Sex Ethics   Hodder   1963
Edward Carpenter
   Common Sense about Christian Ethics   Gollancz   1961
Sherwin Bailey
   Common Sense about Sex   Gollancz   1962
J. V. Langmead Casserley
   Morals and Man in the Social Sciences   Longmans   1961
A. R. Vidler
   Christ's Strange Work (on the moral law)   SCM   1963

Roman Catholic Books

B. Häring
   The Law of Christ   Newman   1961
G. R. Hagmaier and R. Gleason
   Moral Problems Now   Sheed & Ward   1959
N. St John Stevas
   Life and Death and the Law   Eyre & Spottiswoode   1961

Other Books of General Interest

REINHOLD NIEBUHR
    An Interpretation of Christian Ethics (available in Meridian Books)

The Children of Light and the Children of Darkness	Scribner	1944
Moral Man and Immoral Society	SCM	1963

PAUL RAMSEY

Basic Christian Ethics	SCM	1953

EMIL BRUNNER

The Divine Imperative	Lutterworth	1937

D. BONHOEFFER

Ethics	SCM	1955

JAMES PIKE

Doing the Truth	Gollancz	1956

PAUL LEHMANN

Ethics in a Christian Context	SCM	1963

WALDO BEACH AND RICHARD NIEBUHR

Christian Ethics (an anthology)	Ronald Press, New York	1955

T. E. JESSOP

The Christian Morality	Epworth	1960

S. CAVE

The Christian Way	Nisbet	1949

ALAN BOOTH

Christians and Power Politics	SCM	1961

CHARLES C. WEST

Communism and the Theologians	SCM	1958

R. H. BAINTON

Christian Attitudes to War and Peace	Hodder	1961

PAUL ABRECHT

The Churches and Rapid Social Change	SCM	1961

DANIEL JENKINS

Equality and Excellence: A Christian Comment on Britain's Life	SCM	1962

Reports

The Era of Atomic Power (British Council of Churches)	SCM	1946
Christians and Atomic War (British Council of Churches)	BCC	1959
The Valley of Decision by T. R. Milford (British Council of Churches)	BCC	1962
Christians and the Prevention of War in an Atomic Age (World Council of Churches)	SCM	1961

The British Nuclear Deterrent (British Council of Churches) SCM   1963
The Family in Contemporary Society   SPCK   1958
Human Reproduction   British Council of Churches   1962
Sterilization   Church Information Office   1962
Artificial Insemination by Donor   Church Information Office   1959
The Church and the Law of Nullity of Marriage   SPCK   1955
See also *Crucible*, the journal of the Church of England Board for Social
Responsibility

Philosophical Background

P. NOWELL-SMITH
    Ethics (available in Penguin Books)
R. M. HARE
    The Language of Morals   Oxford   1952
S. TOULMIN
    The Place of Reason in Ethics   Cambridge   1950
C. D. BROAD
    Five Types of Ethical Theory   Routledge   1930
D. M. MACKINNON
    A Study in Ethical Theory   A. & C. Black 1951
W. D. ROSS
    The Foundations of Ethics   Oxford   1939

New Testament Studies

C. H. DODD
    Gospel and Law   Hodder   1951
T. W. MANSON
    Ethics and the Gospel   SCM   1960
W. LILLIE
    Studies in New Testament Ethics   Oliver & Boyd 1961
L. H. MARSHALL
    The Challenge of New Testament Ethics Macmillan   1947
A. WILDER
    Eschatology and Ethics in the Teaching of Jesus SCM 1954
C. A. PIERCE
    Conscience in the New Testament   SCM   1955
J. KNOX
    *The Ethic of Jesus in the Teaching of
        the Church*   Epworth   1962

Encyclopaedia of Religion and Ethics (13 volumes) T. & T. Clark
A Dictionary of Christian Ethics, ed. John
    Macquarrie (in preparation)   SCM
Dictionary of Moral Theology   Burns & Oates 1962

INDEX